"*Military Ministry* describes the role and office of military chaplains, which is dynamic and complex in nature.... I highly recommend this book to students, ministers, churches, and others who are thinking about chaplaincy or supporting chaplaincy."

—SAM LEE,
Director of Chaplaincy, Southern Baptist Conference, North American Missions Board

"This is the book I wish I had twenty-three years ago!... *Military Ministry* is a must-read for any person considering the call to the military chaplaincy or already actively serving.... This should be required reading for every chaplain serving in the Department of Defense!"

—PETER E. KEOUGH,
Senior Pastor, Simpson Baptist Church

"This new book is a superb tool for understanding what the American chaplain ministry is all about.... Especially unique to this book are the personal anecdotes of actual chaplain ministry—a writing touch that draws one into the real life of a military chaplain. This will be the go-to book for anyone considering military ministry."

—DOUG LEE,
Brigadier General, U.S. Army, retired

"Military chaplaincy is a uniquely challenging, crucial, and compelling ministry. Linzey and Travis understand it as well as anyone. You will be informed and inspired as you read their book!"

—RICHARD BLACKABY,
President, Blackaby Ministries International

"Linzey and Travis have hit a grand slam! *Military Ministry* deals with legal, moral, ethical, spiritual, and personal aspects of military ministry. Filled with history, facts, research, inspiration, motivation, and personal anecdotes, this book fills a need for an academic resource on military chaplaincy and chaplaincy as a ministry calling."

—NAOMI KOHATSU PAGET,
Gateway Seminary

"A helpful introduction and overview of military chaplaincy for those considering this ministry, for those already in it, and for those—like me—who support chaplains in education or otherwise. I have had the privilege of teaching many chaplains in my doctor of ministry courses—including Dr. Linzey—and am grateful to now have this resource to recommend to them and to continue to learn from myself."

—DAVID A. CURRIE,
Gordon-Conwell Theological Seminary

"Paul Linzey and Keith Travis speak to the heart of chaplaincy: caring for those for whom Christ cares, with a focus on the military. The text is engaging and practical, addressing the foundational dynamics of military chaplaincy.... They speak in theological, practical, and caring terms for carrying out the Christian mission of loving others through the work of the Spirit in the uniqueness of military communities."

—ZACHARY M. TACKETT,
School of Divinity, Southeastern University

"Keith Travis and Paul Linzey served their nation with distinction as army chaplains. They have provided an excellent, much-needed resource for those interested in military chaplaincy and/or in serving as a military chaplain.... This is not just a textbook, but an inside look at serving as a military chaplain. I commend this book to you."

—RON CREWS,
Chaplain (Colonel), U.S. Army, retired

"A lot of people have questions about how to minister in the military today. *Military Ministry* offers insight about the how-to of ministry in the military context. A must-read for anyone considering the call to military chaplaincy, this book provides practical help for chaplains. It will challenge you to think through how to minister effectively and reach this generation of men and women in the military."

—ROBERT HART JR.,
Chaplain Corps Branch Chief, Office of the Army Chief of Chaplains

"Keith Travis and Paul Linzey have provided a great resource for those discerning a call to become a military chaplain, for current chaplains who need to refresh their understanding of this unique ministry, and for civilian pastors who want to know more about the challenges of serving in the armed forces. . . . It is a must-read for those thinking about service as a chaplain!"

—**David Reese,**
Evangelical Seminary

"Paul Linzey and Keith Travis have provided a much-needed volume. They draw from deep research and their own experience as military chaplains, in addition to that of several wise colleagues. This should become the primary textbook for courses training future military chaplains and a treasured handbook for those already ministering those protecting us in uniform."

—**Alan J. Ehler,**
Southeastern University

"*Military Ministry* is a must-read for military chaplains at any stage in their career. . . . This book provides a road map for successful ministry in today's environment. The firsthand experiences are inspiring and an encouragement for chaplains to bring the hope of Christ to those they serve!"

—**Matt Spurgeon,**
U.S. Air Force

"*Military Ministry* is the book every chaplain should read and keep as a resource. . . . Read this book if you want to grow as a chaplain. Ridiculously superb job by Paul Linzey and Keith Travis! This is a game changer! They crushed it!"

—**Keith N. Croom,**
Chaplain (Colonel), U.S. Army, retired

"Excellent read from start to finish. This book captures the essential elements that a military chaplain must possess to be successful in life and military ministry. . . . Current chaplains, military endorsers, families, students, churches, and many others will benefit from the wealth of knowledge contained in this book."

—JUSTIN GREENE,
U.S. Air Force

"This book is a refreshing and welcomed resource, providing the skills for chaplains to pivot with changing times while remaining true to their calling. . . . This mentor-in-a-book will serve as a vital reference for years to come."

—JOHN STEVEN EVANS,
Captain, Chaplain Corps, U.S. Navy, retired

"Building on decades of knowledge and personal experience, Travis and Linzey have woven together a highly readable and practical guide to the unique challenges and blessings of ministry in the pluralistic environment of chaplaincy. I highly recommend this book to those exploring the potential of chaplaincy ministry or those just starting out who need a trustworthy guide to navigate this complex but rewarding ministry."

—KENNETH W. BUSH,
Director of Training, Programs and Research, The National Conference on Ministry to the Armed Forces

"Time-tested precepts, themes, and praxis make *Military Ministry* an absolute must-read for every discernment-oriented inquirer. Rarely does one get to know an individual in multiple realms validating the information shared in a book, but I have known the author as a military chaplain, university professor, and friend."

—EMILE H. HAWKINS SR.,
Air National Guard, Assistant to the Commandant,
Air Force Chaplain Corps College

Military Ministry

MILITARY MINISTRY

Chaplains in the Twenty-First Century

PAUL E. LINZEY
B. KEITH TRAVIS

Foreword by Jeff Iorg

WIPF & STOCK · Eugene, Oregon

MILITARY MINISTRY
Chaplains in the Twenty-First Century

Copyright © 2022 Paul E. Linzey and B. Keith Travis. All rights reserved. Except for brief quotations in critical publications or reviews, no part of this book may be reproduced in any manner without prior written permission from the publisher. Write: Permissions, Wipf and Stock Publishers, 199 W. 8th Ave., Suite 3, Eugene, OR 97401.

Wipf & Stock
An Imprint of Wipf and Stock Publishers
199 W. 8th Ave., Suite 3
Eugene, OR 97401

www.wipfandstock.com

PAPERBACK ISBN: 978-1-6667-3593-2
HARDCOVER ISBN: 978-1-6667-9359-8
EBOOK ISBN: 978-1-6667-9360-4

MAY 13, 2022 2:50 PM

Cover photo by Pixabay. Used with permission.

Excerpts from *Safest Place in Iraq* are used with permission.

Government documents written by government employees are in the public domain.

Unless otherwise noted, all Scripture quotations are taken from the Holman Christian Standard Bible®, Used by Permission HCSB ©1999,2000,2002,2003,2009 Holman Bible Publishers. Holman Christian Standard Bible®, Holman CSB®, and HCSB® are federally registered trademarks of Holman Bible Publishers.

Paul dedicates this book to the following Chaplains:

My father, Stanford E. Linzey Jr. (USN)
My brother, George W. Linzey (USN)
My son, Christopher J. Linzey (USN)

And to Rob E. Noland (USA)
Mentor, Friend, and Brother

Keith dedicates this book to the following Chaplains:

Douglas L. Carver (USA)
Steve E. Keith (USAF)
Dave Mullis (USN)

My childhood friend, John E. Armitstead (USA)
who passed away in 2007

And to my wife, Pam
She is the best part of Team Travis

Contents

Guest Anecdotes | xi

Foreword by Jeff Iorg | xiii

Acknowledgments | xv

Introduction | xvii

SECTION ONE | BACKGROUND OF MILITARY MINISTRY

Chapter 1   Historical Perspective | 3

Chapter 2   Constitutional Basis | 8

Chapter 3   Legal Grounds | 13

Chapter 4   Biblical Foundation | 17

SECTION TWO | BECOMING A MILITARY CHAPLAIN

Chapter 5   Ministerial Calling | 27

                Guest Anecdote Number One:
                Conflict on the Way to Answering the Call | 33

Chapter 6   Family and Emotional Readiness | 35

                Guest Anecdote Number Two:
                God Had Planted Me Right Where I Was Meant to Be | 41

| Chapter 7 | Requirements and Qualifications | 43 |

> Guest Anecdote Number Three:
> *A Call for the Entire Family* | 50

| Chapter 8 | Initial Chaplain Basic Training | 52 |

> Guest Anecdote Number Four:
> *I Felt I Was in Hell* | 59

SECTION THREE | BEING A MILITARY CHAPLAIN

Chapter 9	Relationship with Your Endorser	65
Chapter 10	Self-Care in the Military	72
Chapter 11	Wearing the Uniform	81
Chapter 12	The Role of the Chaplain in the Unit	89

> Guest Anecdote Number Five:
> *Boom! Wounded by an IED* | 98

| Chapter 13 | The Religious Support Team | 100 |

> Guest Anecdote Number Six:
> *Unity in the Religious Support Team* | 106

| Chapter 14 | Chaplain Tasks | 108 |

> Guest Anecdote Number Seven:
> *Kosher Meals for a Jewish MP* | 115

| Chapter 15 | Family Support Groups | 117 |
| Chapter 16 | Pluralism and Religious Liberty | 122 |

> Guest Anecdote Number Eight:
> *Pluralism at its Finest* | 130

| Chapter 17 | Personal and Professional Growth | 133 |

> Guest Anecdote Number Nine:
> *Change in Plans that Worked Out Well* | 138

Chapter 18	Comparing Reserve & National Guard to Active Duty Chaplaincy | 140
Chapter 19	Managing Your Career | 147
	Guest Anecdote Number Ten: *Chaplain Moses* | 154
Chapter 20	Why Chaplains Get in Trouble | 157
Chapter 21	Having Fun | 160

Section Four | Bearing Fruit as a Military Chaplain

Chapter 22	Incarnational Presence | 169
	Guest Anecdote Number Eleven: *The Hardest, Most Rewarding Thing I Have Ever Done* | 175
Chapter 23	Personal Life of the Chaplain | 177
Chapter 24	Spiritual Disciplines | 182
Chapter 25	The Ministry of the Chaplain | 186

Section Five | Building the future of Military Ministry

Chapter 26	Understanding Culture | 195
Chapter 27	Controversy and Criticism | 199
	Guest Anecdote Number Twelve *Understanding Culture* | 211
Chapter 28	Diversity | 213
Chapter 29	A Recommended Strategy | 223
Chapter 30	What's at Stake? | 230

**Benediction: A Prayer for Men and Women
　　　　Serving as Chaplains | 233**

Author Bio for Paul E. Linzey | 235

Author Bio for Brandon Keith Travis | 237

Bibliography | 239

Department of Defense Publications | 245

United States Law | 248

Index | 249

Guest Anecdotes

Guest Anecdote Number One: Conflict on the Way to Answering the Call
CH (MAJ) Lisa Northway, USA

Guest Anecdote Number Two: God Had Planted Me Right Where I Was Meant to Be
LT Chris Linzey, CHC, USN

Guest Anecdote Number Tree: A Call for the Entire Family
CPT (CH) Keah Humphrey, USA

Guest Anecdote Number Four: I Felt I Was in Hell
Ch, CPT Brandon White, USAF

Guest Anecdote Number Five: Boom! Wounded By an IED
CMDR Robert Nelson, CHC, USN

Guest Anecdote Number Six: Unity in the Religious Support Team
SGT Robert Rosenthal, Chaplain Assistant, CA ARNG

Guest Anecdote Number Seven: Kosher Meals for a Jewish MP
Anonymous Military Chaplain

Guest Anecdote Number Eight: Pluralism at its Best
CH (COL-Ret) Ron Casteel, USA

Guest Anecdote Number Nine: Change in Plans that Worked Out Well
CH (COL-Ret) Keith Travis, USA

Guest Anecdote Number Ten: Chaplain Moses
CH (COL-Ret) Rob Noland, USA

Guest Anecdote Number Eleven: The Hardest, Most Rewarding Thing I Have Ever Done
CH (CPT) Daniel Garnett, USA

Guest Anecdote Number Twelve: Understanding Culture
CH (COL-Ret) Keith Travis, USA

Foreword

WARRIORS NEED WORSHIP! They have the awesome responsibility of defending freedom, while grappling with their mortality and the full knowledge of their limitations—both personal and professional. Warriors need spiritual guidance, emotional support, and help answering the thorny questions related to modern warfare. They need help holding their families together and maintaining mental health. For all these reasons and many others, the military needs chaplains to lead Soldiers, Sailors, Airmen, and Marines to worship the True and Living God.

Yet, contemporary culture is making it harder and harder for chaplains to serve. The complications of religious pluralism, rising secularism, the pragmatism of military officers, and apathy from other Christian leaders are making it more and more difficult to find chaplains, and for chaplains to do their job. While the challenges are formidable, the opportunities for eternal impact are even greater.

Keith Travis and Paul Linzey understand that the military needs chaplains. They also believe chaplains must learn new skills and develop better approaches to handling the modern dilemmas of chaplain service. This book is a field guide to enhancing the work of chaplains and to calling more men and women to this important task. The authors take on problems chaplains face—ranging from First Amendment concerns and legal opposition, to developing the inner personal disciplines chaplains must have to survive their stressful job. Without shirking difficult topics or compromising their Christian convictions, Travis and Linzey provide the guidance needed to promote effective service by chaplains in the twenty-first century.

One strong feature of this book is the personal experience of the authors and the many guests who contributed their personal stories. These anecdotes give the book an authenticity other academic writings on this subject often lack. This book reads like a report from the front-lines, not arm-chair quarterbacking from people who have never been in the game.

Another strength of the book is its comprehensive nature. It includes insight about strategic ministry challenges chaplains face, a global overview of what chaplaincy must become in this generation, and reasoned answers to those who oppose chaplains as part of a state-sanctioned military. It also includes personal counsel for chaplains about maintaining spiritual vitality, protecting their families, and balancing career concerns with responding to God's call. The broad range of issues covered in this book make it a compendium of remarkable insights across the full spectrum of chaplaincy issues today.

Some may read this book as a textbook or as a continuing education tool. While that will be helpful, my hope is some will read it as part of considering God's call to serve as a military chaplain. If you are considering that ministry assignment in your future, you are considering an honorable vocation with the potential of both patriotic and eternal impact. Serving God and country is a high honor. May God use this book to lead many to accept their unique commission as a chaplain as part of fulfilling the Great Commission!

Dr. Jeff Iorg, President
Gateway Seminary

Acknowledgments

PAUL WOULD LIKE TO THANK:

I want to thank Linda Linzey, my wife, reader, and editor whose input and encouragement have been priceless.

I have had some wonderful mentors. My father, Stanford E. Linzey Jr., modeled effective chaplain ministry throughout his life. My very first chaplain supervisor, Don Wright in the California Army National Guard, taught me that ministry follows friendship. Ron Casteel was the class leader at the Army Chaplain School Basic Leaders Course who became a lifelong mentor and friend. Doug Lee took me under his wing when I was a rookie on Active Duty, and helped refine and shape me as a chaplain.

My own endorsers from the General Council of the Assemblies of God were extremely helpful to me. Jim Denley, Scott McChrystal, and Chuck Marvin—you were there every time I needed you.

The early readers who provided input and suggestions for improvement cannot be thanked enough.

My friend, Mack Griffith, modeled professionalism, integrity, and attention to detail.

This book would be incomplete without the Chaplains who provided guest anecdotes. Your stories made this book much richer.

Matt Wimer, George Callihan, and the rest of the staff at Wipf and Stock were wonderful to work with.

Acknowledgments

KEITH WOULD LIKE TO THANK:

First, I want to thank my wife Pam. She is my best friend, supporter, and the person who strengthens me. Without her, I could not have written this book, or accomplished the things I have done.

Second, I want to thank some important friends who believed in me: John Armitstead, Larry Marlin, Doug Brown, Sean Lee, and Blair Stone. All of these mentored me and helped shape me into the person I am today. I would like to thank my parents who believed in me, loved me, and shaped me, even though I know it was a difficult assignment for them.

My early endorsers, Huey Perry and Pat Davis, were wonderful role models for me in my work as the endorser for the SBC. Later, Dave Mullis was not only my endorser for a season, he was also my friend when we worked together at the North American Mission Board.

I also want to thank Dr. Jeff Iorg for his forward in the book, along with all of the guest writers.

David Reese, for your friendship and investment in our book. You helped us shape some areas that needed some additional work. Thank you!

Thank you all for your part in turning this idea into reality. We are grateful.

Introduction

PAUL'S PERSPECTIVE

The government and the Department of Defense want chaplains who will be a source of encouragement and hope to people of all faiths. The Church wants chaplains who will lead people to faith in Christ and disciple them. This book shows readers how to do both. By deftly navigating the issues of the twenty-first century, today's chaplains can fulfill the mandate of the government and live up to their divine calling.

When I wrote the book *Safest Place in Iraq*,[1] I asked my friend Keith Travis if he would provide an endorsement blurb. After he sent it to me, he called and suggested that I write another book specifically to train people for military chaplaincy. My immediate reply was, "I'll do that on one condition . . . that you write it with me." He agreed, and this project got started.

Keith teaches graduate-level courses on chaplaincy. I served as an advisor at a school of theology when they developed their Master of Divinity program for chaplains. Keith had been a chaplain and an ecclesiastical endorser before becoming a professor. I had been a chaplain, a chaplain trainer, and a chaplain recruiter before becoming a professor. We both had a need for a better textbook than we had seen.

In a sense, we have been preparing to write this book for a long time. We've read everything we can get our hands on that relates to military chaplaincy. We've lived as chaplains, we've trained and recruited chaplains, and we've taught and advised ministerial students. Before we started writing, we created a project charter that included the following:

1. Linzey, *Safest Place in Iraq*

Introduction

The Need: There are books that introduce the variety of chaplaincies, and others that provide memoir or testimony. But there isn't a comprehensive book about the nuts and bolts of serving as a military chaplain. This book will fill the void. The most widely-used book that deals with chaplaincy issues was written in 2006, and it is barely an introductory glimpse covering a variety of chaplaincies. Many Seminaries are in the process of implementing or revising their chaplaincy training programs, and there is a need for a better, more current look at this topic because a lot has happened in the ensuing years and the chaplain's ministry and role in the military have changed.

Vision Statement: To have the most up-to-date, informative, inspirational, and comprehensive book on military chaplaincy on the market. It will provide a biblical foundation and historical perspective on military chaplaincy, and incorporate the guidelines and regulations from denominational endorsers, the Bible, the Department of Defense, and the Constitution of the United States.

Project Description: This is a book written by two military chaplains who have devoted their lives to military ministry. Between them, Keith Travis and Paul Linzey have completed over 60 years of effective ministry with the military. This book contains the who, what, where, when, why, and how of ministry in the United States Armed Forces. It offers instructional material plus pertinent anecdotes and illustrations from the lives of the authors and other military chaplains.

With the project charter in place, we launched into writing the book, which is structured in five sections. Section one is called *Background of Military Ministry* and provides a foundation from history, the U.S. Constitution, our laws, and the Bible. Section two focuses on what it takes to become a chaplain, looking at the divine calling, emotional readiness, and the specific qualifications. The third section is the largest because it deals with the many tasks, responsibilities, roles, relationships, and dynamics of serving as a chaplain in the Air Force, Navy, and Army. Section four highlights the reason most Christian chaplains are in the ministry. The emphasis is on real-world ministry and bearing fruit for the Kingdom of God. Section five examines the culture, controversies, and criticisms military chaplains live with and provides a recommended strategy as we look to the future.

The narrative includes dozens of anecdotes and stories about serving in the military, including several contributions from other chaplains. The appendices provide invaluable assistance for further research. The reader will gain an understanding of what it takes to become a military chaplain, what is needed to serve successfully, and helpful insights into maintaining an effective ministerial presence throughout a chaplaincy career.

KEITH'S PERSPECTIVE

I've had a friendly or professional relationship with more than a thousand chaplains, but one who stood out was Paul Linzey. When we met, I felt a kinship with him. Every year I saw him at chaplain training events. After I retired and became the endorser for the Southern Baptist Convention, Paul and I kept in touch, never even thinking that our friendship would lead us to co-author a book on an all-consuming call that God placed on both of our lives.

Then a couple years ago, we were talking about a book he had just written, and we joked about writing a book together. I was thinking more about Paul writing the book. However, we both realized it was not a joke, and that God was leading us to write a book to train and prepare chaplains. So we began the adventure of writing this book—Paul the writer and Keith the storyteller.

This book developed from our experiences as chaplains, Paul as a professional writer and educator, and Keith as a long-term endorser and educator. We think we have put together a good book that will help in multiple fields: education, church ministry, personal spiritual journey, and God's Call to ministry, especially the call to military ministry.

One question that always arises is why there's a need for another book about chaplaincy. The simple answer is that there aren't any books that provide a comprehensive look at the role of military chaplains from a ministerial perspective. There are some from a negative slant toward one form of chaplaincy or the other, but having a positive book from a Christian point of view was important to us.

This book truly is a labor of love, and our love is multifaceted. God called us to be chaplains, and naturally we have a strong affection for our fellow chaplains. Also, since we are both educators, we have read a lot of books on chaplains and chaplaincy. There are very few, if any, up-to-date books on military chaplaincy that approach the work from a practical, "ministry-now" perspective. What do I mean by "a labor of love?"

1. *It is a labor of love for chaplains.* Both Paul and I became chaplains because we felt God called us to this ministry. It was a command that we followed. In the process, we have encountered many chaplains, and came to love every one of them. Many were well trained and doing an outstanding work for the Lord and for the people they served. Too many, however, were unprepared for the task and ill-equipped for the roles they needed to play. This book is for them.

2. *It is a labor of love for chaplaincy.* There are some who would say chaplaincy is moving in the wrong direction and that there is a lack of understanding about working together across denominational lines among clergy from different faith groups. I would challenge those people to attend a National Conference for Ministry to the Armed Forces (NCMAF) and see over 200 faith groups that gather together to make sure ministry in the military actually works for the good of all. NCMAF represents our society. Each of those 200+ faith group endorsers love their god and their faith. They love chaplaincy ministry, what it accomplishes, and how it brings diverse practitioners together. Every faith group that is represented by the Department of Defense is there because they love chaplaincy.

3. *It is a labor of love for the military.* Paul and I both come from military families. Our dads were Sailors in the Navy during WWII. Both dads served in the Pacific at the same time. In fact, Paul's dad was on the USS Yorktown when it sank during the battle of Midway. My dad was on the USS Seminole, a sea going tug, that was dispatched to help the sinking Yorktown. It did not arrive in time. Both Paul and I have a love for the military that was instilled in us as young boys. I suspect that God placed that love there to use it for our call to the military. It is something that is in our blood. We know Chaplains are a strong part of the military and that, in many ways, chaplains help the military stay true to a moral compass.

4. *It is a labor of love for the church.* A lot of people are ignorant about what it means to be a chaplain. In fact, questions like "Why did you leave the ministry?" "Will you be able to preach about Jesus?" "Can you pray in Jesus's name?" are heard weekly, if not daily, among good Christian people who attend good churches.

Introduction

My response is that chaplains are "pastors on steroids." The military is looking for pastors who will represent their faith group well, and who will get along with others. We hope the church will read this book and have a better understanding of the role their pastor will have in the military. It is also important for chaplains to know that they don't leave the church when they put on the uniform, because chaplaincy is an extension of the local church. It doesn't matter if the chaplains are in Korea, Okinawa, Abu Dhabi, Ft. Bragg, Minot AFB, or Tidewater, VA, they are an extension of the church. These pastors in uniform represent the churches that sent them to wear the cloth of our nation.

We mention other books in the narrative and in the bibliography. Most of them have a narrow scope, focusing on one aspect of chaplaincy. Others present chaplain ministry in general and include clergy who work in prisons, hospitals, industry, first responders, and other settings. Some were written a long time ago. We believe a new book is needed right now, a book that is up to date on policy, culture, regulations, and religious liberty issues that each chaplain will have to deal with day in and day out, a book whose mission is to focus solely on military ministry.

Therefore, our attempt in this book is to look at what it's like to minister in the military and prepare good people for successful careers and fruitful service for the Kingdom of God. You can find books written on specific issues, but there isn't one book on the shelf that is as comprehensive as this one in terms of dealing with the issues of modern-day military chaplaincy.

We are excited about this project because it offers solid, practical advice on just about every issue a military chaplain might encounter in day-to-day ministry. Each page covers an important issue that every chaplain will face.

When I went into the chaplaincy at age 26, I had no idea what it meant to develop a strategy. In fact, for many ministers, developing a 52-week plan for preaching is about as deep as a strategy goes. However, in the military, it is important to successfully build a strategy early on and continue shaping it as you move through the ranks. This book will help you do that.

Who will benefit from reading this book? Who will it help? We think that list is long. First is the individual who is in seminary preparing to be a chaplain. Second, this book will benefit the junior chaplain who wants to continue growing professionally. Third, seasoned chaplains who may want to mentor those they supervise will find depth and continued guidance for themselves, too. Fourth, denominational leaders and endorsing agents will be better able to assist their chaplains. And fifth, ministerial professors at universities and seminaries will be better prepared to train their students who are called to serve as chaplains.

We also think the church will benefit. This is an excellent book for preparing pastors and ministers who want to live incarnationally in their communities, their parishes, and their congregations. Finally, this book will help chaplains stay centered in the church as well as their ministry in the military.

SECTION ONE

Background of Military Ministry

Chapter 1

Historical Perspective

Military and religion have been essential components of just about every civilization, on every continent, during every era. Almost just as pervasive is the fact that security forces have always allowed representatives of religion to access soldiers and facilitate their desire to worship, pray, or otherwise engage in religious rites.

The practitioners of religion have gone by various names, depending on the culture and the religion they represented. The terms include priest, monk, imam, pastor, chaplain, rabbi, and prayer leader. Often, they are civilian clergy who provide religious services for the people in uniform, but many nations have used religious professionals who are members of the military.

Ancient Rome sent religious personnel to battle fields and foreign lands with their soldiers. These "chaplains" tended to emotional and spiritual needs of the military and leaders within the government. Doris Bergen, in her book *The Sword of the Lord*, says "as *pontifex maximus*, or chief priest, the emperor had supreme responsibility for maintaining the *pax deorum* (peace of the gods) and ensuring that the gods who oversaw the welfare of the state continued to do so. This was particularly important with regard to the army, which was the most significant institution of the Roman state."[1]

Bergen goes on to say that from the eighth century through the crusades, men acting as chaplains heard confessions, assigned penance,

---

1. Bergen, *Sword of the Lord*, 29.

celebrated mass, led worship, and provided last rites on the battlefield. They were not yet referred to as "chaplains," however.

The background of the word "chaplain" provides an important lesson about caregiving. The word itself traces back to Bishop Martin of Tours. According to tradition, in the fourth century, while he was still a young soldier, Martin shared his cloak with a beggar. The cloak became a reminder of this simple act of compassion and kindness. Martin later became a bishop, and upon his death, his cloak (capella) was enshrined as a reminder of his compassion for a fellow human being.

Centuries later, Charlemagne appointed priests to care for his relics. One of the relics was believed to be St. Martin's cape, and the priests became known as the "cappellani," or "keepers of the cape." The cape and other relics were housed in a small room connected to a cathedral, and the room itself was termed the "capella" or "place of the cape." This came into English as "chapel." Gradually, the term "chapel" came to mean a small place for worship or prayer other than the main church, and a priest who served in a chapel was called a "chapelain" in French, which is the immediate source of the English word "chaplain."

Today in America, a clergy who ministers in any context outside a traditional congregation may be called a chaplain. There are chaplains serving in hospitals, prisons, factories, and corporations. Police and fire departments may have chaplains. There are chaplains ministering to truckers and motorcyclists. Others may be found at rodeos, fishing tournaments, campgrounds, and many other places where people gather. Similarly, someone who provides religious ministry for military personnel is typically called a chaplain, regardless of the faith group he or she represents. Interestingly, many service personnel call their chaplain "Padre," which is the Spanish word for "Father," and comes from the Catholic tradition.

In much of the Middle East, the dominant religion is Islam, so the chaplains are Muslim imams. Many Asian nations are Buddhist, so the majority of their religious leaders are Buddhist monks or priests. Many European nations are Lutheran or Catholic, and their chaplains reflect this. Israeli chaplains are Jewish rabbis, and most British military clergy are Anglican priests.

The military chaplaincy in the United States has long consisted of predominantly Christian clergy from a variety of denominations. But because the nation has diversified, so has its chaplain corps. Today, America is comprised of every people group and religion; therefore, there's a

Historical Perspective

conscious effort to meet the spiritual needs of those in the military regardless of their faith background.

There were chaplains who ministered during the skirmishes with the French and Native Americans before America became a nation. During the Revolutionary War, chaplains were known to be aboard naval ships as well as with many militia units. Often, the chaplain was a local pastor who went with the men from his community. At first, each colony determined how they would provide chaplains, but by the end of the war, the process was becoming systematized, including how much the chaplains would be paid.

By 1818, there was a chaplain at the Military Academy at West Point, and by 1838, Congress passed a law that Army posts should have a chaplain. During the Civil War, there were regimental chaplains and hospital chaplains. In addition, thousands of civilian volunteer ministers followed the troops and ministered as the war and circumstances allowed.

At the beginning of WWI, the Army had seventy-four chaplains, with another seventy-two in the National Guard. During the war, however, the Army added more than twenty-three hundred chaplains.[2] At the end of WWI, the government realized the importance of having military chaplains, started building post chapels, and further established the rank and pay structure. The Navy Chaplain Corps developed during the same time frame.

In 1917 Congress passed a law allowing clergy from religious minority groups to serve as military chaplains. That same year the Navy established the office of Chief of Chaplains. The Army followed suit in 1920, and the Air Force in 1949.

During WWII, there were 8,141 chaplains who served with the Army and 2,981 who saw action with the Navy.[3] Many of these military ministers were cited for their bravery and outstanding service. One example of this took place in February of 1943.

The USS Dorchester was on its way to Greenland with more than nine hundred men on board. Captain Hans Danielsen, aware of German U-boats in the area, had ordered the men to stay ready and keep their life jackets on, but many of the men disobeyed the order because the life jackets were uncomfortable and impossible to sleep in.[4]

---

2. *Military Chaplaincy*, 7.

3. *Military Chaplaincy*, 8.

4. Linzey, "When the Ship Sinks," *CBN*, https://www1.cbn.com/devotions/when-the-ship-sinks.

Four Army chaplains were on the ship: a Methodist minister, a Jewish rabbi, a Catholic priest, and a Reformed pastor. All four had been Boy Scouts. All four were brand new lieutenants in the Army. All four were ready to serve their soldiers, their country, and their God. All four were prepared to give their lives if necessary. The four chaplains are often referred to as the Immortal Chaplains of the Dorchester, and symbolize the ethos of sacrifice in the military chaplains corps.

When a torpedo hit the ship, the lights went out. A lot of people died instantly; more died in the water. Others were injured. Men who were trapped below began to panic, looking for their life jacket, trying to find a way to the top deck so they could abandon ship.

As soon as the chaos began, the four chaplains sprang into action. They encouraged the frightened young men, guided soldiers towards the upper deck and the lifeboats, and helped them find life jackets. When there were no more life preservers to be found, they took off their own and gave them away in order to save the lives of a few more men, knowing that it certainly meant they themselves would die.

Two hundred and thirty men made it into the rescue boats that night. As they looked back at the sinking ship, they saw the four chaplains standing on deck, arms linked, praying and singing in Hebrew, Latin, and English.

There are many such stories of bravery, service, sacrifice, and ministry among military chaplains in every time period and every military conflict. Though it is true that not every chaplain was a person of bravery and integrity, the vast majority have been people who were faithful, honorable, and dedicated to serving God and their troops.

Since July 1949, the three Chiefs of Chaplains serve together to form the Armed Forces Chaplains Board. In addition to providing leadership for their own chaplains, as a Board they advise the Secretary of Defense and the Under Secretary of Defense for Personnel and Readiness on religious, ethical, and moral issues. They speak to issues and policies affecting ministry, morale, and leadership in the Armed Forces.

Today, U.S. military chaplains represent over two hundred faith group endorsers. We have Jews, Muslims, Buddhists, and Christians from almost every denomination. These chaplains manage to work together to provide moral and ethical guidance to the command, minister to military personnel and their families, and fulfill the duties of their calling.

We've come a long way, and there have been many challenges as the climate has evolved and changed in the military and American culture in general. Our task is to understand our past, navigate our present realities, and discern with wisdom how to prepare for the future of ministry in the military.

Chapter 2

Constitutional Basis

Throughout most of the twentieth century, understanding the United States Constitution and how it affected the work of chaplains didn't seem all that important. Today, however, it is imperative for every chaplain in the Armed Services to fully understand the Constitution, the Establishment Clause, and the Free Exercise Clause because there is so much at stake.

The Establishment Clause prohibits the government from creating an official state religion. Although the precise definition of "establishment" is unclear, historically it referred to government-sponsored churches or religions, such as the Church of England, or any of the other officially recognized national religions throughout the world.

Whittington and Davidson, in their book *Matters of Conscience*, explain that "the Founders believed the government should not be entangled in the affairs of the church, but their initial intent was to protect the church, not the state."[1] The Establishment Clause created a barrier of protection between religious groups and the government. The Free Exercise Clause, on the other hand, extended religious protection to individuals, giving them the right to practice the religion of their choice without fear of punishment or negative consequences.

As part of the Bill of Rights, the First amendment of the Constitution was ratified in 1791. "Congress shall make no law respecting an establishment of religion or prohibiting the free exercise thereof, or abridging the freedom of speech or of the press, or the right of the people peaceably

---

1. Whittington, *Matters of Conscience*, 45.

to assemble and to petition the government for a redress of grievances." While the freedoms of speech, assembly, and redress are important, our concern in this book focuses on the two sides of the religious issue: Free Exercise of Religion and Non-Establishment of Religion, because these are the bases of religious freedoms and limitations in American society and in the military.

> *Congress shall make no law respecting an establishment of religion or prohibiting the free exercise thereof.*

What do these statements in the Bill of Rights say about religion, separation of church and state, and freedom? And why are they relevant to the military, and specifically the chaplaincy? These questions need to be discussed adequately because although the Constitution deals with religious freedoms for all citizens, it doesn't specify or authorize a military chaplaincy. Our government and military leaders have decided that having military chaplains is the best way for the constitutional rights and privileges of military personnel to be guaranteed, implemented, and supervised. In essence, citizens of the United States don't lose their constitutional rights when they enlist or become an officer in the military.

What constitutes an "establishment of religion" is typically judged by the three-part test set forth by the U.S. Supreme Court in Lemon v. Kurtzman, 403 U.S. 602 (1971). Under *the Lemon test*, the government can assist religion only if (1) the primary purpose of the assistance is secular, (2) the assistance must neither promote nor inhibit religion, and (3) there is no excessive entanglement between church and state.

The Free Exercise Clause protects citizens' right to practice their religion as they please, so long as the practice doesn't run afoul of "public morals" or a "compelling governmental interest." For instance, in Prince v. Massachusetts, 321 U.S. 158 (1944), the Supreme Court held that a state could force the inoculation of children whose parents opposed such action for religious reasons. The Court maintained that the state had an overriding interest in protecting public health and safety.

In 2013, The Family Research Council (FRC) released its first publication concerning religious liberty in the military. It was entitled, "A Clear and Present Danger: The Threat to Religious Liberty in the Military."[2] The FRC has updated this list annually since its inception. Over the last several years, the number of legal and constitutional issues involving religious liberty and military chaplains has risen at an alarming rate. These

---

2. Tony Perkins, www.frc.org/clearpresentdanger.

issues include discrimination in the selection of chaplains, promotions, and other legal and constitutional matters.

These issues might seem benign, but in the late 1990s the Navy Chaplain Corps was accused of discriminating on the basis of religion because it seemed that quite a few conservative Protestant chaplains were not selected for promotion when less-deserving "high church" chaplains were promoted. In 1997, five "low church" chaplains filed a class action lawsuit against the Navy. The court battle lasted more than twenty years. Then, in 2019, this same group of Chaplains refiled their case in the Norfolk, VA Federal Court, except by this time, twenty-seven chaplains signed on to the class action lawsuit. The litigants claim they were discriminated against because of religion.

Sometimes the Establishment Clause and the Free Exercise Clause come into conflict. At other times, the Establishment Clause and the Free Exercise Clause seem to be so tightly woven together that they can't be figured out. When either of these issues happens, the federal courts are called on to help to resolve the conflict, with the Supreme Court being the ultimate arbiter. There are several past court cases that help the government work out the issues.

One such case was Abington School District v. Schempp (1963). In an article in *The First Amendment Encyclopedia*, Emilie S. Kraft quotes Justice William J. Brennan Jr., who wrote, "State and federal courts have recognized, however, that the chaplaincy is one area in which the free exercise rights of affected prisoners and military personnel outweigh any potential establishment clause violation."[3]

Kraft also cites the conclusion of the case, which says, "Since government has deprived such persons of the opportunity to practice their faith at places of their choice . . . government may, in order to avoid infringing the free exercise guarantees, provide substitutes where it requires such persons to be."[4] She then adds the comment from Justice Brennan that not to provide chaplains "would signal hostility toward religion rather than neutrality."

Another case is Marsh vs Chambers in 1983, where the Supreme Court upheld the constitutionality of Nebraska's state chaplaincy in its legislature. The decision, in part, was based on the long-standing history of the military chaplaincy.

---

3. Kraft, *First Amendment Encyclopedia*, para. 2.
4. Kraft, *First Amendment Encyclopedia*, para. 3.

A third case was Katcoff v. Marsh (2d Cir. 1985), which concluded that the military chaplaincy doesn't violate the establishment clause.

There have been many challenges to having chaplains in the military and there will be more, but each case inevitably comes back to the Constitution's Establishment Clause and Free Exercise Clause. In a nation where people of many faiths live side-by-side, the First Amendment's free exercise clause protects individuals from government interference in the practice and expression of their faith. The government cannot target laws at specific religious practices or place undue burdens on its citizens who want to worship.

Constitutional authority travels in a direct chain of command from the Constitution, to the President, to the Secretary of Defense, to the Pentagon, to the Branches of Service, on down to the unit Commanders. The chaplain is the commander's personal staff officer who is delegated the task of implementing and supervising the constitutional religious freedoms, restrictions, and opportunities. In essence, the religious program in the military belongs to the commander, and the chaplain works for the commander to make sure it is done properly and legally. That's why every chaplain must understand the constitutional issues.

An important consideration to keep in mind here is that it's the government that is specifically limited by the constitutional amendment. Because religious freedom is an important part of our national values, the government isn't allowed to restrict those rights or to infringe on the individual's free exercise of religion. Nor can the government impose religion onto the individual. This is particularly relevant to commanders and chaplains in the military.

The commander has legal and constitutional authority; the chaplain is the subject matter expert who provides ministry for those of his or her faith group, facilitates meeting the religious needs for those of other faith groups, and ensures that all personnel have the opportunity to practice their constitutional freedoms. And because of the Establishment Clause, the chaplain also makes sure nobody is coerced or forced to worship, and that nobody is subjected to presentations of religion against his or her will.

It's important to note that the Constitution is the authority that gives chaplains the right to express their faith in a secular and pluralistic environment. But it also provides limitations that chaplains must respect. Otherwise, it is possible for chaplains to find themselves literally caught between the Establishment Clause and the Free Exercise Clause.

The Establishment Clause was written into the constitution to protect churches from government, and also to protect individuals from religion, because freedom to worship also includes freedom not to worship.

Christians have freedoms, yet so does everyone else in the Armed Forces, and those freedoms are guaranteed. Chaplains have a crucial role in how religious rights play out in the military, and we need to know our role.

CHAPTER 3

Legal Grounds

BEFORE HE BECAME OUR first president, General George Washington was keenly aware of our need for military chaplains.[1] He understood that chaplains, through their life, influence, and preaching, could help his men morally and ethically. He knew the impact chaplains would make by instilling courage and discipline. And he wanted chaplains to counsel the soldiers, visit them when they were sick or wounded, honor the dead, and write letters home for those who could not write.

Apparently, the Founding Fathers didn't question whether a military chaplaincy was needed. It seems they merely adopted the British practice without debate. On July 29, 1775, the Continental Congress authorized a chaplaincy for the Continental Army and decided that the chaplains would be paid. In 1777, Congress authorized a chaplain for each Army brigade. By 1791, the First Amendment of the U.S. Constitution was ratified, guaranteeing free speech and freedom of religion for every citizen, including people serving in our military.

These early actions by the United States Congress in the late 1700s served as the legal foundation and paved the way for further refinements as we shaped the military chaplaincies. When he was a congressman, James Monroe had voted in favor of a military chaplaincy on several occasions. Then as president, in 1814, he signed the explicit authorization for military chaplains. In 1818, a chaplain was authorized for the U.S. Military Academy at West Point. Then in 1838, congress passed more sweeping legislation providing military chaplains at frontier forts,

---

1. Randy Murray, Fort Stewart Public Affairs.

military hospitals, and other military schools. Also included were chaplains for the Navy and for Congress itself. By that point, the legal grounds for a military chaplaincy were firmly in place, and they endure to this day.

Congress in 1861 directed military commanders to weed out undesirable or unqualified chaplains because not everyone serving as a chaplain was qualified or was behaving properly. We'll discuss these problems in later chapters.

It wasn't until 1917 that Congress authorized religious minority faith groups to send their clergy into the military. Previously, all military chaplains were Christians, the vast majority being Protestant. This new legislation, however, allowed Jewish rabbis to serve as military chaplains, and eventually let representatives of other minority religious groups serve as well, such as Buddhists and Muslims.

Following WWII, the Geneva Convention established the Law of Armed Conflict, which designated chaplains as noncombatants who are not allowed to fight, and who should be protected during battle. The United States was one of the first to sign the agreement to the Geneva Convention guidelines.

By 1956, Title 10 of the United States Code had been approved. This important legislation significantly expands and identifies the roles and functions of military chaplains. Because of the scope of this legislation, anyone interested in the military chaplaincy should read it thoroughly. What follows here is an abbreviated list. According to Title 10, the military will fund and maintain a military chaplain corps and retain chaplains with these stipulations:

1. Preach in weekly divine services and public worship according to the manner and forms of the church of which the chaplain is a member.

2. Honor and bury the dead according to military protocol.

3. Chaplains are military officers, having rank and pay, but without command authority.

4. Commanders will furnish facilities, funds, and transportation for the chaplains, as well as for chaplain-led programs in support of members of the armed forces and their families.

5. Chaplains serve in the Army, Navy, Air Force, Reserve Components, and Civil Air Patrol.

6. Chaplains may be separated from service for loss of professional qualifications, substandard performance, or other reasons.
7. The Service Academies will have chaplains.
8. The Army, Navy, and Air Force will each have a Chief of Chaplains.
9. Chaplains may retire after qualifying service.
10. Chaplains may participate in education loan repayment programs.
11. Chaplains may not be required to perform any rite or ritual that is contrary to his or her conscience, moral principles, or religious beliefs.
12. Chaplains will be protected from discrimination or adverse personnel action on the basis of their refusal to comply with requirements that violate their conscience, moral principles, or religious beliefs.
13. Chaplains must be endorsed by a recognized faith group approved by DOD.
14. Chaplains are considered to be first responders in emergency situations, along with firefighters, medical personnel, law enforcement, criminal investigators, and judge advocates.
15. Chaplains will be trained to respond to domestic violence situations.

We also need to be aware of Title 14, which covers the United States Coast Guard, and Title 32, which covers the National Guard. In addition to the Constitution, Bill of Rights, Geneva Convention, and various laws passed by Congress, there have been some significant policies, instructions, manuals, pamphlets, memos, and regulations prepared by the Department of Defense and the various military departments that shed light on the role, function, and tasks of military chaplains. We will refer to many of these in subsequent chapters as they relate to the topics under discussion, and you may see a list of many of the DOD documents at the end of this book. However, it would be appropriate here to cite one official memo in particular.

In September 2011, General Norton A. Schwartz, Chief of Staff for the Department of the Air Force, sent a memo to every major Air Force command. The subject of the correspondence was "Maintaining Government Neutrality Regarding Religion." The gist of the memo was that senior officers and commanders should not be the ones to promote religious programs and events. They must maintain an official neutrality. Instead, the chaplains and chaplain staff are the appropriate persons to inform and notify airmen regarding religious programs. Here's part of what the general wrote in that memo.

> Chaplain Corps programs, including activities such as religious studies, faith sharing, and prayer meetings, are vital to commanders' support of individual airmen's needs and provide opportunities for the free exercise of religion. Although commanders are responsible for these programs, they must refrain from appearing to officially endorse religion generally or any particular religion. Therefore, I expect chaplains, not commanders, to notify airmen of Chaplain Corps programs. Our chaplains are trained to provide advice to leadership on matters related to the free exercise of religion and help commanders care for all of their people, regardless of their beliefs.[2]

While this particular memo is from the Air Force Chief of Staff to his downtrace commanders, the essence is equally applicable in the Navy, Marines, Army, and Coast Guard. Commanders are responsible for every program in their command or unit, but they are obligated to remain neutral when it comes to religion. Yes, commanders may be people of faith, but chaplains are assigned the task of implementing the religious program and are responsible to promote it.

Therefore, chaplains have to know the law. They've got to understand current policy, and must build a good working relationship with the commander and command staff, as well as with officers, enlisteds, and NCOs. All commanders are well trained and knowledgeable when it comes to issues related to religion. However, some of them are "antireligion," while some go overboard promoting religion. Others don't care at all about religion, and want to take funds earmarked for religious programs and use the money for other priorities. Therefore, chaplains have to be well informed and strong enough to tell commanders what is right or wrong when it comes to implementing their religious programs.

If we do our homework and maintain proper relationships, we will have an open door for an incredible ministry, and have an opportunity to impact countless lives on behalf of the kingdom of God. How exciting it would be for the Lord to say to military chaplains, "I have placed before you an open door that no one can shut."

2. Schwartz, "Maintaining Government Neutrality."

Chapter 4

Biblical Foundation

Some people, wanting to establish a biblical foundation for military chaplaincy, have tried doing a word search of the scripture. However, they won't find the word *chaplain*. It isn't there. Since that's the case, where do we start? Some proponents of making a biblical case for the chaplaincy begin in the Old Testament.

For example, Exodus 17 tells the story of the Israelite Army engaged in battle with the Amalekites. According to the narrative, as long as Moses held his hands up, Joshua and the Israelites prevailed. However, when Moses grew tired and lowered his hands, the Amalekites started winning the fight. Aaron and Hur saw what was happening, arranged a stone for Moses to sit on, and held his hands up until the battle was over. This guaranteed a victory over the enemy.

In Joshua 6, a messenger of the Lord directed Joshua to place seven priests in front of the Ark of the Covenant, carrying trumpets while circling the walled city of Jericho. Armed soldiers led in front, and a rear guard followed the priestly procession. At the appropriate time on the appointed day, Joshua gave the command, the priests blew the horns, the walls came crumbling down, and the soldiers rushed in to conquer the used-to-be-fortified city.

The book of Joshua also tells stories about Gideon, Caleb, Jephtha, Samson, Deborah, Othniel, Ehud, and others who led the fight and won the victory for the people of God. In fact, the pattern that played out over again went like this: (1) The people of God turned their backs on God. (2) God sent judgment, usually in the form of a foreign oppressor. (3) The people repented. (4) God sent a deliverer who led Israel to victory and ended the oppression. (5) God's people lived in obedience to the Lord. After a generation or so, the pattern repeated.

The situation was similar after the Lord gave Israel a king. When the king and the nation were faithful to the Lord, they prospered and enjoyed peace. When they fell into sin and worshipped the gods of the peoples around them, the Lord punished them. This cycle, of course, culminated in the Babylonian exile and eventual return to the Promised Land, with a new emphasis on the prophetic message about the coming of the Anointed One, the Messiah, who would bring permanent, eternal deliverance and salvation.

It's tempting to see these Old Testament examples of priests, prayer, and piety as a guarantee for victory in battle and apply them to our nation and our military today, thereby proving the need for a good strong chaplaincy program. However, the scriptures are not meant to be used that way.

First, the people of God in the Old Testament were a theocracy. Their nation, their identity, and their religion were inseparable. They were the chosen people to whom God had determined to reveal himself, and through them, to communicate his plan of redemption for all people.

Second, those stories should be applied today with a spiritual meaning. The Lord wants his people to win battles in the spiritual realm. We are to overcome sin and temptation. We need deliverance from the forces of darkness. Life is hard and we face struggle after struggle, but the Lord will help when we turn to him. There are many ways to understand and apply the lessons in those stories as we follow Christ and as we disciple others.

Third, America is not a theocracy, and Americans are not the chosen people. The promises and prophecies about Israel don't automatically apply to North America any more than they apply to any other part of the word today.

It is true, on the other hand, that every nation will reap what it sows, and every people group that practices godliness, holiness, justice, and mercy will be blessed by the Lord. Therefore, we need to be faithful to God, and do what we can to share the good news with as many as we can. We have to make sure we are a people of compassion who care for the poor and the oppressed, and who love all people equally. It is crucial that we consistently represent Christ. But we need to look elsewhere for a biblical foundation for a modern chaplaincy, not the Old Testament stories where God granted victory to Israel over its enemies.

In 1 Timothy 3:1–7 and Titus 1:5–9, we discover Paul's teaching about the qualifications for pastors and Christian leaders. These verses describe someone who is above reproach, maritally faithful, temperate, self-controlled, respectable, hospitable, able to teach, not an alcoholic, not violent but gentle, not quarrelsome, not greedy but generous. In addition, a Christian must manage his or her own family well, and live a life worthy of respect. A pastor or church leader must not be a recent convert, and must have a good reputation with outsiders. We suggest that these scriptures apply to military chaplains also.

Moreover, we would be wise to consider the scriptures that talk about the Great Commission, the Great Commandment, and the Great Call of God on one's life. But first, let's take a look at two stories in the New Testament involving a soldier.

Matthew 8 and Luke 7 tell about a Roman centurion who came to Jesus, even though Jesus was not in the Roman army and did not routinely go out of his way to minister to soldiers. This is an interesting scripture that we should consider. Jon Bloom, a staff writer for an organization called *Desiring God*, wrote that this soldier amazed Jesus with his faith. Bloom makes the following observation:

> Both Luke (Luke 7:9) and Matthew (Matthew 8:10) use the Greek word *thaumazo* (thou-mad-zo) which we translate "marveled" or "amazed" to describe Jesus's response to the centurion's faith. The only other time this word is used to describe Jesus's response to others' faith is in Mark 6:6, when he marvels at the lack of faith in the people of Nazareth, where he grew up.
>
> The centurion was one of the most unlikely persons to amaze Jesus. He was a Gentile. Doubtless he had a pagan upbringing. He was a Roman, stationed in Palestine to subject the Jews to the Emperor's rule. He was a man of war. He achieved the rank of centurion by distinguishing himself above others in the brutal Roman martial arts. Not exactly the résumé you'd expect for becoming one of the Bible's great heroes of faith.
>
> So, what in the world had happened to this man? We don't know. But there he is in Capernaum, a miracle of God's marvelous grace. And he's a firstfruit and a foreshadow of what Jesus had come to bring about. He was a living illustration that "many [would] come from the east and west and recline at table with Abraham, Isaac, and Jacob in the kingdom of heaven" (Matthew 8:11).[1]

---

1. Bloom, "Centurion," https://www.desiringgod.org/articles/the-centurion-faith-that-made-jesus-marvel.

Bloom calls this man a "firstfruit and a foreshadow of what Jesus had come to bring about." It may be that Jesus himself was the first in the New Testament to minister to people in the military, and the "firstfruit and foreshadow" refers to thousands of Soldiers, Sailors, Airmen, Marines, and Coast Guardsmen who will come to faith in Christ through the message of the gospel.

Peter also had an encounter with a centurion. Acts 10 presents Peter's vision about eating unclean food. In the dream, the Lord told him to stop calling something impure if the Lord himself declared it clean. Peter woke up and was thinking about the experience when Cornelius's representatives arrived. The Lord told Peter to go with the men, so he went to the home of the centurion and proclaimed the good news of Jesus Christ. Acts 10:44 says everyone who heard Peter's message received the Holy Spirit and became believers in Jesus.

In this account, the representative of Christ went to where the soldier was in order to minister to him. This is exactly what a chaplain does: after praying, going to where the people are, spending time with them, and paying attention to the leading of the Holy Spirit, who opens a door for sharing the message of the Savior.

The significance that Peter attributes to his experience, and that Luke attests to in writing the book of Acts, is that the Lord has opened the door for Gentiles to come into the kingdom of God. But there's another, more subtle significance that we can't afford to miss. In the same way that the church must no longer think of the gentiles as bad people who are outsiders, the church must not think about people who serve in the military as being unclean or bad. It's not an accident that the gentile who Peter visited was a military man.

Peter understood that from this point moving forward, Christians would accept, love, and serve all people, all demographics, and all ethnicities. Nobody is to be considered inferior, less valuable, or unworthy. The same is true for those serving in the military. They are people who need God, need to be loved and accepted, need someone to tell them about Jesus, need someone who'll be an example of Christian faith and lifestyle.

How does the modern-day military chaplain focus on the Great Commission? Faith group endorsers should spell this out from their theological and ecclesiastical perspective. But here is one way of looking at the issue.

In giving his disciples the Great Commission, Jesus tells them to "Go, therefore, and make disciples of all nations, baptizing them in the name of the Father and of the Son and of the Holy Spirit, teaching them to observe everything I have commanded you." Military chaplains have an opportunity to do this just about every day. They can speak about faith, hope, love, and the grace of God. They develop relationships and friendships with the people in the command, and let their light shine. Chaplains come from all backgrounds and all walks of life. This allows for a wide variety of methods and opportunities to teach, disciple, and represent the Lord.

Despite the fact that the military chaplaincy has a lot of detractors, chaplains have an opportunity to represent the hope of the Gospel to all kinds of people almost every single day. The chaplain in the twenty-first century needs to be able to filter through the minutia and the plethora of critics to remember why he or she is serving in this capacity. The Great Commission is a mission within the mission of being a chaplain.

At one point in Jesus's ministry, some Pharisees and Sadducees came to question him. As they planned and plotted, a person who was knowledgeable of the Mosaic law asked which was the greatest commandment. Jesus responded with what we call the Great Commandment: *love your neighbor as yourself.*

How does this Great Commandment work into the daily life and ministry of a chaplain? Loving our neighbor is the essence of what a military chaplain in the twenty-first century is all about. It's what we do. It's our driving force. Our Soldiers, Sailors, Marines, Guardians, and Airmen, regardless of their faith tradition or no faith tradition, are our neighbors. Despite their particular life choices and hang ups, they are our congregation, our mission field, and we love every one of them.

When one pastor was being interviewed for accessioning into the Navy Chaplain Corps, the committee asked how he felt about gays and others from the LGBTQ+ community serving in the Navy. His answer revealed a powerful understanding of the Bible and the message of Jesus. He told them, "As a chaplain, I am called to love all of my sailors and Marines, no matter who they are." He gave the right answer, and is now serving as an Active Duty Navy chaplain, loving every one of his sailors and Marines in the name of Christ.

Jesus didn't approve of the lifestyle of the sinners he had dinner with at the home of the tax collector in Mark 2, but he loved them and spent time with them. That's what a good chaplain does, and that's what a good Christian does. Just because we serve in the military doesn't mean we like everything the military does, nor do we have to agree with the lifestyle choices many of the personnel will make. But we are there to love them, serve them, and care for them regardless of who they are and what they represent. That's because of who we are and who we represent.

Another way the Great Commission may be fulfilled is that because of the nature of the military, chaplains travel all over the world. In most cases we are not allowed to hand out Bibles or other religious items to people from other nations. However, military chaplains might be asked to participate in humanitarian projects. As chaplains work alongside Marines, soldiers, or airmen to clean up after disasters, dig wells, or complete other tasks, they wear the cross. They may not always be able to speak words of faith directly, but they are often allowed to pray before events. At some level, this contributes to the fulfillment of the Great Commission.

The next chapter talks more about the specific call of God on the life of a chaplain. The individual call of God might be to function as a Servant, Missionary, Prophet, Provider of Love, Pastoral Care Giver, Evangelist, or one who is Present. However, in this chapter, we mention the call of God because it is part of the biblical foundation for the military chaplaincy.

Being a chaplain is much more than a nine-to-five job. It is a divine calling on the lives of men and women to serve in this ministry context. This means it's not for everybody, and nobody should apply without experiencing a specific call to be a military chaplain. It's too important, and too much is at stake. One of the ad slogans used by the military is, "The Marines are looking for a few good men." Similarly, we might say the Lord is looking for a few good chaplains.

The call of God will take you places you might not want to go, but you go anyway. In the past twenty years, chaplains have gone to the battlefields of Iraq, Afghanistan, and many other places around the world. Some have died. Many have been wounded, and are now wearing the nation's symbol of love and sacrifice, the Purple Heart, as witness to this calling.

As we will discuss in the next chapter, the will of God compels you to accept difficult challenges and hardships, but in every one of those situations, you will have an opportunity to bring glory and honor to the Lord Jesus Christ as you bring his hope into the lives of men and women in some pretty tough circumstances. Therefore, you have to be 100% certain that ministering in the military is God's will for you personally. If you're married, it is crucial that your spouse is just as sure, and in agreement.

We want to end this chapter with one final thought. The Psalmist David, in Psalm 61:2 wrote, *Lead me to a rock that is high above me.* As chaplains in the twenty-first century, that should be our prayer. We will face difficult days as we struggle with our identity, our biblical mandate, and our calling. We might find ourselves in desperate moments asking God to *Lead me to the rock that is higher*. When that happens to you, our hope is that you rise up with this certainty—there is no better foundation than that rock.

SECTION TWO

BECOMING A MILITARY CHAPLAIN

Chapter 5

Ministerial Calling

KEITH'S CALL TO MINISTRY AND CHAPLAINCY

When I was in college, God had already called me to pastoral ministry. I was going to be a preacher. I remember it like it was yesterday. While attending Carson-Newman University, I was walking around Jefferson City, TN, one night, when God spoke to me. He told me he wanted me to be a military chaplain. I weighed two hundred and forty-four pounds and had a forty-two-inch waist, but I told God I would do whatever he asked me to do. I also asked him if he would help me get in shape to do it. It was late April, and I was ready to go home for the summer, but during that summer of 1977, I dropped more than fifty pounds, and eight inches off the waist. I came back to school in the Fall and joined ROTC to better prepare myself for the military chaplaincy.

    Years later, while serving beside chaplains of many different faith groups, I learned that not every chaplain experienced a "call experience" from God. After I retired and was serving as the endorser for the Southern Baptist Convention, I was guest speaking about military chaplaincy at a seminary. Between sessions, a guy walked up to me and told me he became a military chaplain to please his mother. His call was obviously different than mine. My mother was happy that I became a chaplain, but that was not my reason or motivation. I became a chaplain because I heard God's voice say that was what he wanted me to do.

PAUL'S CALL TO MINISTRY AND CHAPLAINCY

When I was in high school, I experienced a definite call to ministry during a Sunday evening service at our church, so I attended a Christian college to prepare for ministry. My father was a Navy chaplain, and I assumed that's what the Lord wanted me to do, too.

One day, my fiancée and I were in the library, supposed to be studying, but doing a lot of talking instead, and she asked, "So what are you doing after college?"

"I'm going to seminary so I can be a Navy chaplain."

She replied with two words that would change my life direction... "Not me."

Instantly, I had a problem. Either I misunderstood what God wanted me to do for a ministerial career, or I was wrong about wanting to marry Linda Smith, because there has to be unity in the marriage when someone wants to go into ministry. We got married a year later, and after graduation, I stayed involved in civilian church ministry, but deep down inside, I still felt the Lord wanted me to be a Navy chaplain.

Ten years later, I was praying on a Thursday. "Lord, if you want me to be a chaplain, I need two things. I need my wife to be in agreement, without me trying to persuade her. And I need $15,000 to finish seminary." I didn't mention this prayer to anyone else.

One week later during dinner, out of the clear blue, Linda said, "If you still want to be a chaplain, I'm OK with that, but part time, as a Reservist." I was so stunned that I literally dropped my fork. But that was only half the answer to my prayer.

Another week went by, and, again on a Thursday, after dinner I was cleaning up the kitchen when the phone rang. It was my mother. "Honey, if you had the money, would you finish seminary and become a chaplain?"

Had she called before my wife changed her mind, I would have said no. But since Linda had already said she was OK with my being in the Reserve, I said, "Yes, Mom. I would."

"Well, I'll see what I can do."

A couple weeks later, and at the start of every term for the next two years, Mom sent a check to cover expenses for that quarter. It was pretty clear to me that the Lord had given a green light for me to become a chaplain, so I applied, was approved, and was sworn in as a Naval Reserve chaplain.

Two weeks after the swearing in, I was at my church, preparing for Sunday worship services, when a kids' Sunday school song started going through my head, and I actually sang out loud as I walked down the hall, "I'm in the Lord's army. I'm in the Lord's army."

This was followed by a distinct impression that the Lord was speaking to me, "I want you in the Army, not the Navy." I went back my office, sat in the chair behind my desk and began to argue with God. "Sorry, Lord. I'm already in the Navy. You're wrong." Again, it seemed the Lord was telling me that he wanted me in the Army, so I looked up toward the heavens and said, "Lord, It's too late, I'm already in the Navy."

Have you ever argued with God? Something strange was happening, and it felt weird.

Just then the phone rang, and the voice on the other end of the line said, "This is Commander so-and-so from the Pentagon. DOD just changed the Navy's budget, and I'm calling to tell you that you can't come into the Naval Reserve this year. But, the Chief of Chaplains convened a special board and approved you for Active Duty in the Regular Navy."

"But my wife doesn't want to go Active Duty."

"Then wait til next year to come into the Reserve. Your authorization will still be good."

"But next year I'll be past the Navy's age limit. I'll be too old."

"Then call the Army. They have a higher age limit." And he hung up.

I was in shock. My dream of being a Navy chaplain was dead.

However, God was leading, and I was glad that the Holy Spirit had spoken to me before the call came from the Pentagon, because it was now clear that God wanted me in the Army instead of the Navy. Previously, I had no desire to be in the Army. But the call of God changes situations, and changes people.

In fact, the call of God is one of the most important points in your thinking about becoming a military chaplain, and this call has professional, personal, and spiritual dimensions.

The *professional side* of the call has a lot to do with how the military looks at you and your work as a chaplain. When a minister goes to an accessioning board to apply for a billet for Active Duty, Reserve, or National Guard for the Army, Air Force, or Navy, one of the topics each candidate will have to respond to is "Tell us about your call." This may be asked verbally or in writing. Either way, an applicant should be able to communicate a definite experience when the Lord called him or her to become a military chaplain. At the least, you should be prepared to explain convincingly why you decided to be a chaplain and why that particular branch of the Armed Forces.

There is also a *personal side* to the call to military ministry. Fulfilling the call of God on your life isn't easy. There will be tough days. There may be times you feel like quitting or throwing in the towel. You have to do physical training when you'd rather be relaxing with your family or spending time with friends.

Somewhere along the way you will have a commander who doesn't like chaplains. You might even have a Supervisory Chaplain who doesn't like you because of your church, your theology, or your endorser. There might be personality conflicts or any number of reasons for being disliked or persecuted. You might even have some dark situations in ministry that will cause you to think, "Is this really what I want to do?" It might be the tragic death of someone in your unit, or a mass casualty that stretches you beyond your ability to minister, or even a transfer to a place where you really don't want to be.

Several years ago, Keith was invited to speak at a seminary on what the church expects of its military chaplains. After an hour or so, he concluded the presentation and asked if there were any questions. One person asked what his toughest day of ministry was as a military chaplain. There were a lot of stories he could have told because there were quite a few difficult days. But his mind reflected back to his first duty assignment.

KEITH'S STORY:

Fort Bragg had a policy that ninety days after arriving on post, chaplains were required to be put on the after-hours duty rotation. When my turn came up, I was handed the logbook and beeper. I didn't have any specific reason or experience to base it on, but I just expected the night to be long. I had absolutely no idea it was going to be as hard as it turned out.

I got home about 1630 (4:30 p.m. for non-military folks). I planned to eat an early dinner, and then anxiously wait for the beeper to go off. Well, no sooner had I walked in the door than the beeper sounded the alarm. I called the staff duty NCO, and he told me I needed to go to Womack Hospital. I jumped in my car, prayed on the way, and got there fairly quickly because I was traveling opposite the heavy traffic.

When I walked into the Emergency Room, the nurse told me there was a young couple in the room whose baby had died, and the medical staff needed my help getting the mother to give the baby to them. *What?* So, I walked into the room, shut the door, and encountered a sobbing young woman, holding a lifeless little baby in her arms. It took several hours, but I was finally able to get her to give her baby to the nurse. We cried together, and I reassured the young couple many times. After what seemed like forever, I went home about 1:00 in the morning.

As I walked into the house, I looked in on my own daughter, asleep in her crib, and about the same age as the baby who died. I went into her room, knelt beside the bed, thanked God for her, and cried for a long, long time. Before this night, I couldn't even imagine what it felt like to lose a child. Now, it tore me up just thinking about it.

I finally got to sleep around 2:00 in the morning, but about an hour later, the beeper went off again. I needed to go back to the hospital. As I walked in, the nurse told me, "Chaplain, we have a lady who miscarried, and she wants to speak with you."

In all honesty, I felt drained with nothing more to give. But I stood there with that young lady, wept with her, then prayed with her. It seemed like I was running on empty.

That night and the next day, I wondered what I had gotten myself into. I didn't think about quitting or walking away, but I could have. Instead, I reflected back on that night in Jefferson City, TN when God called me to be a Chaplain. I remembered the moon that night as I heard God's voice telling me what he wanted me to do. I had no doubt that God called me to this ministry, and that he would provide the stamina to continue.

There is also a *spiritual side* to the call. In 1994, Christian musician Steven Curtis Chapman wrote a song titled "Burn the Ships."[1] The song tells the legendary story of Hernán Cortés, the Spanish conquistador who sailed from Spain with a fleet of ships to conquer the Aztecs in Mexico. After arriving, some of the men were homesick, fed up with being away from family and the life they knew, and threatened to return to Spain. Cortés responded by ordering the ships to be destroyed so his men had no way to leave. The lyrics include the devotional application that when we make a decision to follow Christ, there's no going back. In essence, sometimes we have to "burn the ships" in order to remain faithful to the Lord and his call on our lives.

The point is this: if you obey the call of God to minister as a military chaplain, the Lord will strengthen you. God called you to the work, God

---

1. Elliott and Chapman, "Burn the Ships."

will prepare you for the work, and God will sustain you in the work. You have to believe this.

As you can see in both Keith's and Paul's "call experiences," a specific divine call will change the direction of your life. It will motivate you and lead to new behaviors and habits. It will give you the strength, stamina, and tenacity that you're going to need if you're to run the race and finish the course. And just as important, the call will come with a divine anointing, and the promise that the lord will be with you every step of the way.

The call of God, therefore, is undoubtedly one of the most important points in thinking about becoming a military chaplain, and this call includes the professional, personal, and spiritual dimensions of your life. If you aren't sure, then take more time to pray and seek God until he confirms his call for your life's work. There must be no doubt. There's no room for wondering whether this is where you are called to serve. You don't have the luxury to guess or assume. You have to be certain.

Guest Anecdote Number One

Conflict on the Way to Answering the Call

The day I graduated from seminary was especially sweet. My Master of Divinity program was a decade-long process that included numerous jobs and moves, while raising an energetic only-child. I was the only U.S. Army chaplain candidate in my graduating class because, due to their pacifist beliefs, the seminary didn't attract many students who were called to military ministry. In fact, there was only one other chaplain candidate in the history of the seminary.

Family and friends from near and far gathered with joyful enthusiasm for the long-awaited commencement service. After a shared party with a classmate and a missionary friend who was headed back to Ireland, my husband, son and I headed home after the celebration. But my husband seemed depressed. I suggested to him that he was probably still grieving the recent, unexpected death of his brother.

His response was embroiled in a deep anger. "You may have just graduated from seminary, but you are not my therapist!"

From that moment on, he shut me out emotionally for months. Nothing could have prepared me for his harsh and heartbreaking response. After all, it was only hours earlier that he spontaneously shouted "Hoooooaaaah!" as he stood alone during the commencement service when my name was called.

He had been angry many times over our nearly fifteen years of marriage, but this seemed different, and it felt even more difficult in light of what I thought was a shared victory. This incident occurred a few weeks before I was to leave for a much-anticipated chaplain candidate training at the Presidio of Monterey in central California. My husband was mostly silent about my plans, and I wondered how I could proceed in good conscience with the scheduled training, since our marriage was not doing well. I sought godly counsel from a wise woman at my church who spoke to me about the importance of sustained obedience to following God's call. She encouraged me to continue stepping out in faith as I had been doing for nearly two decades while pursuing the Army chaplaincy. She prayed with me that my husband would continue to agree with me in this pursuit.

It was a long summer. The time apart, while awaiting my ordination and denominational endorsement, allowed me to grow personally and professionally. When my husband came to visit for a long weekend, he noticed I had grown in self-confidence. He also noticed in me an ability to be appropriately playful while showing him around my new military community. I believe that particular combination of spiritual resiliency was attractive to him, and helped soften his heart. Later he mentioned he had missed seeing me that way. In addition, knowing that he had missed me helped us to rejoin the path to answering the call together.

CH (MAJ) Lisa Northway, U.S. Army

Chapter 6

Family and Emotional Readiness

KEITH'S STORY:

My wife and I had dinner with a young couple just before the husband became a chaplain. We talked about what the coming days would be like for them as a chaplain, a military spouse, and a family. When we mentioned that deployments are a normal part of being in the military, even for chaplains, and what separations might mean for the family, the young wife leaned back in her chair and said, "I'm not sure I am ready for this!" Her words and facial expressions indicated there were serious red flags. After further conversation, however, she had a better feel for what was going to take place, and a more realistic expectation of what she was getting into.

This is just one example of how important it is for the family to share a sense of divine calling to the military chaplaincy. It also points out the need to be fully prepared emotionally and spiritually for what this new life is going to be like.

KEITH'S BACKGROUND:

I grew up in a military family. My dad was a career naval officer who entered the Navy in 1940. He and my mom married after WWII, and he didn't retire until 1970. He was a sailor for over thirty years.

It was tough on our family because Dad was often at sea. My parents were married in the old days of the military when the thought was "if the military wanted you to have a wife and family, they would have issued you one." There was very little care for the family, and almost zero attention to Family Readiness. However, there was a lot of "adapting and overcoming" as a family. The long deployments were not easy.

There were many birthdays, Christmases, Easters, and other family celebrations when my dad was gone. I also remember the two-year period when he chose to be a geographical bachelor because he didn't want to move our family to New York City. Instead, he was away during the week, and came home on weekends. Because of my personal experience as a child, I never recommend being a "geo bachelor." The military will separate the family often enough; there is no reason for you to choose separation. As a military chaplain endorser, I saw many chaplains do this. In my opinion, rarely is it the right thing to do.

PAUL'S BACKGROUND:

My dad was a Navy chaplain. We moved so often that by the time I graduated from high school, I had attended eleven different schools. To this day, I can develop friendships quickly, but I have a tendency to be superficial in relationships, and have a tough time maintaining long-term friendships.

When I had an opportunity to go Active Duty as an Army Chaplain, my two older sons told me, "Don't do it, Dad. You'll ruin our lives." So, I didn't. I remained in the church I was pastoring at the time, and stayed in a Reserve unit. After they left home to go to college, I had one more chance to request active service. When I asked my youngest son, his response was, "Anywhere you wanna go, Dad, I'm with you." The difference in the two attitudes was huge for us, because we strongly believe in unity in the marriage and in the family. When I finally got orders, we moved to a different state. Our son finished high school, and we moved again.

I like moving around, and after a couple years in one place, start to get the itch to move again and start fresh. My wife, on the other hand, prefers to stay in one place long-term, and she misses having deep friendships that can only develop with time. But she understands and agrees that this was God's calling on our lives for a season.

For my wife, perhaps more difficult than moving around, was when her son and then her husband deployed during the war in Iraq. I asked her after I returned from being overseas, "Which was worse? Knowing your son could have been killed? Or your husband?" Without hesitation, she answered, "It was worse knowing my son might be hurt or killed."

Readiness is a key word for the military, nowadays. It includes training that prepares you for whatever is to come. The military also uses the term *Family Readiness*. This training helps the family prepare for the impending weeks or months of deployment and separation.

An important part of *Readiness Training* is the phrase *Adapting and Overcoming*. As a chaplain family, there will be times you are forced to adapt and overcome. Like everyone else in the military, chaplains may experience back-to-back deployments. Some go to a new unit because they were told to "take a knee," only to find out the new unit had deployment orders, and they have to leave their spouse and kids again. One young chaplain told me that in a five-year span, he was away from home for three years.

KEITH'S EXPERIENCE:

I knew that the first step towards Readiness was getting my own family ready for military service. I had to make sure my wife shared my call not only to ministry, but to military chaplaincy. I believe God prepared both of our hearts for serving him in the Army.

I learned from our experience in the military and as a chaplain endorser that being ready helped keep our emotions in check. Were there tough times? Yes! Did I miss birthdays, anniversaries, holidays, and other special days? A *lot*! However, our readiness as a family helped us overcome much of the anxiety.

One method of overcoming was our ability to adapt and compensate for the time we were apart. For instance, one year we celebrated Christmas in the fall. Another year, Pam and I celebrated our planned (and paid for) twenty-fifth anniversary to Hawaii on our twenty-seventh anniversary. Two years later! But it was still fun!

As a chaplain endorser, I saw many chaplains and families go into the military unable to handle the dynamics and the tensions. It seems the common denominator for those who didn't make it as military families was the lack of readiness to face the hard days of being apart, which included days, weeks, and months of loneliness, frustration, anger, hardship, and temptation. Separation will come. It is not a matter of if; it is a matter of when.

Why does the DOD move people around a lot? That's a great question, and you need to know the answer. There are three reasons.

First, the realities of military action require our personnel to quickly develop teamwork and relationships with a wide range of people and personalities. Second, the Department of Defense wants to build leaders who can thrive and succeed in any environment. This means they need to see how people handle the full spectrum of challenges and situations. Third, with the need to be ready for emergency action at any time, we have to be able to "plug and play" at a moment's notice, and this takes practice. So, we move around a lot, gaining a ton of experience and knowledge in the process. Unfortunately, a lot of families suffer and fall apart.

Separation isn't the only issue you'll face, however. Some military spouses feel called to a career, but it might be hard to find a meaningful position in their specific line of work when they have to relocate every two or three years. One chaplain's wife was a university literature professor, but couldn't always find a teaching job where her husband was stationed. Many spouses were highly involved in ministry in the local church while they were pastoring, but when they left the church to go into the military, they didn't have as many meaningful opportunities to participate.

Depression can be a result of the military lifestyle. You leave friends and family behind. You give up your home. Your kids won't have a hometown. You basically become a family of nomads, traipsing around the globe throughout your military career. Sometimes you'll be in a great location with a lot of friends, and sometimes in a pretty bad place with very few friends. All of these dynamics affect the psyche, and it takes a while to adapt.

In addition, being in the military is dangerous. People get hurt, not only during battle, but during training. This, too, is something we have to prepare for.

Because Soldiers, Sailors, Airmen, Coast Guardsmen, and Marines spend considerable time away from home and family, there is a tendency to grow distant from each other. There are temptations, and we have to plan in advance how to respond appropriately. Another dynamic is that we don't always have the same kind of support system like we had back home before going into the military.

For these and many more reasons, the calling has to be shared. You have to know this is God's plan. And you have to be ready for anything. Each chaplain and each couple will have a unique story and journey, with one-of-a-kind experiences and challenges. The key is to count the cost and think through the issues in advance so you're not caught off guard or taken by surprise. You need to pray together before you make the decision to sign up, and then continue praying together after you begin serving in the military. Spiritual and emotional unity is essential for maintaining readiness as a person, as a couple, and as a family. It's also a prerequisite to seeing the kind of effective, fruitful ministry that the Lord has in mind for you.

PAUL'S STORY:

Several years ago, when I was a brand new Active Duty Army Chaplain, I got a call from an Army chaplain recruiter. A pastor of a Baptist church in Southern California had called to ask about becoming a chaplain. Although the pastor was in a wonderful church and was doing a great job as their pastor, he felt that the Lord might be leading him to redirect his pastoral and discipleship efforts to soldiers, instead of among civilians.

I asked the recruiter why he was telling me about the pastor, and he said, "The guy's wearing me out with his questions. He literally calls every day of the week with another couple of questions. And after I answer the question, he has ten more. I'm not exaggerating here!"

I agreed to take on the challenge of staying in touch with the pastor, and I called him. He admitted that he always has lots of questions, even to the point that while he was in seminary, classmates referred to him as "Captain Interrogative."

"Here's the deal I'd like to make with you," I said.

"Deal?"

"Yes, deal. I'm willing to answer every question you come up with, on two conditions."

"Conditions?"

"Yes, conditions."

"OK, what are they?"

"First, you may call me or email me up to three times a week, Monday through Friday during the workday. Second, you will keep a record of every question you ask and every answer I provide."

"Oh yeah? Why?"

"You have a right to know everything you possibly can know before making the decision to transition from your church ministry to the military. Since you and your wife need to pray over this potential move together, you need to keep a notebook that you can both review from time to time. And after you have the answers to all your questions, you'll have a large notebook full of information about ministry in the military, and who knows, maybe you'll be able to help someone else someday."

The guy agreed, and boy did he have a ton of questions. In the process of Q&A, he and I became good friends. My wife and I even visited his church to see him in action and meet his wife. After about six months, he had a fat notebook filled with everything he needed to know about military chaplain ministry. He made the decision to apply, and was selected.

It's important to keep in mind that ministry in the military is in many ways the same as ministry in a local congregation. Men and women in the uniformed services have the same needs as those who are schoolteachers, plumbers, mechanics, or salespersons. The context is different and there are some issues particular to the military, as there are in any field. But Soldiers, Sailors, Airmen, Coast Guardsmen, and Marines need someone to teach them the Bible, provide pastoral counseling, visit them when they're sick, model effective relationship styles, and set an example for how to live for Jesus, just like anyone in any town in America.

Guest Anecdote Number Two

God Had Planted Me Right Where I Was Meant to Be

Gearing up to be an Active Duty Navy Chaplain was quite an experience. In essence, it was a journey of becoming. You see, I had not planned to walk that particular road at any time of my life. Years back, I was a civilian pastor in a local church and an Army Reserve chaplain. That meant I was in my Army uniform one weekend a month and two weeks a year. The rest of my ministry was done in the church. As happens to many pastors, I had a negative experience with a church and found myself without a pastorate. The Army Reserve was my only ministry outlet. At the time, feeling burned by church members and church leaders, my wife told me that she had absolutely no desire for me to take another pastorate. She was fine with ministry, but not leading a local congregation.

Right around that time, I received a call from a chaplain mentor of mine who said, "The Navy is looking for qualified chaplains for Active Duty. Have you ever considered a lateral transfer from the Army Reserve to the Navy?" I had not, and I thought there was no way on Earth my wife would go along with the idea, but I said I'd talk to her. I didn't even finish telling her my whole thought when she exclaimed, "Yes, this is the door that God wants us to walk through!" Without my knowing about it, she had been praying for several years that I would sense the leading of the Lord to go into the Navy instead of the Army. When it finally happened, she was ready.

The next seven months were filled with paperwork, interviews, and preparation. Long story short . . . I was accepted by the Navy and made the shift. In those seven months, I was ecstatic. I felt as though I was right where I was supposed to be. It was odd for me, because the path towards Navy chaplaincy meant I had to go through some pain and devastation, both personally and professionally. Without the negative experience at the church, however, I might never have pursued the Navy. But God took a lousy situation and made something beautiful of it. I was nervous, for Active Duty was a brand-new experience for me. What would my first command be like? What would my boss be like? Would I be able to handle ministry in a pluralistic environment?

During my first year as a Navy chaplain, I felt confirmation that God had planted me right where I was meant to be. One of the major sources of affirmation was the recurring sense that even on my worst days as a chaplain, I still loved my job! Sure, there were elements that didn't appeal to me, but the excitement and joy of ministering to sailors and Marines never faded. It's been about six years since taking the Oath of Office, and my experiences have varied widely. Through it all, the excitement and anticipation I felt leading up to becoming a Navy chaplain still remain with me. I love my job, and wouldn't trade it for any other.

LT Chris Linzey, CHC, USN

Chapter 7

Requirements and Qualifications

The phone call was from the pastor of a large church on the West Coast, who felt the Lord was calling him to become a military chaplain. He wanted to know how long it would take to get in, so he could notify his church board. After getting acquainted a bit, Paul started asking him about his qualifications. He had more than eight years of full-time ministry experience, was in pretty good physical shape, with no criminal history or use of drugs. It was looking like he might be a great applicant for the military chaplaincy . . . until he was asked about his education.

"What do you mean I have to have a Master of Divinity? I have a B.A. in Theology & Ministry from a great university, and I got an A in every single class, and the Lord is calling me to become a chaplain NOW. I don't want to go back to school."

"Well, brother, sounds like you're a great pastor, but you're just not qualified without an M.Div. If the Lord is calling you, then you need to obey, and the first step is to get into seminary and complete the degree."

His anger took over from there, and the rest of the call wasn't pleasant. Apparently, he had gotten into some sort of trouble, and needed to leave his church immediately. Going into the military would have been a perfect "out."

A few weeks later, Paul got a call came from another pastor who felt called to the chaplaincy. When she was told there was an age limit, she asked, "But I heard I could get an age waiver. Can't I get an exception from the Chief of Chaplains since I'm a bit over the cut-off?"

"Well, ma'am, the current guidelines from the Office of the Chief of Chaplains says he'll consider age waivers up to forty-six years of age if you have prior military experience, but you're already fifty with no previous time in service, and though you seem like a fantastic minister of the gospel, there's no way you can begin a military career at age fifty."

"Oh, I see."

As the officer in charge of Army chaplain recruiting at Fort Knox, KY, Paul met a lot of pastors, priests, rabbis, imams, evangelists, theology students, and seminary professors who inquired about becoming an Army chaplain. Almost all of them were good people, effective in service and ministry in their congregations and organizations. Many of them applied and were accepted, completing the process to become a chaplain. A lot of them, however, didn't meet all the criteria. Therefore, it's important to understand what is required.

There are seven qualifications for every applicant who desires to become a military chaplain: Education, Citizenship, Ministry Experience, Security/Background Check, Medical Exam, Ordination, and Physical Fitness. Every one of these is also a potential disqualifier, which means as far as the military is concerned, it doesn't matter how good a preacher or counselor you are, if you don't have all seven qualifications, you're not going to be a chaplain in the military.

The three military Chiefs of Chaplains have the authority to grant waivers or exceptions for faith groups that have a shortage of chaplains, but those faith groups tend to be Jewish, Roman Catholic, and Muslim. The rest of us need to make sure we understand and match up in the following seven ways.

EDUCATION REQUIREMENT

The standard degrees for all military chaplains are the Bachelor degree and the Master of Divinity. Historically, the M.Div. was a three-year degree requiring at least ninety semester hours, which has traditionally been the ordination requirement for many main-line denominations. However, because many faith groups don't require the M.Div. for their clergy, the minimum number of units has changed to seventy-two semester hours, even for those whose faith groups and endorsers that don't have an education requirement.

The qualifying degrees have to be from regionally accredited universities, or seminaries accredited by the Association of Theological Seminaries (ATS). Therefore, it's important to make sure of the accreditation status before enrolling in a degree program. If you're already in a non-accredited degree program or have already finished, please call a military chaplain recruiter to see whether you qualify for a "Wash Letter Waiver" and find out what's involved. Clergy who immigrate after completing their theological education outside the United States will have their transcripts and institutions examined to make sure they are equivalent to the education standards in the United States.

Another factor to keep in mind is whether your degree was done online or in residence. Many traditionalists and older clergy have a bias for a degree program completed in residence in a "brick and mortar" institution, where you have face-to-face, in-person interaction with the teachers. However, the advent of online degree programs is changing the way we think about education.

At the time of this writing, the three military chaplaincies allow clergy with online degrees to apply for service. What is unknown, however, is whether the traditional bias for residential degree programs might come into play, even subconsciously, when the environment is competitive, a limited number of chaplains can be approved, and the selection board has to choose between two applicants. You want your packet to be the best it can be.

CITIZENSHIP

All members of the Armed Forces of the United States have to be citizens or lawful permanent residents with a green card. This is an important consideration that must be settled before an applicant can be approved to serve as a chaplain.

MINISTRY EXPERIENCE

The Navy, Air Force, and Army chaplaincies need clergy who, from the first day on the job, can handle themselves with professionalism, dignity, and confidence. We don't have the luxury of thinking we can ease into the tough aspects of being in the military. As Keith mentioned in an earlier chapter, the very first day might throw a tough situation at you, and you have to handle it appropriately. This might be a death, a child with a serious injury, a suicide attempt, a budget meeting, a crisis, mass casualties, or a difficult counseling issue. The possibilities are endless.

Each candidate is required by the DOD to have a minimum of two years ministry experience, typically subsequent to completing the M.Div. But if an applicant has the right amount of ministerial experience before or while completing the education requirements, sometimes the DOD may allow the faith group endorser to write a letter saying the applicant has met the ministry requirement. Nevertheless, the Accessioning Board will scrutinize the ministerial record and select those who have the best experience and record in civilian ministry.

One young pastor was interviewed by a retired Navy chaplain, who asked, "Have you had any conflict or tension in your last pastorate?" The minister said "Yes, I have. In fact, it was quite a painful experience." After discussing the details, the interviewing officer made the comment, "That's wonderful. You're ready to be a chaplain."

The bottom line is that the military wants its chaplains to be seasoned clergy who have extensive pastoral experience. We have to be able to handle all aspects of ministry: preaching, counseling, visitation, funerals, baby dedications, baptisms, weddings, budgets, sacraments or ordinances, socializing. We have to be ready to deal with stress, conflict, criticism, and uncomfortable circumstances. In the opinion of the military chaplaincies, the more experience you have in civilian ministry, the more qualified and competitive you will be.

SECURITY/BACKGROUND CHECK

Every officer in the military has to maintain at least a "Secret" security clearance. Therefore, part of the process is to undergo a thorough background investigation. This will include employment history, financial situation, criminal record, personal relations, and international travel. You'll be fingerprinted, and they'll ask about the use of any drugs. Then they'll do a credit check and an FBI screening.

Some activities in your past might disqualify you from ever serving as a chaplain. On the other hand, many aspects of your past will not prevent you from serving. It's better not to lie or try to hide anything. Instead, be honest and up front. Some offenses can be forgiven or waived, but if you lie about your past and it ever comes out that you were devious or dishonest, your story won't have a good ending.

MEDICAL EXAM

Because of the demands of military lifestyle and activities, it's important for people in the Armed Forces to be healthy, in shape, and that they maintain certain physical capabilities. This is true for chaplains, too. To come into the military, you will have a complete medical exam. They might even ask you to provide your medical and dental records. Some preexisting conditions will disqualify you from serving, but others might not.

Another way of looking at it is that the Department of Defense is going to provide complete medical care once you're in, so they want to make sure you have no preexisting debilitating conditions. If you develop medical problems after accessioning, you're covered.

PHYSICAL FITNESS.

The standard physical fitness test varies among the services, but all of them test your strength, stamina, agility, weight, and general fitness. We've mentored a lot of clergy from many faith groups who balk at this, but listen. If you feel God's calling on your life to be a chaplain in the military, then you have a responsibility to stay in shape. If you don't, then either it's not God's calling, or you are disobeying the Lord, because it's one of the requirements for serving. Get out there and run. Do the push-ups. Do the sit-ups. Or get out of the military and serve the Lord somewhere else.

When Paul deployed to Iraq, he was fifty-two years old. The Blackhawk dropped him and his Chaplain Assistant at a landing pad in the middle of the desert, on a pitch-black, moonless night, about a quarter mile from the Flight Ops center. He had to carry all his personal gear plus crates and boxes of supplies and equipment. Making that round-trip hike four times that night added up to a total of two miles. To do that requires health, strength, and stamina.

ORDINATION

Every chaplain has to be ordained and endorsed by a DOD-approved ecclesiastical organization, but the government is not in the business of religion. It's aim is to take care of its personnel and guarantee their constitutional rights, so the military asks faith group endorsers to provide qualified clergy. It's up to the faith groups to monitor their own clergy and to send qualified men and women who represent the organization. We'll discuss this further in a later chapter, but for now, keep in mind that your goal should be to stay in good relationship with your faith group and your endorsing agency if you want to serve as a military chaplain.

Keith was the faith group endorser for the Southern Baptist Convention for eleven years, and then he became the assistant endorser for Liberty Baptist Fellowship. As the endorser, he looks for candidates who are above reproach. He and his staff take the scripture seriously, and want candidates who are people of integrity and faith.

He's had many candidates who wanted to have a waiver for ministerial experience. Some of them didn't qualify for the waiver because they didn't meet the requirements and qualifications. Some taught Sunday School or led a small group ministry. One applicant actually tried to use bus ministry as his qualifying ministerial experience.

Many will ask what qualifies as ministry experience? Each denomination will have its own qualifications or expectations. For most faith groups, the applicant should be a preacher, teacher, and counselor. It's also important to see how the applicant plans and implements programs. Every applicant for the chaplaincy has to have completed at least one funeral and a wedding, which are requirements by the DOD. The military also wants its chaplains to have some experience with budgeting and leading meetings. Basically, the process will discern how well the candidate performs a wide variety of pastoral duties.

It is important for chaplains and chaplain candidates to know that there will always be requirements from both the DOD and the faith group endorser. You should do your best to know the requirements and understand them before moving forward in the process of becoming a chaplain.

Once it is determined that a minister meets all of the requirements for the chaplaincy and is endorsed by a denomination or independent endorsing agent, the chaplain recruiters of the desired branch will assist in building an application packet to present to the next Accessioning Board. The Accessioning Boards are convened periodically throughout the year by the Chiefs of Chaplains of the various branches of service, and they are told how many clergy of each faith group are needed, along with the current waivers that are allowable.

The members of the board will examine each application, scoring them according to the criteria provided by the Chief's office. The applicants who are qualified, who raise no red flags or concerns, and who score the highest, will be notified the next day that they were selected for the military chaplaincy. The others will be told what they need to do to improve their packet in order to be competitive. Or they may be told that they'll never qualify.

Here's the bottom line: Conservative Christian pastors are a dime-a-dozen in the military, so you have to be extra diligent, making sure you understand the requirements, and then endeavor to go above and beyond in order to be competitive. If you'll do that, you can travel the world. You can have a good income and medical coverage for you and your family. You can have a life better than you ever imagined. Most importantly, you can have a fantastic experience as a pastor to Soldiers, Sailors, Coast Guardsmen, Airmen, or Marines, leading many of them to faith in Christ.

Guest Anecdote Number Three

A Call for the Entire Family

My call to military chaplaincy was unique. I was a full-time high school English teacher and my husband was pastoring a church we founded in a suburb of Atlanta. I had been teaching for thirteen years and we had been pastoring for about ten. Our children were seventeen, eleven, nine, and three. At the time, we had a church member who had served in the National Guard as a chaplain's assistant. He suggested that my husband and I look into the chaplaincy and we did. This was the beginning of my call to the military. In a matter of weeks, I found myself enrolled in seminary at Liberty University and a second lieutenant chaplain candidate in the Army reserve.

I had truly found something that I enjoyed doing. I was able to serve one weekend a month and occasionally on a few special assignments. It broke up the monotony of teaching school and gave me something to look forward to each month. Fortunately, I had a supervising chaplain who allowed me to operate in my gifts and who was very supportive of me. I was able to do a different kind of ministry with different kinds of people.

A couple of years later the time came for me to attend Chaplain BOLC at Fort Jackson, SC. This is where the challenge began. My family could deal with me being gone for a day or a weekend or even a couple weeks for training, but when I was going to be gone for six weeks (which turned into three months because I loved being on active orders for school), then we had a problem. Although I visited home on some weekends and the family came to visit me some, it was not the same. My husband was left with three minors who had a variety of sports practices to attend, and a church to pastor without me. I handled all the financials for home, and was the praise and worship leader for the church. He was overwhelmed, but I was enjoying being away from the stress of home and having the freedom to move when and how I wanted with no children in tow. It was the best and worst three months of my life. Days of happiness and joy would end in nights filled with tears. I found a new me and realized how much I enjoyed and needed time away. Meanwhile, my husband was left juggling all the responsibilities of family and church while not really knowing what I was doing day by day. This was not what he had signed up for.

My husband did not take this "new me" too well and blamed this change on the Army. He would really struggle a year later after I graduated seminary and decided to submit my packet for Active Duty. He agreed with my decision to go active but still did not understand how the military worked. It would be a difficult transition for the entire family.

Today, I have completed one year of Active duty in which I have spent a few months as a geographical bachelorette, a few months as a "single mom," and some time with the whole family in South Carolina. If I could offer advice to anyone who decides to take this path, I would suggest a lot of family counseling prior to coming onto orders, especially if the family is new to the military. Although my husband knew this was a call from God, it has been difficult for him to make the transition and find his place. It has also been difficult for my middle children who are 13 and 15 to adjust to the move. Sports and the youth centers on post have been instrumental in helping the kids make the transition.

Family and emotional readiness are essential to the military chaplain. Take time to count up the cost of the call, not just for you, but for everyone involved. This is a call for the entire family and oftentimes that means letting go of what is familiar in exchange for the land that God will show you. It takes time and adjustment, but God always makes a way.

CH (CPT) Keah Humphrey, Battalion Chaplain, US Army

Chapter 8

Initial Chaplain Basic Training

WITHIN A MONTH OF being notified that you are selected to become a chaplain, the military will send you orders indicating when and where you have to go for initial officer training. The locations change from time to time, but as of right now, Air Force chaplains go to Maxwell Air Force Base in Montgomery, Alabama. Navy chaplains do their training at Naval Station, Newport, Rhode Island. And the Army sends its chaplains to Fort Jackson, in Columbia, South Carolina.

Every chaplain already has the required ministerial experience, education, and other qualifications, so the initial officer training is designed to prepare you mentally, emotionally, and tactically for the service you have entered. Each armed service has its own culture, worldview, and language, and these are important. Therefore, chaplains must get ready to live, work, and minister in that environment. There are some cross trainable tasks for all of the Armed Services chaplaincies, but the important thing is that you learn these tasks best within the backdrop of the service God has called you to.

Ever since the 1950s, there's been a desire in Congress to merge the chaplaincies, because some people think there's no difference in how you would minister to people in the different services. Therefore, for several years, all military chaplains trained at Fort Jackson. Most people in the military, however, agree that was not a good idea, so the three chaplaincies returned to their respective service branch's training location. It matters to the people in uniform that their chaplain is a member of their branch of service. There's more trust, respect, and openness, which are vital for establishing effective relationships, and relationships are key to ministry.

When Paul was a rookie chaplain, his first chaplain mentor said to him, "Here's my philosophy of serving as a military chaplain: ministry follows friendship. If you love your soldiers and spend time with them and they know you like them, then they'll come to you when they want to talk about their spiritual need. Just love them, spend time with them, and trust the Holy Spirit to draw them. When they are ready to talk about the Lord, they'll know who to go to."

In the same way pastors and missionaries have to learn the cultural context of the people they're called to serve, chaplains need to understand the new world they're going to be living in and ministering in for the next twenty years. You need to know the mentality, the lingo, the expectations, and the dress code. You have to know what you can and cannot do, the limitations of your authority, and the freedoms you have in ministry.

Sometimes, there's a fine line between behavior that earns a medal, and activity that gets you in trouble, so you have to be able to discern the differences, and know who you can go to for guidance and accountability. Initial officer training is where this part of your education begins. If you do it right, you'll set yourself up for a successful career of effective ministry, while meeting new people and making friendships that'll last a lifetime.

US ARMY INITIAL TRAINING

Every new Army chaplain has to attend the Chaplain's Basic Officers Leadership Course (CHBOLC) at Fort Jackson. The following information comes from the United States Army Chaplain Center and School's website.

The CHBOLC Vision:

"To transform civilian religious leaders into influential, adaptive, and critically thinking military religious leaders capable of meeting the religious support needs of the Army."[1]

---

1. US Army Chaplain Center, https://usachcs.tradoc.army.mil/courses/chbolc/.

The CHBOLC Mission:

To train students to become religious leaders who demonstrate the core competencies of nurture the living, care to the wounded, and honor the fallen while advising Commanders and providing religious support to the Army family.

Course Overview:

CHBOLC is an intensive, outcomes-based, entry-level, initial military training process for newly accessioned chaplain and chaplain candidates. The training and special activities during this course provide unique opportunities for professional, physical, academic, and spiritual growth.

Chaplain Initial Military Training (CIMT).

This is the "basic training" phase in which Army Basic Officer Leader Course common core, Army Warrior tasks, and orientation to the U.S. Army Chaplain Corps are trained. After CIMT, you'll start Phase 1, which focuses on developing the essential staff officer skills needed to function in the Army. Phase 2 provides basic chaplain ministry and pastoral skills necessary to function as a chaplain at the battalion level. And Phase 3 training brings together leadership, professionalism, and functioning as an officer in field, garrison, and social environments. The main focus of this phase is the one hundred and eight hour field training exercise (FTX).

For many students, CHBOLC is the first opportunity to work as a member of a multi-faith team providing religious support and services to a diverse community. The Chaplain School's CHBOLC program stresses teamwork to accomplish the religious support mission. The program helps you integrate into the Army Community and its customs, courtesies, ethics, and traditions. You'll see how you can adapt your civilian education and experiences to the Army environment, learn to perform the critical staff officers' skills necessary to work in collaboration with other battalion staff officers and NCOs, and find out how you can advise unit leaders on the impact of religion on the military community and tactical operations.

You can expect a vigorous Army physical education program and adherence to Army standards for physical fitness. You and your classmates will be working in multi-faith teams to solve religious support problems and implement effective solutions. It'll be an interactive and challenging academic program requiring critical thinking and decisive action. But you'll be under the guidance of faculty who have successfully done what they are teaching, are committed to the Chaplaincy's mission, and are trained to teach, coach, and mentor students.

Part of the curriculum and experience is an immersion in the digital tools used by the Army. You'll become familiar with systems that simulate operational religious support scenarios. Plus, you'll spend time in the field, experiencing Army life in a military operation.

All of these tasks are crucial for the mindset of chaplains and chaplain candidates. Even more importantly, chaplains and chaplain candidates will learn basic military training that will enculturate them into the Army environment and attitude. As a part of that enculturation, students will do physical fitness (PT) almost every day. Drill and Ceremony (D&C) is another key part of the curriculum. Yes, even chaplains have to be able to march in step, understand the various commands and cadence calls, and be prepared to do it right. There are many common-core soldier tasks and experiences in store for you, all designed to help you understand the people you'll be ministering among, and preparing you for the situations that you will inevitably encounter personally, politically, and professionally.

US AIR FORCE INITIAL TRAINING

Before starting any chaplain-specific training, every Air Force chaplain will attend the Air Force's Officer Training School (OTS). The purpose of the officer training course is to train and commission new officers to fulfill Air Force Active Duty, Reserve, and National Guard requirements, in partnership with the U.S. Air Force Academy and Air Force Reserve Officer Training Corps. The training aims to instill high standards of conduct and provide officer trainees with the essential military knowledge and skills needed for effective performance as Air Force leaders.

Judge advocates, chaplains, doctors, dentists, hospital administrators, and medical scholarship recipients will attend the first five weeks of the training. After completing OTS, these officers move on to their specialized training. The information in this section comes from the US Air Force Chaplain School website and the Officer Training School website.

AIR FORCE CHAPLAIN CORPS COLLEGE

The four-week Basic Chaplain Course is the Air Force Chaplain Corps' skills-set training for newly accessed chaplains. Chaplains are required to attend the course within twenty-four months of graduating from Officer Training School.[2]

The course provides the foundation new chaplains need to deliver spiritual care and advisement to leaders in the Air Force context. Topics covered in the course fall within seven areas: leadership, staff development, advising leadership, resource management, readiness and chaplain skill-set training. The course also upgrades the chaplains' official status, making them worldwide qualified and able to deploy.

Mission:

Provide education, training and resources that promote professional excellence and enhance the free exercise of religion for the Air and Space Force professionals and their families.

Goals:

Achieve vocational excellence, professional integrity and service to others by providing relevant knowledge, skills and resources for students to better perform their duties; attracting, mentoring and recognizing quality people; ensuring that faculty and course directors properly apply instructional system development principles; securing resources to support mission requirements; improving information flow and ensuring effective communication; and monitoring the quality of support services and seeking necessary improvements.

2. Air University, https://www.maxwell.af.mil/News/Display/Article/2170882/chaplain-corps-college-continues-chaplain-training-providing-resiliency-profess/.

Other lessons include instruction of enlisted students in crisis intervention skills, trauma, pastoral care, and pluralism. Faith group support requirements will further their professional abilities to support chaplains in peacetime and contingency operations. State-of-the-art integrated technology mediums have enhanced world-wide Chaplain Corps training efforts in readiness, mentoring, and global ministry efforts. Officer and enlisted evaluation systems have been added to all levels of instruction, ensuring that chaplain and senior enlisted support personnel will use evaluation and supervisory skills appropriately.

NAVY CHAPLAINCY

Serving full-time as a chaplain in the Navy will begin with five weeks of Officer Development School in Newport, RI, and end with seven weeks at the Naval Chaplain School, also in Newport. Active Duty chaplains normally complete their training within three months of commissioning. This information may also be found on the Navy Chaplain School website.[3]

The Chaplain School program includes four weeks of introductory training, which covers professional chaplaincy, working in a pluralistic environment, chaplain corps history, ethics, ship visit, and religious ministry team training with a Religious Program Specialist. Chaplain School also includes three weeks of Religious Ministry Team Exercise (RMTEX); field exercise for religious ministry teams; Tools, Empowerment and Ministry Skills (TEAMS); pre-marriage training; suicide prevention; and more.

The combination of classroom instruction and on-the-job training that you receive in the Chaplain School program offers leadership and professional development while also preparing you to provide religious ministry wherever Navy Chaplains serve, whether at sea, at home, or in a foreign land.

The initial course is designed to provide the religious ministry training necessary to prepare chaplains to serve the Navy, Marine Corps, or Coast Guard. The course challenges the mind, the body, and the soul. Plus, there is an emphasis on leadership, spirituality, and fidelity. Ministry in the Sea Services is dynamic, demanding, and requires dedication;

---

3. "Navy Chaplain brochure," *Navy.com,* https://www.navy.com/sites/default/files/2018-03/chaplain-brochure_0.pdf.

the Professional Naval Chaplaincy—Basic Leadership Course is designed to bring a grounded awareness of these realities so students are well-prepared as they enter into their ministry settings.

After Chaplain School, you can continue your education throughout your career as a Navy chaplain. There are opportunities for continuing education through the funded Graduate Education Program, while being paid full-time as a Navy Officer. Plus, Navy chaplains may participate in Clinical Pastoral Education (CPE) and receive tuition assistance for other off-duty educational programs.

Because the military environment is a strange world to a lot of clergy, and because the regimen is rigorous and demanding, many who come to the basic chaplain and officer training schools are intimidated or nervous. That's fairly normal. Any time you begin a brand-new endeavor, there's going to be a learning curve. There's a lot to absorb as you immerse into your new life as a military chaplain.

Our advice is to work hard getting in shape before you get there. Pay attention while you're there. Read everything they give you. And take advantage of all the training and social opportunities. You're already a good pastor, or the military wouldn't have selected you. Your endorser believes in you, or wouldn't have recommended you. And, you have a divine calling. In other words, you already have what it takes to succeed.

So, if you've disciplined yourself, if you are a good minister who likes people, and if you're sure this is the direction you're called to go, then you can arrive at the chaplain school and the officer training course with confidence. Chances are, you're going to fit in really well, make some great friendships, learn what it takes to succeed in the military, and then transition to a dynamic and effective ministry career.

Guest Anecdote Number Four

I Felt I Was in Hell

I had heard that COT, or Commissioned Officer Training, was easier than the enlisted side's Basic Military Training (BMT), or even the Officer Training School (OTS), because we were the professionals (lawyers, doctors, chaplains, and nurses). In fact, I heard some stories that included tales of playing golf that made COT seem like an officer's club, complete with housekeeping and gourmet buffets. However, for this thirty-six-year-old who had been in full-time ministry for nineteen years, had a full staff of employees, preached to an average of six hundred to eight hundred people every Sunday, and ministered around the world several times over, this was a huge hardship, and I learned quickly that those narratives were considerably false.

I remember waking up on the fifth day thinking to myself, "What have I done? I definitely did not hear from God!"

The previous night I almost cried myself to sleep from the stress of not eating normal food, only MRE's (Meals Ready to Eat), not sleeping enough, the high-pressured, extreme environment, missing my wife and four children (whom I had never been gone from more than one night), feeling total isolation, and having serious caffeine withdrawals.

We had an alarm clock every morning at 0430 that consisted of about five MTI's (Military Training Instructors) and five officers who from a loudspeaker would say, " *Wake up, wake up, wake up*, it's 0430" while at the same time kicking on the doors and yelling at the top of their lungs at anything breathing. They gave us a total of ten minutes to put on a uniform I had no idea how to wear, while I also had to make sure my bed was made, and the room was in order.

I felt I was in hell and that I was emotionally, mentally, and physically being broken apart. My mind would continually go back to the scene in my hotel room the day before training began: drinking coffee, facetiming with my family, hearing my kids tell me they loved me, and having the freedom to do whatever I wanted. I had no idea what to expect when I arrived at COT. I actually thought there would be a full day of getting to know everyone, checking-in like one would at a hotel or conference center, with identification and paperwork needed, room assignment, and a restful night's sleep to start a fresh day of training in the morning. My assumptions were far from reality.

I pulled up in my taxi at Maxwell Air Force Base in Montgomery, Alabama, during June's summer heat to some of the most organized chaos I had ever seen. As I attempted to pay for my taxi, three MTIs walked over to me and calmly waited for me to finish paying and grab my bag. Immediately when I was done conducting my business with the civilian driver and my bag was in hand, a switch flipped in those MTIs, and reality quickly sank in. The entire day we were yelled at, taught how to reply when spoken to, given the rules of the land, how to stand at attention, and how to somewhat march together as a group. At no time were we allowed to speak, laugh, or even move, unless given permission.

Our first lunch was served as we all were told to sit in our civilian clothes on the concrete, at least four to six feet apart from each other, and thrown an MRE. There were no instructions. All we had was a basic instinct on how to eat this food made to survive a nuclear holocaust. We had to wear Camelbacks, and were told to drink at least four or five full Camelbacks of water a day while in the one hundred and five degree Montgomery heat. I was the only person in our squadron that tried to heat up my MRE with the water from my Camelback, and I remember numerous people watching me with speculation that I was doing something wrong.

In retrospect, I should have just eaten the MRE cold since half my Camelback's water spilled onto the concrete, wetting half my jeans, and I wasn't able to move for fear the hovering MTI would make a huge spectacle of my mistake. So, for the next two hours, I had to practice standing at attention and marching with the group, with a tucked in shirt and jeans that looked like I peed myself. I am sure others around me thought the pressure of the first day had really gotten to me.

Nonetheless, after that first week, the training became easier. New relationships had formed as we were put into flights of sixteen individuals. We learned to "embrace the suck" and get through the training as a team. It was still hard, but we learned how to maintain military bearing; understand the need for standardization, procedures and protocols; and follow instructions.

Yes, there were several other times that I wanted to quit, like waiting in the hot sun while standing at attention for thirty minutes in front of the dining facility, soaked in my own sweat, and trying not to squint, while both the sun and sweat were stinging my eyes. And once you were in the dining facility, you had ten minutes to eat while sitting at attention and not being allowed to talk to one another.

I now know that there was a purpose to the madness. The training was designed to break us down and rebuild us as leaders, enabling us to serve effectively as strong officers in the United States Air Force.

On the fifth day, I was certain that I did not hear from God and that I had made a huge mistake, but that was far from the truth. Less than a year later, at my first station, I had six suicide interventions, hundreds of counseling sessions, preached to thousands of people, shared the gospel message, and met and served with the best people in the world. I realize that God called me to this position, not for me to change anything specifically, but for God to change me and to change others through me.

CH, CPT BRANDON WHITE, USAF

SECTION THREE

Being a Military Chaplain

Chapter 9

Relationship with Your Endorser

When Keith was a young chaplain, his endorser went to Germany to visit him. Keith was impressed that the denominational rep would come all that way to spend time with him, and he learned an important lesson: "My endorser cared about me. I knew from that moment that I was not just a number. I might have been one of many, but I was loved and cared for."

He was fortunate. Not every endorser is as compassionate and caring as that, but many are. They are there to help you, encourage you, and go to bat for you. That's why it's so important to stay in touch with your endorser throughout your military career, and to do whatever it takes to maintain a good relationship.

You see, a chaplain endorser sits in a pivotal position and is aware of every topic, debate, and challenge facing the military chaplaincy. In a nutshell, the endorser helps the military in three ways: (1) Provides a faithful voice of the church to the Department of Defense regarding First Amendment issues. (2) Serves as a solid advocate for chaplains in an era of extreme cultural change. (3) Establishes spiritual, moral, and ethical standards for chaplains.

A good endorser also serves the church, as well as the individual chaplain, and can make a powerful difference in your life and career.

A senior level Army chaplain was accused of hate speech and bias against an LGBTQ+ service member, and was under investigation by his command. The media carried the story about "another Christian chaplain with homophobia, who should be booted out of the military." It was getting ugly, and didn't look like it would end well for the chaplain, the church, or the military chaplain corps in general.

But the chaplain had maintained a good relationship with his endorser, who knew the chaplain well enough to figure out that the accusation probably wasn't true. The endorser went to the installation where the chaplain was stationed, met with the commander, talked at length with the chaplain, and interviewed others who were in the Bible study when the alleged hate speech happened. The endorser was able to provide sufficient evidence that the accusation was unfounded, and was influential in getting the charges dropped. In essence, he saved the chaplain's career and restored his reputation.

Another endorser found out that one of his Navy chaplains had an ongoing conflict with the ship's captain. The chaplain's superior officer actually said he didn't like chaplains, and ordered him to go clean the deck plate with a toothbrush. As the chaplain turned to leave, the captain shouted, "And no one better help you either!"

After hearing about the situation, the endorser called the Chief of Chaplains. The Chief's office had heard about it, and did not want to get involved. But after the call from the endorsing agent, the Chief of Chaplains did respond and saved the chaplain from a toxic command that could have sabotaged his ministry and ruined his career, leaving him disillusioned and demoralized. Instead, that chaplain was able to continue in an effective and fulfilling ministry. Later, he was promoted and stayed in the Navy quite a bit longer, instead of getting out because of a terrible experience on that particular ship.

There are times, however, when an endorsing agent needs to mentor a chaplain, or even provide correction, redirection, or discipline. One chaplain was overweight, couldn't pass the physical fitness test that every service member has to complete, and was in danger of losing his commission. His endorser mentored him, helped him with a weight loss and workout plan, and checked in on him from time to time. The intervention process worked, and the chaplain is enjoying a great career as a military chaplain. He's keeping the weight off and staying in shape.

Endorsers are willing to walk through personal crises and tragedies with their chaplains. Some chaplains suffer from PTSD, burnout, marital issues, difficulties with their children, death of family members, or other tough situations. We know denominational reps who spent time with a chaplain's family, helping them heal after a tragic accident took the life of their husband/father.

During one denominational conference, the wife of a chaplain walked up to the endorser and, referring to her spouse, said, "I'm not sure who that man is, but I want my husband back." When the endorser approached the chaplain later, the chaplain said he was not going back to Iraq. Strangely, it seemed like he was implying that he was going to kill himself, so the endorser took him to the nearest military hospital, where he stayed several months, getting the care he needed. In this case, because a courageous wife told the endorser what she observed, and a caring endorser followed up with the chaplain, they saved his life and their marriage.

The role of ecclesiastical endorsers began in 1917. At that time, there were only three endorsing agencies: the Federal Council of Churches (Protestant), The National Jewish Welfare Board, and the National Catholic War Council. The role of the chaplain endorser has changed drastically through the years, and today there are nearly two hundred faith group endorsers that send chaplains to the military. In most cases, each endorser represents a denomination, but there is an increasing number of independent organizations that endorse clergy for the military, which means a chaplain might be ordained by one organization and endorsed for chaplaincy by another.

The Department of Defense cannot choose a chaplain for induction to the military because that would be like choosing a religion, and would be a violation of the Establishment Clause. Instead, the DOD asks each qualified faith group to give them the names of ministers who meet the standards.

It's important to know that a clergy entering the military as a chaplain or chaplain candidate will have several lines of authorities to answer to. First, of course, is the military chain of command. The chaplain always works for the commander as the commander's personal staff officer. In this way, every chaplain is held accountable to military standards. Second, the chaplain works for the installation chaplain or the next higher command chaplain. In other words, the chaplain has a technical chain that begins with a senior supervisory chaplain and goes directly to the Chief of Chaplains, ensuring that every chaplain is held accountable to Chaplain Corps standards and methodology. Third, the chaplain has an endorser or denominational "chain of command." This relationship ensures that the chaplain maintains the theological and lifestyle standards as a representative of his or her faith group.

Most commanders and military personal outside of the chaplain corps don't understand the unique relationship between chaplain and endorser. In fact, most don't even know what an "endorser" is, and they probably don't care. For this reason, it's important for the chaplain to educate the chain of command about the role of the endorser.

With the ever-changing culture in our world and in the military, the endorser should communicate often with his or her chaplains. Endorsers can relay important information about the denomination in regard to religious liberty and first amendment issues, as well as the variety of issues that come up in the churches. Every chaplain should look for this communication, read it, and understand the issues being discussed because they'll most likely come up again somewhere along the way, while serving in the military.

As an endorser, Keith received many calls and emails from chaplains at the basic and career courses who wanted to know what was being said about particular issues. This is good, but it made him wonder why they didn't already know? In most cases, he had already sent them that very information, so they could have read it if they had paid attention.

But the communication between chaplain and endorser has to be a two-way street. One endorser had a senior-level chaplain who was getting ready to retire and felt he needed to "reconnect with his denomination" in order to get a good pastoral position as a civilian minister. The denomination told him it was already too late. Why? Because he had abandoned his church, had severed all ties with the denomination, had gone his own way, and done his own thing, totally ignoring the church's efforts to keep in touch. Now that it was convenient or important to him, he wanted to reconnect. But it doesn't always work that way.

It's important for you as a chaplain to remember your roots. The chaplain comes from the church, and will more than likely want to return to church ministry at some point. So, you can't afford to lose touch with your denomination. Communication is crucial.

One of the ways many endorsers and denominational offices attempt to stay in touch with their chaplains is by asking the chaplains to send a monthly, quarterly, or annual report. Too many chaplains won't submit the requested information. Here's a hint: make up your mind from the start that you will send whatever report they ask for.

Keith was a Southern Baptist chaplain for twenty-eight years, and was never ashamed of denominational affiliation. He always looked to his endorser for help, always filled out the periodic reports, and always tried to attend the annual conferences sponsored by his faith group. Paul was endorsed by the Assemblies of God for his twenty-four years in the Army. In addition to filling out and submitting the reports to denominational HQ, he emailed the endorser several times a year to let him know what was going on, wrote articles for the denomination's magazine that went out to all the pastors and churches, and attended district and General Councils as often as possible. When it was appropriate, he even invited the endorser, who was a retired military chaplain, to speak at prayer breakfasts and other special events.

Because they kept in touch with the church during their military service, Keith and Paul had opportunities for service and ministry after getting out of the military.

KEITH'S STORY:

While I was the Southern Baptist endorser, many chaplains fought the idea of doing the reports. In fact, only about 6% of our chaplains filled out a report when I started. Reports are important because they let the faith group know what's going on. Church leaders get a clearer understanding that they are represented well, that the chaplain is making a difference for the Kingdom of God as well as for the faith group. Reports provide accountability for the chaplain, and also for the endorser. When I left the endorser's office after eleven years, about 30% of the chaplains were reporting, and the church-chaplain relationship was much stronger and healthier.

Another crucial concept is that although culture changes, the gospel does not. Ministerial methods may change, but the message we are trying to communicate to those we serve does not change. The endorser provides leadership for those representing the church in the military, and chaplains need to walk within the guidelines of their particular faith group.

Over the past few decades, several significant issues changed because of culture and politics. Denominational leaders are usually aware of the changes before the boots-on-the-ground chaplain hears about them, and the leaders can adopt policies to deal with these changes for their chaplains. But it is up to the individual chaplain to stay within the intent of the polices, and a few chaplains don't want to do that. Some choose to leave their church and move to other endorsing agencies and faith groups because they have different policies or doctrinal statements.

One chaplain was a personal friend of someone on the denomination's leadership team. He called the friend, and told him he did not agree with the policies, that he was going to do whatever he wanted to do, and didn't have to abide by the directive. Please listen up and understand: it doesn't work that way. When you are endorsed by a faith group, it's no longer about you; it's about your faith group. You represent your church, your denomination, and your endorser. The minute you don't represent them adequately, they can terminate your endorsement, and you are no longer qualified to be a chaplain. If that happens, the military can evict you from the service. It happens more often that you'd think.

Endorsers help chaplains maintain a proper focus on the work being done, assisting them to achieve the high standards of the military and the kingdom of God. The values and ethics that endorsers and faith groups demand are important for both the chaplain and the endorser.

As an endorser, Keith has had to cancel a number of endorsements. Most of the endorsements that he pulled were for what he refers to as SPAM, which stands for sex, pornography, alcohol, and money. There are other disqualifiers that could be added to the list, of course, such as a chaplain no longer agreeing with the church's theological positions. But most of the problems involved one or more of these four issues.

In today's ever-changing environment in the military, it is extremely important that chaplains and endorsers communicate regularly. There are many ways this communication can take place. Some endorsers conduct periodic Zoom, FaceTime, WebX, or Google meetings with their chaplains. Many send out newsletters, while others use social media to connect with chaplains, and chaplains with endorsers. We have to remember that communication is the key. When we communicate with each other, we provide a layer of accountability that endorsers and chaplains need in their ministry.

As mentioned earlier, there are approximately two hundred faith group endorsers that provide chaplains to the DOD. These endorsers do not receive financial help from the DOD or the government. Some denominations fully fund the ministry of the endorser, others partially fund this crucial ministry, while a few faith groups rely completely on contributions from their chaplains to maintain an endorser.

The Southern Baptist Convention's chaplaincy department is fully funded. They have the money to pay for retreats, reunions, travel, and other important ministry programs. The Assemblies of God Chaplaincy Department pays for its chaplains to participate in their annual chaplain conference. Other endorsing agencies do not receive any monies from the church or other organization. Their entire budget is received from their chaplains. Whatever the budget and method of support, the key for endorsers is to maintain good communication in order to serve, love, and care for chaplains and their families, which is the aim of most endorsers.

When you serve as a military chaplain, make it a priority to stay in touch with your church, faith group, and endorser. Send in the reports on time. Live up to your ordination vows. Pay your tithes or dues. If your endorser or faith group doesn't require these actions, consider doing them anyway. You'll be amazed at the love and the support you get in return. There are many ways of expressing this principle:

Pay it forward.

You reap what you sow.

What goes around comes around.

Cast your bread upon the water, and it'll come back to you.

There's a return on your investment.

You get the idea.

Chapter 10

Self-Care in the Military

Make no mistake about it, the biggest problem among chaplains today is the lack of self-care. This is true among ministers in general, but especially so for clergy in the military. Self-care is talked about at many conferences and by almost every denominational endorser, but few chaplains have an intentional plan or a personal strategy for effective self-care, and this failure is taking a serious toll on our chaplains, their families, and the people they're called to serve.

We've actually heard people say, "Be honest now: isn't self-care overrated? After all, pastors, chaplains, and others involved in ministry are called, anointed, and led by the Spirit. Doesn't the Lord watch over them?" Indeed, there are many who say that self-care is a non-issue, and that Christians don't need to worry about it. But they are 100% wrong. We definitely own the responsibility for taking care of ourselves, and we need to get back to the basics.

Jesus set an example of self-care. The Gospels talk about him getting away by himself, apart from the crowds. He frequently took time to pray. He spent time with friends. He exhibited a sense of humor. And he made sure he was worshipping on the Sabbath. To put the Lord's intentional self-care in different words, Jesus knew how to set boundaries. He spent a lot of time giving of himself in many ways, but he knew how to balance that by spending ample time alone, time with close friends, and time with the heavenly Father.

The Old Testament also demonstrates the importance of self-care when it lays out the Sabbath principles. No matter how busy life got, the people of God understood that they had to set aside time for restoration, regrouping, and focusing on what matters most. The Lord intended for his people regularly to stop the busyness, set aside their work, spend time with loved ones, worship the Lord, and relax . . . and it wasn't optional.

There's a good reason for the Sabbath: the God who created us knows that if we don't care for ourselves, we will run ourselves ragged to the point that we are less effective in our lives, in our relationships, and in ministry. It seems we have forgotten this principle.

Why are ministers often so bad at self-care? Precisely because we want to help people. We like being the under-shepherd, caring for and tending the sheep, and we get a good feeling from doing it. We find meaning, purpose, and a sense of fulfillment. So much so, in fact, that we don't want to let go and take care of ourselves. Another problem is that a lot of people in the caring professions are people pleasers who can't say "no." This in itself is a form of sickness.

But there's a bigger problem than the minister's personal health or effectiveness. A clergy's lack of self-care almost always has an impact on other people, too. For example, it almost always hurts the family, those who are closest to the chaplain. It's like the ocean: the waves keep rolling toward the shore. In this analogy, the wave represents the problem that comes to the minister. It hits him or her, and then keeps rolling until it drowns everyone in its path.

One particular chaplain took vacations with his family, but every single time, something tragic happened among his congregation or in the command, and he canceled his vacation to return to the people who he felt "needed him." Never once did he spend the entire planned vacation with his family, and they got the message: other people are more important. That is a powerful, devastating statement to the family. They needed him, but he refused to be there for them. He preferred to be on the job caring for others.

It's crucial that we understand what happens to a minister who doesn't take care of himself or herself. The chaplain who doesn't care for the self becomes less effective, and that's not fair to the people we serve, or to the kingdom of God, or to our own ministerial career. The Lord empowers us, encourages us, strengthens us, prepares us, and anoints us so we can be highly effective in the ministries he called us to. He wants us to be at our best. But we sabotage the work of the Holy Spirit in our own lives by failing to practice self-care.

One chaplain who never said "no" to people outside the family, was always there for his troops, regardless of his own family events, needs, or desires. He would often get sick and be in bed for a week or more at a time, as if his body was trying to catch up with his inability to say "no." Not only was he not at his best in service to the Lord, but he was not at his best for his wife and children, either. He ended up losing his family because his wife grew tired of life on the back burner. That's not what she bargained for, so she asked for a divorce.

Taking care of the self, the marriage, and the family, versus caring for the flock, is like a balance beam at times. If your values and priorities aren't right, the results will show up in your health, your relationships, and your career. Too many good clergy end up losing their families and their ministries. The risks are so high that only a fool would dare ignore the dangers.

There are many methods of caring for oneself, and every individual has to find out what works personally. It's not a one-size-fits-all operation. We are unique. Our needs are particular to our personality, relationships, and circumstances. Therefore, we have to experiment a bit until we discover what it takes to recover, restore, and refresh ourselves. But there are some general categories of activities that we should consider.

Interestingly, though perhaps not surprising, is the fact that the self-care methods that are most effective will inevitably be related to one of the four aspects of our humanness: body, mind, spirit, and relationships. Those who are really good at self-care will intentionally include the entirety of their being in their care plan. A good way to start would be to ask yourself what it takes for you to feel at your best in each area of your life.

- What does it take for you to be at your best physically? Your care plan should include making sure you get enough rest, enough exercise, and that you maintain a healthy diet.

- What does it take to be at your best emotionally, mentally, and intellectually? Your care plan should include experiences designed to nourish your intellectual and emotional well-being.

- What does it take to be at your best spiritually? Here's where the spiritual disciplines can make a huge difference in your life. The basics include prayer, worship, and Bible reading. But there's so much more you can do.

- What does it take to be at your best in your important relationships? This should include quality time together that is uninterrupted, prioritizing one another, and staying loyal to each other.

In all four areas of your life, you might want to start with the basics, the obvious elements that form the foundation of your care plan. But if it's going to be effective and make a difference for you long-term, you might consider being creative, doing something out of the ordinary from time to time. This will keep life, relationships, and your walk with the Lord fresh, enjoyable, and meaningful over the course of your life and career.

If done right, there are some wonderful results of self-care? You'll experience a deeper sense of fulfillment and meaning. People will want to be around you. Your family will be glad you are in their lives. And the people you work with and minister to will respond positively to you. In essence, the result of living your life the way the Lord wants you to will empower you to be much more effective in what matters most. The bottom line is that you'll be happier. You'll reap the benefits of having a clear mind, a physically prepared body, an unbendable spirit, and a better prayer life. You'll be rested and stronger mentally, physically, and spiritually. And your personal life will be sweeter.

The painful truth is that those who don't take care of themselves will experience the opposite dynamics. The risks are high, and the choice is yours.

One chaplain regularly practiced the spiritual disciplines as part of his self-care. He fasted, prayed, and spent time in meditation. Because of this attention to spiritual self-care, he was better prepared to serve as a chaplain. Another chaplain's self-care was quite impressive. He asked the Lord to give him a scriptural theme for the year, and God always did. That Scripture verse became part of his self-care. He also participated in a Lenten fast every year to help him stay on the right path. But it was the scripture theme that he built his self-care around. Keith adopted this strategy about five years ago, and it has made a powerful difference for him.

Faithfully practicing the Sabbath one day every week is a crucial part of the care plan for many chaplains. This is true for both Christian and Jewish clergy. Right after Hurricane Katrina, Keith assisted a senior rabbi chaplain as he moved into his lodging. He was part of the ministerial team that responded to the devastation and homelessness in many parts of the Gulf Coast, providing food, clothing, shelter, and counseling for thousands of people. The rabbi began preparing for each Sabbath well in advance, making sure he had the scriptures, enough food, and a lot of reading material. It left an impression on Keith about the importance of preparing for the Sabbath and taking it seriously.

Unfortunately, there are many stories of chaplains who fail to practice appropriate self-care, resulting in some rather tragic consequences. A hospice chaplain who was around death all the time was really good at caring for others, but because he wasn't careful and intentional about what was happening in himself, he burned out. His ministerial presence would grind to a halt, making him unable to continue. Because of the goodness of God, the man's obvious anointing, and the divine call on his life, he came back after recovering. But had he engaged in effective self-care all along, he wouldn't have had to reach the point of burnout over and over again. One Navy chaplain burned out. When he left the Navy and the ministry, he was bitter and felt like a failure. He never did come back to ministry.

An Army chaplain returned from a combat deployment suffering from PTSD and admitted that he did not practice good self-care. He almost lost his family, his faith—everything. He left the military, determined to take care of himself, get healthy, find a good counselor, and try to fulfill the call of God on his life. Four years later, after much counseling and personal healing, he returned to the Army chaplaincy as a new person, better prepared to take care of himself. His ministry was much more effective this time around. He came to realize that just like the Sabbath was not optional for the Old Testament people of God, self-care is not optional for people in ministry today. It is essential.

KEITH'S PERSPECTIVE

As a representative for two endorsing agencies, first the North American Mission Board of the Southern Baptist Convention, and more recently the Liberty Baptist Fellowship, I've interacted with thousands of chaplains, so I've seen the full spectrum: from those who do self-care extremely well, to those who are literally killing themselves, their marriage, their family, and their ministry.

Two of my chaplains killed themselves. I saw others spiral down into suicidal ideations. Several chaplains returned from combat and were not the same. In fact, there were some good chaplains who either lost their families, or almost lost them. Some left the military because of the stress of ministry and combat.

A number of our chaplains experienced moral failures, many of them resulting in my having to remove their ecclesiastical endorsement.

Almost all of the moral failures were because of sex, pornography, alcohol, and money (SPAM) combined with poor or nonexistent self-care. In some cases, the memories of combat brought back latent psychological issues. Having to stand with chaplains who came under some type of official military disciplinary action isn't fun, but it's part of the role of an endorser. I am certain that all of these moral failures were the effects of burnout in ministry, combined with poor self-care.

Several years ago, we hired a person whose role was to be a pastor to the chaplains. He helped our chaplains find a sense of equilibrium in life, ministry, and family. He sat down with each chaplain and spouse who came to our conferences: loving them, caring for them, providing counseling when needed, sharing the scriptures, praying for them, and later, calling on those who needed follow-up care. This initiative was successful because we were able to provide the one-on-one personal attention that everyone needs from time to time—including clergy. It gave the chaplain and the spouse a safe place to open up and talk about what was happening in the inner person, and it gave the pastor an opportunity to speak into their lives about the importance of taking care of the inner person.

PAUL'S PERSPECTIVE (EXCERPTED FROM THE BOOK, *SAFEST PLACE IN IRAQ*)[1]

> The generic issues that everyone faces have been well chronicled. What's different is what goes on in the mind of each one of us. There are some common themes, of course, but the individual make-up, the personality, the background, and spiritual condition combine to make each story unique.
>
> When I deployed to Iraq, I didn't think I had any issues. I was "prayed-up," well-trained, eager to serve, and excited to be there. However, it didn't take long for the environment and the experiences to start affecting me. Even though the Lord used me to help others, occasionally the stress was overwhelming. I wasn't sleeping well. The daily mortars were taking a toll on my psyche. I started having nightmares. Being far from home, the loneliness was inescapable. Along with loneliness comes sexual temptation.
>
> A lot of people think when they're that far from home, and the circumstances are that bad, they're justified in doing things

---

1. Linzey, *Safest Place in Iraq*, 69–72.

they wouldn't do otherwise. But instead of giving in to the temptations and the opportunities for sex, alcohol, drugs, or porn, I spent time with other Christians, listened to Christian music, and worked out at the gym. I ate pecan pie a la mode and oatmeal raisin cookies, read my Bible and anything decent I could get my hands on. I prayed with some of the men who came to church or to one of the Bible studies. And I called home as often as I could.

I hate to think how bad it might have been if I didn't have some good Christian men to talk with, pray with, and worship with while I was deployed. I am thankful for each of them. I'm thankful for a wife who has been gracious and supportive. And I'm thankful for the faithfulness of God, who promised to never leave me nor forsake me.

ELIJAH'S PERSPECTIVE

One of our favorite Bible stories comes from 1 Kings 18–19. Elijah experienced a tremendous victory on Mount Carmel, where he literally called down fire from heaven, witnessed an exciting miracle, and enjoyed a great triumph for the Lord. By all accounts, he had bested all the prophets of Baal. Perhaps Elijah was tired and wiped out emotionally from the ordeal, because when Jezebel threatened him, he was so scared that he literally fled for his life and hid. Apparently, he went into a deep depression.

It is not uncommon for clergy today who have experienced a season of exciting and successful ministry to have an emotional let-down afterwards. That's why ongoing self-care has to be in place and practiced faithfully. It's not optional, friends.

Many organizations have studied the work and life of people in ministry. One writer went so far to call this type of research "Doomsday Surveys."[2] Most researchers and psychologists agree that approximately one in four ministers suffers from depression.[3] A 2015 survey from Lifeway found that 80% of graduates from seminaries and Bible schools who enter the ministry will leave within the first five years. Then in 2019, further research concluded that approximately two hundred and fifty

---

2. Ed Stetzer, *Head, Heart, Hand*, https://headhearthand.org/blog/2016/02/18/check-out-831/, para. 1.

3. *Lifeway Research*, "1 in 4 Pastors and Congregants Suffer from Mental Illness," https://lifewayresearch.com/2014/09/22/1-in-4-pastors-congregants-suffer-from-mental-illness/, para. 1.

ministers leave the ministry each month. Could an effective self-care plan help prevent this from happening? We think so.

The Barna group recently conducted a study that resulted in a list of eleven indicators of burnout in the life of the minister.[4] According to their findings, if a clergy has one of the risks, there's a medium risk of burnout. And if there are three or more of the indicators, the risk of burnout increases dramatically. The eleven indicators are:

- Less confident in their calling today than when they began ministry
- Rate their own mental and emotional health as average, below average, or poor
- Seldom or never are energized by ministry work
- Frequently feel inadequate for their calling or ministry
- Frequently feel emotionally or mentally exhausted
- Have suffered from depression sometime during their ministry
- Not satisfied with their pastoral vocation
- Not satisfied with ministry at their current church
- Tenure at their current church has been a disappointment
- Tenure at their current church has not increased their passion for ministry
- The primary day to day tasks do not fit their calling or gifts

We understand there will always be sacrifices that ministers have to make in order to serve in the kingdom. We all have to count the cost of living for Christ and obeying the call on our lives. But the goal is to stay healthy enough to serve the Lord over the course of a lifetime. We're not just called to minister for two or three years. We want to minister twenty, thirty, or forty years. To do that, we have to be healthy emotionally, intellectually, spiritually, physically, and relationally.

The bottom line is this: self-care for the clergy is not optional if you want to be effective in ministry long-term. A military career can last from twenty to thirty years, and then there's room to serve in a church, mission field, or a parachurch ministry long after retiring from the military. Our goal is to help you prepare for enjoyable, fulfilling, and effective ministry

---

4. *Barna*, "38% of Pastors Have Thought About Quitting Full-Time Ministry in the Last Year," https://www.barna.com/research/pastors-well-being/.

for a lifetime. If you do it right, you don't have to lose your marriage, your family, your health, or your sanity in the process.

Chapter 11

Wearing the Uniform

An invitation to wear the uniform of the United States military should not be taken lightly. It is an open door to a world of challenges, opportunities, dangers, friendships, personal growth, and ministry. But with these dynamics comes an array of obligations that must be considered as you count the cost of ministering in the military.

Wearing the uniform is significant on two levels. It begins with the superficial issue of wearing the uniform correctly and then transitions to the deeper issues of what it means to represent the government, the constitution, and the people of the United States. Even more significantly, every Christian chaplain wears the cross, which means you also represent your church, your endorser, and the Lord Jesus Christ when you wear the uniform as a Navy, Army, or Air Force chaplain.

Paul's father and another Navy chaplain were having lunch in town one day, both in uniform, when his dad noticed the other man's shoes were scuffed and dirty. Dad asked his friend why he didn't shine his shoes. With an air of self-justification and spiritual superiority, the man replied, "Man looks at the outward, but God looks on the heart." Paul's dad replied, "That's true, and that's exactly why I polish my shoes." Dad tried to explain what he meant, but the other chaplain didn't seem to agree or understand. When it came time for the next promotion board, Dad was selected for advancement, and the other man was not.

In the military, as in much of life, how others see us will often determine what they think of us, how they treat us, and whether they trust us. Right or wrong, these factors add up, so that some people are promoted to the next higher rank, while others are "non-select."

It feels great to be promoted. The pay is better. You get more respect. Your family is proud of you. And you feel good about yourself. On the other hand, when you are not on the promotion list, the rejection feels personal and hits you deep down in your gut. You feel like a failure. Even some good people become bitter and angry and want to quit. They have to wait a full year before going to the next promotion board, wondering every day whether they'll be selected. They don't feel good about themselves or their career, and unfortunately, their ministry can suffer. Some even blame God.

Dr. Toni Pfanner is the head of the International Committee of the Red Cross (ICRC) Legal Division. When he was the editor-in-chief of the International Review of the Red Cross, he wrote an article titled "Military Uniforms and the Law of War" in which he says,

> The use of uniforms is found everywhere. School children often wear uniforms distinguishing them from pupils of other schools; boy scouts proudly don military-like uniforms with insignia indicating membership and rank. Bus drivers, sportsmen and women, milk deliverers, monks, nurses and security personnel of private companies all wear clothes identifying them as belonging to a particular group, service, firm or profession. They may wear uniforms of plain fabric or of a distinctive design. By its lack of variation and diversity, the uniform promotes a sameness of appearance and brings homogeneity to an otherwise heterogeneous group of people.[1]

He then points out that the word uniform literally means "one form," and refers to the significance of everyone in a military organization dressing alike.

> The military uniform is a form of clothing with a particular symbolism and a long history and tradition. . . . It also calls for respect and fear and symbolizes strength and power. . . . Finally, it helps to create an identity of appearance and an esprit de corps and is thereby conducive to the bonding process.[2]

Each of the armed services of the United States has policy manuals and regulations covering the appropriate wear of the uniform. An example of this is Army regulation 670-1, "Wear and Appearance of Army Uniforms and Insignia," which says in Chapter 7, Art. 1:

---

1. Pfanner, "Military Uniforms and the Law of War," 93.
2. Pfanner, "Military Uniforms and the Law of War," 93–94.

> The Army is a uniformed service where discipline is judged, in part, by the manner in which a soldier wears a prescribed uniform, as well as by the individual's appearance. Therefore, a neat and well-groomed appearance by all soldiers is fundamental to the army and contributes to building the pride and esprit essential to an effective military force. A vital ingredient of the Army's strength and military effectiveness is the pride and self-discipline that American soldiers bring to their Service through a conservative military image. . . . Soldiers must take pride in their appearance at all times, in or out of uniform, on and off duty.

Commenting on this Army reg, Pfanner says that the reason for insisting on the precise and correct way to wear the uniform is to "keep up the military uniform's traditional functions, such as identification, maintaining discipline, taking pride in wearing the uniform, and creating bonds and an esprit de corps."[3]

The uniform is important. Most types of chaplaincy have them. Corporate Chaplains often wear a shirt, sweater, or jacket that has the logo of the corporate chaplain company. A hospital chaplain usually wears a badge and a name tag. Chaplains with police, firefighters, and other first responders all wear a uniform that represents their particular organization.

When speaking about the uniform worn by military chaplains, one person mentioned that chaplains "wear the nation's cloth." Keith was taken aback by this description at first, but the more he thought about it, he realized that is exactly what the military chaplain is doing. Whether she wears an Army, Navy, Marine, Coast Guard, or Air Force uniform, it is the "nation's cloth."

KEITH'S STORY:

For me, wearing the "nation's cloth" was an honor. I wore it for over twenty-eight years, and, frankly, whenever I can, I still wear it as a retiree. The cloth comes in many colors and styles, and it changes every so often, but it is still the nation's cloth.

I conducted our unit's remembrance of the National Prayer Breakfast one year, and had invited a dignitary as a speaker at the breakfast. One of the chaplains who worked for me in the Division came to the

---

3. Pfanner, "Military Uniforms and the Law of War," 99.

prayer breakfast looking rather disheveled. His uniform was a mess. Our speaker, a highly decorated veteran, pulled the chaplain aside and fixed his uniform. It was definitely an embarrassing moment.

The regs of each of the Armed Services spell out the appropriate way to wear the uniform and provide the exact measurements where the ribbons, name tag, and other insignia should be placed. If you care about your career and ministry opportunities, you can't afford to get it wrong. Plus, you have to keep in mind that different situations call for different uniforms and uniform configurations.

There are PT (physical training) uniforms, work uniforms, and dress uniforms. Some events require the formal dress uniform, while others call for the daily duty uniform. Which color shirt and pants, which jacket, which shoes? Long sleeves, short sleeves, hat or no hat, name or no name, tie or no tie? Ribbons, no ribbons, or just the top row of ribbons? The Navy probably has more uniforms and combinations than the other services, but in all of them, it's crucial to understand what's expected in each setting and for each occasion.

At some installations, wearing the uniform off post is forbidden except on your way to work or on the drive home. Even with that policy in place, soldiers can often be seen walking around the mall in uniform. Invariable, a senior NCO will walk up to those young soldiers and correct them.

It's never good for the chaplain to show up as the only person not in the correct uniform. Normally, there is a published plan of the day or week that has the uniform listed for each event. It is a good idea for the chaplain to see the plan of the day as soon as it is posted, take note, and make sure every uniform is ready in advance. Too many have waited til the morning of an important ceremony, only to discover they don't have the right uniform, or the name tag was missing, or the rank had fallen off without their noticing it.

PAUL'S STORY:

I was at a civilian clergy conference, in uniform, when another chaplain showed up with the wrong color shirt with his uniform. Thinking he'd be the only military chaplain at the event, he thought nobody would know it was the wrong shirt and he'd get away with it. He was humiliated when he saw me. At a military event, I saw an officer in a Major's uniform pull out a black Sharpie and darken his gold leaf to make it black. In essence, changing his rank from Major to Lieutenant Colonel.

"Major, are you promoting yourself to Lieutenant Colonel?" I teased.

He told me that he had been promoted a few weeks earlier, but this uniform was in the laundry at the time, and he forgot to change the rank before packing for this trip. Apparently, he truly was an LTC, and was embarrassed to discover he was wearing the wrong rank.

I was invited to do the invocation for a formal military dinner where the guest speaker was a two-star General from a different installation. He had flown in, checked into the hotel, changed into his Class A uniform, and was in the elevator by himself, when the doors opened, and I walked in. The doors closed, and as we stood there in silence, I noticed he was wearing a pair of dirty, old, brown shoes that looked like they'd been in the mud and hadn't been polished or cleaned in years. Now, I had a choice to make. Do I say something, or keep my mouth shut?

At the time I was a Captain, an O-3, and the officer in the elevator with me was a Major General, an O-8. I fought the urge to make a joke or say something, but finally the sinister human nature got the better of me, and I couldn't take it anymore. I knew if I messed this up, my career could be over before it even got started, but I simply couldn't keep my mouth shut any longer.

"Nice shoes, General," I uttered softly and meekly, trying not to laugh.

"Aw, chaplain! I was hoping nobody would notice! I landed at the airport an hour ago, got a taxi over here to the hotel, and as I was getting dressed, I realized I didn't have my uniform shoes. These are my gardening shoes, and they're all I have with me!"

Here was a General, pleading with a Captain not to tell anyone.

"Tell you what, General. Your secret is safe with me."

"Thanks, chaps. I owe you one!"

We went into the banquet hall together, side-by-side, and nobody noticed a thing. Either that, or they had enough common sense not to say anything about it to a two-star.

When it comes to the ribbons and badges to put on your uniform, a good rule of thumb is to wear only those ribbons and awards that you were officially awarded and have documentation for. That sounds obvious, but apparently not everyone understands this. One chaplain added ribbons to his uniform that he did not earn, and was kicked out of the military.

Once, when Keith was going to a promotion board, his photo didn't match his Officer Record Brief (ORB). He actually took the time to count the stars, ribbons, and oak leaf clusters to make sure they were all correct, and discovered there were a few errors. He had to go home, update the insignia on his uniform, and then return a different day to take the picture because he didn't have enough stars, and a ribbon that he earned was missing. The fact is, paying attention to detail can make or break your career.

One chaplain came out on the promotion list and was so excited that even though he didn't have the promotion order yet, he pinned the next higher rank on his uniform and moved to his next duty assignment to start his new job. The unit records showed him as a Lieutenant Colonel, but he was wearing the rank of a Colonel. When they challenged him about his rank, he had no documentation. He ended up receiving non-judicial punishment for putting the next higher rank on his uniform. With this faux pas on his record, he never got the eagle. He never was promoted.

Wearing the uniform correctly and looking sharp is an important aspect of serving in the Armed Forces. But the issue is far deeper than what your uniform looks like, because at all times you are representing something and someone bigger and higher than yourself. When you put the uniform on, you represent the military, the nation, the law, the president, and the Constitution of the United States. Likewise, when you wear the cross, you represent your church, your endorser, and ultimately, the Lord himself. The motto of the Army chaplaincy expresses it well. *Pro Deo et Patria* means *For God and Country*.

This dual representation is at the very heart of what being a chaplain is all about. One way to look at the role of the chaplain is that the chaplain is "wearing two hats." Half of the job is to be a pastor to the people in the command. The other half of the job is to serve as the commander's staff officer. In the same way that you have to know which uniform is required for each occasion, as a chaplain you have to know in any given situation, whether you are speaking and acting as a pastor . . . or as a staff officer.

Another way of looking at it is this: if you do your job as a staff officer well, you'll maintain the privilege of representing Jesus Christ in the military. You might be a great pastor, preacher, counselor, or evangelist, but if you're not just as good at representing the nation and working for the commander, you might not do very well in the military.

We'll get into these issues in the last section of this book, but let it suffice at this time to make a few brief comments along these lines. Chaplains are obligated to uphold the Constitution and all the laws of the land, to treat all people with courtesy and respect, even when they are non-Christian, even when they have immoral lifestyles. Part of the job as a religious subject matter expert (SME) in the military is to guarantee religious freedom for all people, Christian and non-Christian, people of all faiths, and people of no faith.

The cross lets people know we are Christians, but we are there to love and serve all our Soldiers, Sailors, Airmen, Marines, and Coast Guardians. When leading a Bible study or conducting a worship service, we have the freedom to preach and teach whatever we and the faith group we represent believes. But, when we're not in a religious activity, we have an obligation to be nonjudgmental, affirming, and encouraging to all. John 3:16 says God loves everyone in the world, even the sinners. This is reaffirmed in Romans 5:5–8. "While we were still in our sins, Christ loved and died for us."

When we're in a religious event, we can pray in Jesus's name and do whatever we want. But when praying at a command function or ceremony, we should consider ourselves to be civic functionaries, representatives of the commander, and be inclusive in what we say and how we pray. For example, chaplains who come from a faith group that doesn't endorse women in ministry must accept the fact that the military accepts women chaplains, and we have to be willing to work alongside them. Again, we'll go deeper into these controversies later in the book when discussing the challenges facing the military chaplaincies. But it's imperative that we're aware of these issues at all times.

As a way of summarizing. Your overall appearance lets people know whether they can trust and respect you and what you have to say. Your ribbons communicate at a glance the great work you do. Rank indicates pay grade, but also time in service and influence. By wearing the appropriate uniform, you communicate to those who are paying attention that you are someone they can look up to. The cross lets it be known loud and clear that you represent Jesus Christ, the church, and the Bible. Beyond the wear of the uniform, people will definitely be able to detect your attitudes and values by the way you talk, behave, relate, and live. The ministry of presence is powerful and effective.

Several years ago, Keith had an opportunity to take the trip of a lifetime. He was invited by a chaplain friend to do a Tiger Cruise, when a sailor on a Navy ship invites a friend or relative to accompany him or her on the cruise back to home port. Keith flew out to Hawaii and joined the ship for the fifteen-day cruise back to San Diego. It was a fantastic experience.

During the cruise, the sailors wore the uniform of the day, most of them in a blue jumpsuit. However, on the last day, when they were pulling into San Diego Bay, every sailor on board wore the white uniform, and they stood all around the perimeter of the ship's top deck, an amazing Navy tradition called "lining the rails." Standing behind the chaplain, Keith was wearing jeans, tennis shoes, and nice shirt. He was filled with pride as his friend and the rest of the crew stood there in dress white uniforms. There's nothing like that picture of the ship and her crew returning home to friends and family, each of them wearing the uniform, each of them representing what's best in America, the chaplain also representing the kingdom of God.

CHAPTER 12

The Role of the Chaplain in the Unit

EVERY CHAPLAIN NEEDS TO ask this question, "How important am I to the unit?" Because if you don't understand your own significance, there's no way others will respect you and what you have to offer. In fact, in the course of your military career, you will encounter a lot of people who have no use for a chaplain or religion, including the very people you work for and who write your evaluations.

We've heard some commanders say, "If it isn't about 'beans and bullets' then it isn't important." In other words, they're only interested in military tasks. They'll only allow staff meeting time for discussing the training or fighting mission, and they'll only allocate funds for those purposes. With that mentality, the role of the chaplain is sometimes disrespected and unfunded, and the chaplain may be marginalized. How the chaplain responds in that situation is the key to overcoming the obstacles that hinder effective ministry and impact.

It may be helpful to be aware of a few high-ranking leaders who have a respect and admiration for the role of the chaplain because there may be times you can share that information with people in the command. For example, in the closing remarks of an address delivered at the annual meeting of the General Commission on Army and Navy chaplains in Washington, D.C. on 1 May 1946, Admiral Chester Nimitz made this comment:

> My own esteem for the chaplains is not so much based upon deeds of valor as it is appreciation for their routine

accomplishments. No one will ever know how many young men were deferred from acts of desperation by a heart-to-heart talk with the "Padre."

"Man cannot live by bread alone," to be sure, and neither can man's spiritual needs be wholly satisfied by ritual. By his patient, sympathetic labors with the men, day in, day out, and through many a night, every chaplain I know contributed immeasurably to the moral courage of our fighting men.

None of that effort appears in the statistics. Most of it was necessarily secret between the pastor and his confidant. It is for that toil in the cause of God and country that I honor the chaplains most.[1]

Army Major General John Meyers wrote a book called *The Company Command,* which includes a short chapter on how a good commander and a good chaplain can work together to each other's mutual benefit. In the chapter titled "The Chaplain's Role With Your Unit," General Meyers acknowledges that the "organization and mission will affect how the chaplain functions" with the unit. Then he adds the following descriptions of a good chaplain and a good commander.[2]

A Good Chaplain Will Be:

- Dedicated to one's own faith but tolerant of the views of others.
- Service-oriented. The chaplain's job is to care for the commander, soldiers, and families . . . 24 hours a day.
- An example. Will be a quality soldier and officer, physically fit, and military appearance will match the commander's.
- An excellent communicator. Can relate to the soldiers in the unit.
- An effective counselor. Will listen to problems and recommend real solutions.
- Another set of eyes and ears. Will help the commander focus on all aspects of a problem.
- Seen by the soldiers. Will visit them at home, at the unit, in the hospital, in the field, and in the motor pool.

1. Nimitz, *History of the Navy Chaplains Corps*, 2:308.
2. Meyers, *The Company Command*, 205–6.

The Role of the Chaplain in the Unit

- A soldier's chaplain. Will be tough when required and compassionate when necessary.
- Commander's friend and advisor. Knows the spiritual and physical demands of today's Army.

A good commander will:

- Use the chaplain.
- Seek the chaplain's advice.
- Honor the confidentiality between a chaplain and a soldier.
- Involve the chaplain in unit activities and training events.
- Encourage the soldiers to get to know the chaplain.
- Be a friend to the chaplain.

In 2016, more than two hundred Air Force chaplains and Religious Affairs airmen gathered at the Air Force Chaplain Corps Summit to develop a strategy for the Air Force Chaplain Corps of the future. The Chief of Chaplains at the time, Chaplain MG Dondi Costin, invited the Chief of Staff of the Air Force, General Mark A. Welch III, to speak and the general had some challenging words for the Chaplain Corps. One of his statements was: "What a responsibility you share. What a burden you carry. What joy, comfort, and happiness you bring. And what a gift you are to the airmen and families you serve." He concluded by saying, "Thank you for choosing to serve. Thank you for caring for and leading our people. And thank you for inspiring me."[3]

"Recently, Air Force General Paul J. Selva spoke to a symposium that included chaplains from all ranks and service branches about the need for chaplains to serve not only their troops, but their commanders as well. Selva reflected on the role of the four chaplains on the USS Dorchester. He discussed the faith and sacrifice of "the Four Immortal Chaplains," then went on to talk about the advisement that chaplains offer their commanders at all levels in times of war. He reflected on a specific occasion when his chaplain explained some cultural differences in the country they were serving in, and the General said the input he

---

3. Air Force Chaplain Corps, "Gen Mark Welsh: You Are My Faith," YouTube video, 2:06, https://www.youtube.com/watch?v=7aCErx0iN8s.

received was invaluable. Then he acknowledged the significant impact that a good chaplain has in the military.[4]

In Keith's role as an endorser, he had opportunity to visit and speak with many flag officers. He traveled the world to visit and support his chaplains, and he was almost always able to schedule an office call with area commanders. He spoke with GO's (General Officers) and Flag Officers (Admirals) in Korea, Germany, England, Hawaii, and many posts across the Continental United States.

One such visit was to Paris Island, a training base for Marines that is a tough, hot place. When he met with the commander, a newly selected and pinned one-star General for the Marine Corps, he was told that the meeting would last no more than ten to fifteen minutes, which was normal.

KEITH'S STORY:

When I walked in, I sized him up, as I am sure he did me. His face was like I had imagined. His jaw was tight, and his eyes were steadied on me. I introduced myself to him and explained my role as an endorser. As we talked, time rolled on.

He explained the importance of his chaplain, who had done more Crucible Marches than any chaplain he had ever seen. Then he told me that his chaplain was the most important staff officer he had. In fact, if it wasn't for his chaplain, he could not and would not be able to do his job.

As we talked about the ministry and influence of the chaplain, I realized about forty-five minutes had passed. But, as I looked at this steely-eyed general, I realized he wanted to continue. So, we kept going. After about an hour, I told him that I should let him go, and asked if I could pray for him. He said, "Yes chaplain, please pray for me." So, his chaplain and I laid our hands on him and prayed. At the end of the prayer, I looked up and his once-hardened eyes were now weeping, tears running down his leathery cheeks. He said, "Chaplains, that is the most blessed I have felt in a long time." And with that, we left. What a visit!

When I reported to my first assignment at Fort. Bragg, NC, the senior chaplain asked if I wanted to be a "muddy boots chaplain." I had no idea what that meant, but figured I needed to say yes. It sounded like the right answer. I soon learned that it meant being with the soldiers

---

4. Jim Garamone, U.S. Department of Defense, para. 5.

wherever they were. It meant being at PT, in the field, in the motor pool, and many other places.

In religious terms, we call that "incarnational ministry," and it's often referred to as the "ministry of presence." I learned that living my faith outside the walls of my office and the chapel was just as important—maybe even more important—than what happened during religious services. I was assigned to an old WWII-style chapel that had an office for my Chaplain Assistant and me, but I wasn't supposed to stay there. My job was to be outside—living, breathing, eating, and doing everything my soldiers did. Well, almost everything.

As Paul mentioned in his book, *Safest Place in Iraq*, an effective chaplain will eat what the people eat, dress how they dress, speak their language, learn their culture, live among them, and endure the same conditions, all for the privilege of representing Jesus Christ and speaking into their lives with the gospel.

PAUL'S STORY:

As an Army chaplain, I dressed in the same uniform every soldier wore. When they ate a prepackaged meal, ready to eat, I had an MRE for dinner. I went wherever my soldiers went, even if that meant sleeping on the ground, road marching in the rain, or dodging mortars in the desert. My decision to go wherever they had to go created a lot of opportunities for conversation and ministry.

Colin Powell said one of the things he did was to stop by the mess hall every morning to have a cup of coffee. In some ways, that is what the *incarnational ministry* of the chaplain does. It stops by the mess hall, or myriad other places, to bring the touch of faith. And every once in a while, a whole lot more than just a touch. The impact of a chaplain who is visible, who is a living representative of the risen savior, can be tremendous.

When it comes to the role of the chaplain in the unit, there are many different expectations. The first is from your endorser, who expects you to be a minister from your particular denomination. Chaplains from some endorsers and denominations are expected to be bearers of the hope of Jesus wherever they go. So, in their incarnational work, they should be prepared to share the hope of the gospel with everyone they meet. Does that mean they carry around a big Bible and preach all the time? No. But it does mean they are always ready to share the hope that is within them at any time, day or night. Chaplains from other denominations expect their chaplains to provide the sacraments or ordinances of the church. Others expect the chaplain to be a counselor. You have to be true to your faith group and true to your understanding of the call of God on your life and ministry. This would include your personal lifestyle, as well as the way you conduct worship.

Secondly, there is an expectation from your commander that you be a good staff officer. That means you know what an officer in the United States Military is supposed to be, know, and do. The Army used to have the slogan: "Be, Know, Do." This phrase emphasized three distinct aspects of successful service.

BE:

First, it emphasizes that you are a representative of the military, your family, and your values twenty-four-seven, even when not in uniform, so it implies a consistency.

KNOW:

Second, it focuses on staying current on what you need to know in order to do your job at the highest level. This means reading, regularly completing more training, attending conferences, and adding to your qualifications.

DO:

Third, it stresses action, behavior, and conduct because regardless of what you say you believe, what you do is what matters in the end.

This "Be, Know, Do" mindset is particularly relevant for followers of Jesus Christ, because it closely resembles the discipleship process of the church. Much of the teaching of the scriptures and the church has to do with who you are as a person, increasing in knowledge, and actively conducting your life in a godly, biblical manner.

The Role of the Chaplain in the Unit

KEITH'S STORY:

My first commander at Fort Bragg told me, "Chaplain, you are my pulse finder. Go out and feel the pulse of the unit." I probably gave him that deer in the headlights look because I had no idea what he was talking about. I soon learned that he wanted me to use my "sixth sense" to go out and get a feel for how things were. He wanted me to understand the morale of the unit. He wanted me to see the working conditions, and how the troops were living. In other words, he wanted me to be incarnational.

My wife and I spent a season of life and ministry as foreign missionaries. It was the hardest ministry I have ever done. I found out that missionaries had to learn the culture, worldview, and language of the people they were serving.

We spent about three months at a learning center just outside of Richmond, VA. One day, we were told to go to the library and study the culture and worldview of the people group we were going to serve. I had no idea what this person was talking about. However, I soon learned some very important facts about the people I was going to be ministering with.

After that, we went to school for a year to learn the language. Believe me, it was not a simple task. God did a good job when he tried to confuse man at the Tower of Babel. I was pretty confused at first, but we prevailed.

As an endorser, I saw a lot of new chaplains. I told them that they needed to learn the language, culture, and worldview of the people they were going to serve. Some of them had that same deer in the headlights look I had at first. However, most, if not all of them, worked hard and managed to accomplish the mission.

Language, culture, and worldview: these are the "big three." As a chaplain in the military in the twenty-first century, if you want to be effective and successful, you have to learn the "big three." You can't avoid them, nor should you want to. Each of the armed services has its own culture, worldview, and language. In fact, each unit will have its own unique variety of the "big three."

We've seen chaplains try to buck the culture and worldview of those they serve. When this happens, inevitably they are out of step and less effective than they should be. Chaplains who decide not to learn the "big three" are much like missionaries on the field who maintain an arrogance and a sense that they are better than those they are called to serve. Keith encountered some missionaries who would say, "I don't need to learn the language, I will just love them!" Or "The culture isn't important." And some who actually said, "Why can't they all just be like me?"

It is easy to see how wrong these questions and statements are. However, those missionaries were making a conscious decision in not learning these very important tasks. They were like some chaplains who didn't remain in the military very long because they couldn't communicate and didn't fit in. They were always out of step.

By learning the language of those we minister to, we learn how to talk with them, how to communicate with their souls. We learn how to share the hope that is within us. We learn by speaking their language, and by understanding what makes them tick. By learning their worldview, we know what drives them. We know what they believe about faith, or no faith. We know what they believe about God, or no God. We learn about what provides them hope. It is imperative to listen to them and learn their worldview.

In understanding someone's culture, we go much deeper than just learning where they are from, what their family was like, and what political party they belong to. We gain an understanding of their lifestyle, their values, their tastes, and this will often provide insight about how to relate to them, love them, and share Christ with them.

Keith always loved going to the range with the armored battalion when he lived in Germany. This knowledge allowed him to speak to them in ways that resonated with them on their own terms. He observed and learned about a lot about the skills of the people in the unit: how to drive a tank, how to command a tank, how they fire the main gun. He also learned that going down range you had left and right limits. You were not supposed to go outside those limits, nor fire your weapons outside those limits.

Our culture is similar. We might meet someone whose left and right limits are very narrow. We might say that person didn't get out much. Then we encounter someone who has no left and right limits and is willing to do anything. These two individuals may have vastly different cultural backgrounds. Part of the role of the chaplain is to figure out how to minister to both at the same time.

Military One Source is a site that tries to provide as much help and support as possible for military personnel. Their statement on the role of chaplains says, "Chaplains are the military's religious leaders, responsible for tending to the spiritual and moral well-being of service members and their families. The chaplain's responsibilities include performing religious rites, conducting worship services, providing confidential counseling and advising commanders on religious, spiritual and moral matters."[5]

In a nutshell, the role of the chaplain boils down to who you are, what you know, and what you do. At a very basic level, your role will be built on personal relationships, and will include the following: (1) Advise the command on ethics and morals, (2) provide and facilitate religious services, (3) monitor and enhance the morale of the troops, (4) participate in military ceremonies, and (5) nurture the living, care for the wounded, and honor the fallen.

As you'll see in the next few chapters, however, there are dozens, if not hundreds, of tasks and responsibilities that go into fulfilling the role of the contemporary chaplain. The minister who feels called to serve in the military should make it his or her ambition to find out as much as possible about these roles and tasks, because there is an open door for a ministry experience beyond what you ever imagined.

---

5. "The Unit Chaplain: Roles and Responsibilities," *Military One Source*, https://www.militaryonesource.mil/family-relationships/spouse/getting-married-in-the-military/the-unit-chaplain-roles-and-responsibilities/.

Guest Anecdote Number Five

Boom! Wounded by an IED

There's a certain peace that comes from knowing you are where God has called you to be. Sometimes that peace makes no sense; it surpasses all understanding. I felt that peace very clearly on December 12, 2006, when I was struck by an IED.

I had only been a chaplain for a few months, serving with my first unit—a Marine Infantry Battalion—in combat for OIF. My RP and I had been through other scary situations before that day. Every time we arrived at a FOB where I would deliver services and counseling, the enemy rained mortars down on us . . . every single time. We had also been through several firefights—never as combatants of course—but ministry of presence on a battlefield cannot be done behind the wire. You have to be with your people where your people work, and ours worked on patrol, so on patrol we went.

We hitched a ride that morning with a logistics run, carrying supplies from FOB to FOB, hoping to get to some Marines we'd not seen in over a week. As the only unarmed member of the patrol, they loaded me onto the back of the first vehicle and sat me right behind the driver . . . on top of the fuel tank . . . which is what the IED was targeting. We were rolling down the road, assured it had been cleared by EOD earlier that morning, when *boom!*

The ringing in my ears hasn't stopped since that moment. As we slowly came to, Doc did a quick inventory for immediate casualties, while the rest of the patrol "circled the wagons" to create a defensive perimeter. I remember feeling fuzzy headed; my head, neck, back, and ribs hurt. My RP was unharmed, even though he had been sitting right next to me. A piece of the road sealed up the fuel tank in the blast which miraculously kept it from exploding underneath us.

And then the ministry day began, and we were too busy to think of anything else: civilian casualties, multiple medevacs, another IED attack. A young Marine had to take the life of a civilian, and that sat heavily on his nineteen-year-old soul. Another barely escaped the fireball from the second IED, and he sat next to me reciting "Praise Jesus! Praise Jesus!" while chain-smoking until the helicopter came to take him away to treat his flash burns. We shared feelings of betrayal when no one came to help our patrol, and feelings of pride when the decision was made to finish the mission rather than head home.

Not long after, we finally returned to our home base. My RP asked, "Aren't you afraid to go back out, chaps?" I remember very clearly that I was not. I was at peace, and had been at peace the entire patrol, despite the wounds, because I knew I was right where God had called me to be.

CMDR ROBERT NELSON, CHC, USN

Chapter 13

The Religious Support Team

THERE'S NO DOUBT THAT a good chaplain adds immeasurably to the life of a military unit, whether it's a Navy or Coast Guard ship, an Air Force Squadron, a Marine battalion, or an Army installation. Before discussing the chaplain's tasks and interaction with the Family Support Group in the next two chapters, it's safe to say that the military without chaplains would not be as effective, would not be as humane, would not be as user-friendly, and would not be in line with the Constitution of the United States. In addition to helping maintain religious freedoms for all personnel, the influence of a good chaplain reduces suicides and increases morale. Moreover, there are countless examples of the mere presence of a chaplain preventing criminal activity, stupid decisions, and career-ending behavior. We've seen it all.

When Paul was an infantry battalion chaplain, he kept the commander out of legal trouble several times by providing timely guidance on decisions he needed to make. Sometimes, his input was unpopular with the rest of the command staff, but there are times a chaplain has to have enough guts to stand strong and speak up for what is right. Not every disagreement is worth turning into a showdown, though, so it takes skill and discernment to know which issues are worth fighting for. Then, when the time comes to take a stand, hopefully you've built relationships with key people, established a good reputation, and have enough credibility to pull it off.

Keep in mind, the commander will always outrank the chaplain. Therefore, to be effective, a chaplain can't afford to be intimidated by rank. The chaplain represents ethics and morality, the Constitution, and

God himself. Each of those entities outranks the commander. So, to do your job well, you have to be strong enough to take a stand. Plus, you have to be discerning enough to know when and when not to engage in a showdown.

It's important to take note of the word "good" in the opening paragraph of this chapter, because good chaplains are what our military units need. That's what this book is really all about: helping you to become a good chaplain, or perhaps a great chaplain. Someone who is respected, whose input is requested, whose influence is long-lasting. A chaplain who is loved and appreciated.

However, as the saying goes, no person is an island. Few of us can be as effective on our own as we can be when working with others. People can usually accomplish more and have a greater impact when they're part of a team. Ecclesiastes 4:12 says, "A cord of three strands is not easily broken." This is a powerful statement about teamwork, and a good chaplain is not a loner, but part of a team.

This is why almost every chaplain in the military is paired with a Chaplain Assistant. The terminology changes from time to time, but at the time of this writing, a Chaplain Assistant in the Air Force is called a Religious Affairs Airman, while the Army uses the term Religious Affairs Specialist and the Navy has Religious Program Specialists, usually shortened to RP.

Even though the chaplain and Chaplain Assistant are called to work as a team, there are some significant differences between them. The Chaplain Assistant comes up the enlisted ranks to become an NCO, and the chaplain is an officer. The Chaplain Assistant is weapons qualified, but the chaplain is a noncombatant. The Chaplain Assistant is an administrator, office manager, and problem solver, while the chaplain is an ordained clergy doing ministerial tasks and specialized command assignments. They almost always have different personalities and interests, but they have to work as a team. People in the military occasionally use alternate phrases such as "Chaplain Team" or "Unit Ministry Team," but the new standard terminology is to refer to the chaplain and Chaplain Assistant as the "Religious Support Team" (RST), and sometimes the "Religious Affairs Team."

In team sports, each player has a specific role that helps the team succeed. Whatever the sport, the team that excels in all aspects of the game usually wins the championship. For example, to do well in football, you have to have a good offense and defense. A powerful offense with a lousy defense won't win championships. Neither will a great defense with a terrible offense. Both are needed.

Similarly, the Religious Support Team works together to complete its mission by providing and facilitating religious support for the people in the unit. This is known as the Commander's Religious Program. In order to do this effectively, members of the chaplain team have to know their roles, perfect their skills, and work together in unity. They can't afford to be at odds with each other because infighting or jealousy can lead to ineffectiveness and failure. According to the now famous line from the movie *Apollo 13*, failure is not an option. A successful RST, therefore, takes time to build relationship, develop teamwork, and support each other.

Have you ever noticed that at the end of a sports season, after the champion is crowned, a reporter inevitably asks the winning coach and players what it was that led the team to win the title? Almost every time, the answer has to do with teamwork, camaraderie, team spirit, or chemistry. They'll say things like "We're a family on and off the field." Or, "We love and support each other no matter what we're going through." Or, "We're a band of brothers." Or even, "We have a chemistry." This same dynamic is essential in a ministry team.

Jesus mentions this in Matthew 12:25. "Every kingdom divided against itself is headed for destruction, and no city or house divided against itself will stand." Then in Matthew 18:19–20 the Lord says, "If two of you on earth agree about any matter that you pray for, it will be done for you by My Father in heaven. For where two or three are gathered together in My name, I am there among them." Whether we're talking about a sports team, a business, a church staff, a college faculty, a family, or a Religious Support Team, the principle is true: if you're going to be effective, unity is essential. Unity produces winners.

Interestingly, although the chaplain has to be an ordained representative of an acknowledged faith group, the Chaplain Assistant does not have to be religious at all. We've worked with all kinds of Chaplain Assistants: religious and non-religious, Christian and non-Christian, ministry-minded and non-ministry-minded, personable and standoffish, good and bad, male and female. We know chaplains whose NCOs were LGBTQ+ or nonbinary. Each person is assigned separately based on career progression and other military factors, so unfortunately, you usually don't get to choose who you're paired with in the RST. But you do have to be able to work together.

Chaplain Assistants who are people of faith might choose to be actively involved in the worship, fellowship, Bible studies, and other activities of the religious program. On the other hand, Chaplain Assistants who have no faith, will assist by helping logistically, planning, budgeting, and doing a lot of the behind-the-scenes work, but might not attend worship or fellowship events at all. In this case, the chaplain has to be careful not to impose his or her religious beliefs and expectations onto the Chaplain Assistant. You can hold your Chaplain Assistant accountable for physical fitness, weapons qualifications, military tasks, and job-related performance, but you cannot insist on spiritual conformity or religious beliefs and practices.

One Army Chaplain Assistant got to her new hospital unit in Germany only to discover most of the people had a strong dislike and disrespect for chaplains and anyone associated with the chaplain. Frustrated because there seemed to be no inroad for building relationships and doing ministry, she began to pray more fervently. Lord, show me how to break down the barriers these people have put up. Allow me to share you with them.

A few weeks later, the commander "invited" the whole unit to a command-sponsored 10k run, and she had to participate, just like everyone else. As they got ready to start, she overheard some of the faster runners in the group making derogatory and snide remarks about being saddled with another lame chaplain and Chaplain Assistant. What they didn't know was that this Chaplain Assistant had been a distance runner throughout her life, and was in great shape. To everyone's surprise, she smoked them all, finishing well ahead of even their best runners. Suddenly, she had earned their respect.

There are times when the chaplain needs to go to bat on behalf of the Chaplain Assistant because even though the Religious Affairs Airman, Religious Support Specialist, or Religious Program Specialist is assigned to the chaplain's office, every enlisted person and NCO belongs to the NCO corps and is managed by NCO leadership. Because of this, every Chaplain Assistant may be subject to additional duties away from the RST, and may be called on to take turns doing common tasks, just like every other Sailor, Airman, Soldier, Coast Guardsman, or Marine. However, some senior NCOs don't see the Religious Support Team mission as important as their own agenda, so they try to take advantage of Chaplain Assistants, pulling them away for what they consider essential military or training assignments, and they tend to do this more often than is reasonable. We've seen some units take advantage of the Chaplain Assistants, using them more frequently than personnel from other departments, sometimes to the point of abuse.

When this happens, the chaplain needs to step in and protect the Chaplain Assistant, and in essence, protect the effectiveness and cohesiveness of the team and the religious program as a whole. If the chaplain can't or won't do this, there's a risk of losing people, positions, equipment, and funds because the chaplain is sending a signal that it's okay to take advantage of the RST. Instead, both the chaplain and the Chaplain Assistant have to work and act like their mission is the most important part of the command . . . because it is.

KEITH'S STORY:

During my twenty-eight years as a chaplain, I had some good chaplain assistants. They weren't all Christians, but they all had some kind of faith. When I was stationed in Germany, one of my Chaplain Assistants was a young man straight out of high school. He arrived on a Friday, and the next day he went with my family to Nuremburg to go to a Christmas market. When we picked him up from the barracks, he walked to the car wearing a long black trench coat. There was nothing strange about that, but on the front of the coat were about a hundred pins from his favorite bands. It was hilarious. He was tall and super thin, and I was afraid he might be blown over by the wind. It was a wintry day, with snowflakes the size of golf balls. We all had umbrellas, and the snow attacking our umbrellas sounded like big thuds.

I loved that young man. He was a great Chaplain Assistant, and an excellent member of the team. He always made the chaplain's office better, whether getting ready for Bible studies, worship services, counseling appointments, or other events. He and I had a lot of differences—age, education, and musical preferences among them—and his personality and skills were different from mine, but he was a hard worker and was able to connect with many soldiers. Together we made a wonderful team.

I was at a different installation as the war in Iraq kicked off, and I had two chaplain assistants who couldn't have been more different from each other. One was extremely active in the chapel and was highly involved in helping us accomplish anything that needed to be done. The other, who was the senior NCO, was always fighting against the RST, making it tough to maintain a sense of unity, camaraderie, and good relations with the command staff and other leaders.

One of the command policies was that Senior NCOs would take turns leading PT. But every time it was her turn to lead, she reported to sick call and had the junior Chaplain Assistant lead the PT formation instead. Everyone knew she was shirking her responsibilities as a leader, and her actions did not help build a good reputation for the chaplain team. This was an extremely stressful and difficult time for us because the senior chaplain assistant was not a team player, making it more difficult to provide good quality chaplain care.

The bottom line is that unity produces winners. Unity can be difficult to achieve and then to maintain, especially when each individual has a different reason for being in the RST. That makes it all the more important for the chaplain to take the lead, build relationships within the chaplain staff, and support the Chaplain Assistant. The chaplain needs to set an example for the team, even in terms of arriving to work on time, wearing the uniform properly, and staying physically fit. When the chaplain will do what it takes to build and maintain unity in the RST, fulfilling the mission can be interesting and fun, providing a deep sense of meaning and fulfillment for everyone on the chaplain team, resulting in people being drawn into the kingdom of God.

Guest Anecdote Number Six

Unity in the Religious Support Team

In order for there to be unity in the Religious Support Team, both the chaplain and the Chaplain Assistant must respect each other's beliefs and respect the uniform that is worn. The RST must be willing to spend time together. The chaplain must rely on his assistant to do the job he was trained for, and the assistant must rely on the chaplain's judgment as to the mission to be completed. My own experience as a Chaplain Assistant illustrates this need.

During a field exercise, my chaplain and I had a mission to complete. A chaplain is an officer and has to follow the mission guidelines as well as be responsible for the spiritual welfare of the battalions' soldiers. He or she also has to attend official briefings to discuss the mission's objectives and observations.

My chaplain was doing everything he was supposed to do. As a Chaplain Assistant, I was trained to protect and care for his physical well-being.

I observed that my chaplain was extremely tired, and suggested that he rest and get a little sleep. Because of our close relationship and the unity of the RST, he did rest and take a nap.

Another instance was when I was at an RST conference where there were several chaplains and Chaplain Assistants in attendance. Because of the unique structure of the RST and the respect we had for our colleagues, officer and enlisted, I was asked by a Jewish chaplain who was a Brigadier General to partake in a celebration of a Jewish holiday called *Purim*. It was just the General and I who celebrated it. Because of the unity and respect for each other, I was asked and able to celebrate.

SGT ROBERT ROSENTHAL, CHAPLAIN ASSISTANT

Chapter 14

Chaplain Tasks

So... what exactly does a chaplain do? Title 10 USC 3547 of the US Code says: "Each chaplain shall, when practicable, hold appropriate religious services at least once on each Sunday for the command to which he is assigned, and shall perform appropriate religious burial services for members of the Army who die while in that command."[1]

This original statement contains only two tasks: preach on Sunday and bury the dead. That would be an extremely brief job description for anyone in the military. However, there are regulations, manuals, pamphlets, memorandums, instructions, laws, treaties, policies, and guidelines that add to the duties and spell out the ministry of the chaplain. Therefore, the real answer to the opening question is going to be very long, even if we just listed the tasks without describing or discussing them.

Your training begins in seminary, where you learn the essence of theology, ministry, and representing your denomination or faith group. And you need a minimum of two years of real-world pastoral ministry. The military relies on the seminaries, churches, and endorsers to train and prepare quality clergy before you come into the military because from the get-go through the end of your career, you are required to be a minister in good standing with your faith group. In fact, your mission, should you choose to accept it, is to represent the church you came from. One way of looking at it is that when you come into the military, you are on loan from your faith group.

---

1. Title 10, uscode.house.gov.

Chaplain Tasks

When the Southern Baptist Convention "loaned" Keith to the military, they expected him to be a pastor in uniform. Likewise, when the Assemblies of God "loaned" Paul to the military, they expected him to represent the denomination throughout his career. This is supported by DOD's expectations of a minister who comes into the military. A chaplain does the very same tasks that a pastor in a local church does. This usually includes teaching, preaching, performing weddings and funerals, counseling, administering the sacraments or ordinances of the church, conducting business, preparing budgets, providing strategic vision and leadership, and many other responsibilities. In fact, the DOD insists that a minister must have this experience before being considered for Active Duty military service, which is why a smart applicant will keep track of the number of weddings, funerals, sacrament services, baptisms, and other ministerial actions he or she has conducted.

We said in the beginning that there were a lot of tasks. When you consider that chaplains have three lines of accountability that they answer to, it is easy to understand why the task list is so long. As a chaplain, you are a military officer and a member of the commander's personal staff. As such, you work for the commander, implementing the command religious program and advising the commander on a number of issues. You also work directly for the Chief of Chaplains of your branch of the Armed Forces, carrying out the policies and directives regarding the plans, activities, and programs designed by the Chief of Chaplain's staff. And you mustn't forget your denomination's or endorser's leadership. All of these leadership chains (command, Chief of Chaplains, and faith group leadership) have the right to issue guidance and hold you accountable.

What this means for the average chaplain is that you have several bosses telling you what to do: the authoritative chain of command starting with your executive officer and commander up the chain to the next higher command and beyond, the technical chain starting with your supervisory chaplain on up to the Chief of Chaplains, and the denominational hierarchy. If you are endorsed by someone other than your ordaining organization, then you might have a fourth line of authority to answer to. You have to understand that you have no direct authority, only delegated authority. Therefore, you can't afford to fight against your commander, your Chief of Chaplains, or your church leadership. You have to find a way to be a team player.

A good chaplain has no authority, but a lot of influence. That's enough to get the job done, see some amazing results, and have an outstanding career. Your influence in the command and in people's lives depends on your doing enough of the right tasks well, and staying out of trouble. This influence leads to effective ministry . . . and sometimes it leads to fantastic ministry.

Because the chaplain is part of the commander's staff, you are expected to be at every staff meeting. As a member of the battalion, squadron, or ship's company, you should be at every physical training (PT) event. The commander will expect the chaplain to understand what is going on in the unit. This can only happen when you are actively involved in the life of the command, out doing visitation in work areas and hospitals, planning a dynamic worship service and fellowship program, and participating in leader development events.

One senior leader had a vanity tag on his vehicle that said "UFAL." When Keith asked him what it meant, he looked at Keith as if he should already know. "Chaplain, it means *up front and leading*!" That is exactly what he expected from all of his staff, including his chaplain.

One rookie Navy chaplain visited his Marines regularly and developed an amazing rapport with them. One day the Gunny said, "Hey Chaps! How 'bout you doin' PT with us from time to time?"

"OK, Gunny. I can do that," the chaplain replied.

A few days later, when the chaplain was doing his rounds, the Gunny called him into his office and handed him a personalized USMC PT uniform that said "CHAPLAIN" on the back. The chaplain visited his Marines, worked out with them, attended their special events, counseled them, loved them, and they responded—not only to him, but to the gospel as well.

KEITH'S STORY:

I visited a senior chaplain deployed to a foreign nation who was on the verge of being fired by his command. When I got there, he was leading a community-wide humanitarian assistance effort, which sounded good to me. The chaplain had arranged food distribution to the local population. Service members who wished to participate would have to hike six miles up a mountain.

Upon my arrival, he asked if I would like to participate. Never one to shy away from a new challenge, I accepted, and hiked up the mountain with a bunch of people in the command, carrying food in bags and backpacks. It was a pretty good hike, and when I got to the top of the mountain, the chaplain was already there, high-fiving everyone, congratulating them, and slapping backs. I knew he hadn't passed me on the way up the mountain, so I asked him how he got there. When I heard that he and his chaplain assistant had driven up, I understood the problem right away. His commander expected him to be with his troops, but he wasn't. He should have been sweating, walking, talking, joking, and struggling with his service members going up that mountain. In essence, he tried to appear as if he was with the troops, but he routinely took the easy, lazy way out, and the soldiers in the command saw through his ruse.

The point is this: as a staff officer, you are the eyes and ears of the commander, who wants you to be out and about with the people. On a higher level, as a minister *on loan* from your faith group, your endorser expects you to be the eyes and ears of the church and of God as you are out with the service members in your care. That can't be done inside the four walls of the chapel or office. It's done by going out and spending time with the people in your unit. Don't misunderstand. You will be in your office plenty: counseling, preparing sermons and lessons, planning, budgeting, writing memos, and taking care of business. But the time outside the office complements the work done inside the office. God will give you eyes to see the need and the hurt of those you serve as you walk with them along the journey of life. And that is just as important as the time spent preparing for your next sermon or Bible study, because that is the *incarnational ministry of presence.*

As a retired chaplain and then a denominational chaplain endorser, Keith follows hundreds of military chaplains on social media. He loves seeing what they post, which isn't the four walls of the chapel or an office building. It may be a video or picture of them jumping out of a perfectly good plane. Sitting in the mud or sand, breaking open an MRE. Standing among a group of service members. They might be hanging out of a helicopter window, or on the bridge of a ship, or in the middle of a platoon hiking twelve miles. Those are the views where the chaplain is building his or her congregation and sharing the love of Christ.

Each of the Armed Services has regulations that govern what chaplains do and how they do it. They include worship services and burying the dead. But they go on to include a lot of "ministries" that you might not have studied in Seminary. This list includes the idea of "performing or providing" ministry. This phrase is important, and here's what it looks like.

KEITH'S STORY:

I did not normally do infant baptisms because they were not part of my church's theology or practice. But when someone came to me and wanted me to baptize their baby, I didn't turn them away. I took care of them by finding another chaplain who could do the baptism and meet the family's needs.

The point of the "perform or provide" concept is that no chaplain will be required to do anything that falls outside the parameters of his or her faith group. However, the chaplain is expected to provide a way for the religious needs of the Armed Forces member to be met, even if done by someone else. One chaplain was visiting the offices on the base where he served, and discovered that there were several LDS folks who wished there was an LDS sacrament service on base. Because they worked in different offices in different areas, they didn't even know there were other members of their church in the command. When the chaplain introduced them to each other, they discovered there were two LDS bishops among them, so they organized an LDS worship service. Because the chaplain wasn't LDS, not only was he not expected to lead the sacrament service, he didn't even attend. But he facilitated in such a way that he met their needs.

In addition to performing and providing for the religious needs of the people in the command, chaplains advise the commander and the command staff on religious issues, ethics, and morale. The chaplain provides individual and relationship counseling. Chaplains often work with the personnel section to provide suicide prevention and awareness training. Because people in the military spend a lot of time away from home, chaplains will often prepare couples and families who are dealing with separation issues. They work with the personnel section to provide programs for single service members as well as marriage seminars for couples. All of these tasks and roles require specialized training and positive relationships among the people in the command.

Chaplains should be proactive and aggressive about requesting further training and skills certifications. In fact, we recommend that chaplains request additional training every year. That way, you continue to grow professionally, adding to what you have to offer the command and the people in your area. Additional training might include Critical Incident Stress Management, Advanced Suicide Awareness Training,

Personal and Professional Mentoring, World Religions, Ethical Decision Making, or even an additional graduate degree.

One chaplain became a Master Fitness Trainer because there was a shortage of qualified personnel at his base. Another completed the Navy's personal finance course in order to provide additional guidance for her sailors and Marines.

Official chaplain duties include assisting with Casualty Assistance notifications. When a service member claims to be a conscientious objector, the chaplain interviews the person and prepares a memo to the commander. Chaplains should become experts in religious accommodation, pluralism, and ethical leadership. Sometimes, chaplains might need to complete some extended training to be qualified as a family counselor, resource manager, or hospital chaplain with Clinical Pastoral Education (CPE).

Chaplains also need to understand their role in the Religious Support Team. As a section leader, the chaplain is responsible for training the Chaplain Assistants, ensuring that they pass the common skills tests, PT, and military education requirements for promotion. Chaplains need to understand the evaluation and promotion system, both for themselves and their staff, including the best way to word the evals. They should be competent with the budget process, how to prepare an SOP, and how the command wants them to contribute to the training calendar.

As you can see, there's a whole lot more than preaching once a week and occasionally burying the dead. Nobody can do everything, though, so you need to understand your own calling, your own gifting, your own strengths and weaknesses. A good chaplain will work hard to master the essential skills and knowledge required for the many challenges facing the chaplaincy in the twenty-first century. This can be done by paying attention during training sessions, reading the provided materials, and building relationships with key people so you know where to go and who to contact when you need help. A good chaplain will prioritize building the team and esprit de corps, investing in and relying on each person on the staff to carry some of the load.

As you rise in rank, you'll undoubtedly move into positions of leadership where you will supervise a larger staff and supervise other chaplains. It's a good idea to prepare for this well in advance by reading about leadership and observing others in leadership positions. You might even want to take note of those you consider to be good leaders and those who are bad leaders, and analyze what makes them good or bad.

It's also crucial to maintain your personal relationships and spiritual life, taking time for family, as well as to worship, pray, and read the scriptures, keeping in mind that self-care has to be practiced along the way.

It's easy to become overwhelmed by the enormity of the task of being a chaplain, which is why we have to be sure of the divine call on our lives. This kind of ministry isn't for everyone. But when you know God has spoken to you, when you are certain this is the direction for your life, and when you are committed to representing Jesus Christ in an incarnational ministry of presence, you have a unique opportunity to make a powerful difference in people's lives.

There is still an open door for genuine ministry in the Armed Forces of the United States. But the price to pay for that open door involves a lot besides preaching, praying, and pastoring. Those who are willing and able to rise to the challenge, who stay faithful and consistent, have a chance at witnessing the fulfillment of Ephesians 3:20 in some spectacular ways.

"Now to Him who is able to do above and beyond all that we ask or think according to the power that works in us—to Him be glory in the church and in Christ Jesus to all generations, forever and ever. Amen." To him be glory in the Army, the Navy, the Air Force, the Marines, and the Coast Guard. Amen.

Guest Anecdote Number Seven

Kosher Meals for a Jewish MP

A few years ago, one of our Military Police NCOs had to go out of state for a month of training. He happened to be an orthodox Jew, and his orders said he was to eat in the mess hall at the base. That's where the problem was. The manager of the chow hall told him he could not get kosher food during his Temporary Duty for Training (TDY), so the soldier called me to report what was happening and to ask for my assistance.

I had known the guy for a couple of years. He came to my office to ask for Jewish scriptures, which I provided. On another occasion, I intervened to help his supervisor understand the man's desire to honor the Sabbath and the Jewish calendar. He was a great soldier, a hard worker with an outstanding reputation, and didn't attempt to avoid his responsibilities, so there was never a doubt about his motives or his character. Plus, we became friends. So when I heard how distraught he sounded on the phone, I knew he was being genuine, and I assured him that I would do whatever I could to take care of him.

After hanging up the phone, I called the chaplain at the base to ask for his help, and he sprang into action, because providing for the bona fide dietary needs of religious groups is a serious religious accommodation issue. The chaplain on location called the mess hall manager, who told him the same thing he had said to the soldier: he would not provide any special meals just because the guy was unhappy about the cuisine.

However, this wasn't a situation where somebody didn't like the food. The chaplain had to explain to the mess boss that religious dietary needs are valid military concerns that are explicitly covered in military regulations and policies, and that we are obligated to accommodate religious requests whenever possible. And this certainly appeared to be possible.

After a bit of back-and-forth over the necessity of accommodating the soldier's request on religious grounds, and the chaplain threatening to call the installation commander, the manager of the mess hall agreed to take care of the Jewish MP. Although he didn't have the means to prepare kosher meals, and didn't have any kosher MRE's on hand, he managed to come up with an acceptable solution. He provided vouchers for a nearby grocery story, he secured a vehicle for the soldier to use for shopping, and then had his staff deliver a microwave oven to the soldier's room in on-post lodging.

The soldier was pleased that he now had the means to fulfill his religious commitments. But it required the immediate intervention of two chaplains who understood the validity of his request and who also knew the laws, regs, and policies regarding religious accommodation.

Anonymous Military Chaplain

Chapter 15

Family Support Groups

FAMILY LIFE IS FILLED with challenges, and being a military family is even tougher. Serving in the Armed Forces is a dangerous profession, with built-in health and safety hazards because working with or near explosives can be catastrophic. Death or dismemberment during war is always possible, but sometimes tragedies occur during training exercises, too. You get a feel for this when watching a war movie, but the real-life version of the story is incredibly more heart wrenching. However, the conditions impacting a military family go beyond the physical dangers of the person in uniform. In fact, they are rather far-reaching.

Every year or two or three, the military moves its people to different installations, and there are good reasons for this. We have to be able to work with a wide variety of people in order to truly be ready to "plug 'n play" during a crisis. We need to experience different environments and conditions. Another factor is that in order to be promoted, we usually have to be assigned to a slot rated for the next rank. Also, moving from time to time helps us stay fresh and on top of our profession, rather than becoming complacent or comfortable in what might become a routine or a rut.

The downside of moving, however, is the toll it takes on the family. The spouse and children are frequently saying goodbye to friends and neighbors, which often leaves the family without an emotional support group. Telephones, video chats, and social media can help, but there's nothing like being with your friend in person, hanging out together, or having a cup of tea or coffee together while talking things over. It takes time to build trust with new acquaintances, and in the military, just when that trust is starting to be established, it's time to PCS again. PCS is the acronym meaning "Permanent Change of Station."

PAUL'S STORY:

My dad became a Navy chaplain when I was four months old. Before I finished high school, the family moved ten times. The result was that I attended eleven different schools and lived in four different states. This made it almost impossible to maintain friendships. Twice, we moved on my birthday: no party, no cake, no presents, no friends.

Some people respond well to this constant readjusting to new schools, churches, and other social structures. Others don't do well at all. Moving around makes it difficult for kids who are active in sports programs. For example, when I was a sophomore in high school, I became the starting quarterback on the varsity football team. Halfway through the season, the coach asked me how long my dad would be stationed in the area. When he found out I wouldn't be at the school the next year, he benched me and then demoted me to the JV team. When I got to the next high school, I was an unknown, so it took a while to earn a starting spot on the team.

Another challenge is that the service member may be away from home, sometimes frequently, and for many weeks or months. This puts a strain on the family and on the marriage. The absence of mom or dad throws everything out of kilter, and those at home have to adjust. Then, when the service member returns, they're forced to adjust all over again. From being together as husband and wife, to being away from each other, and coping with life on your own. From shared parenting, to single parenting, and back to being a couple again. The back and forth can be as difficult as the separation itself because you have to keep redefining roles and responsibilities.

If the spouse of a service member wants to have a career, moving around the country makes it harder, especially when it comes to promotions, greater responsibilities, and availability. These moves can lead to problems with personal fulfillment, identity, and loss. It can also be detrimental to finances and retirement planning.

An issue for many people in the early years of a military career is that they are paid less than those who've been in longer. The financial struggle is real because it takes time to move up the ranks. Every two years, there's a time-in-grade pay raise, and every promotion includes an increase in salary. So eventually, the pay becomes comfortable, but getting through the early years is the challenge, especially among enlisted personnel.

Added to these issues is the fact that sexual temptations abound. In addition, many military families deal with loneliness, anger, stress, fear, anxiety, and being far from the extended family, hometown, and lifelong friends.

Because of these factors, most military units have a Family Support Group, sometimes called a Family Readiness Group or a Family Network, and it's really important that chaplains build relationships with the Family Support Group leaders, and participate in their activities. Not only can a chaplain help them reach out and provide significant support to the families, it's a great way for chaplains to be visible, so that when someone wants to inquire about the Lord, they already know who the chaplains is. In essence, participating in the family support group removes potential barriers and obstacles, providing an open door for ministry. Plus, it's just good business practice to support the work of others in the command, especially when there's an overlap in purpose and mission.

The military is often a stand-alone community or city of its own. For example, each installation has a shopping center, gas station, grocery store, movie theatre, gym, community center, hospital, playgrounds, walking trails, sports activities, library, chapels, and its own shoppette, which is similar to a 7/11 or Circle K. But it's the human connection that the Family Readiness Group and command social events try to offer. In a sense, these are the same kinds of needs the church tries to meet through its fellowship activities and small group ministries, so it's natural that a good chaplain will participate in as many of these kinds of programs as possible. The stated purposes for these Family Support Groups are as follows:[1]

1. Distribute relevant command information to the family members of the unit.
2. Act as a support and communication bridge between the command and the family.
3. Connect you to and advocate for the community resources at your disposal.

---

1. Duttweiler, "What the Heck is an FRG?" para. 8.

4. Help solve problems that arise while your spouse is affiliated with the command.
5. Make you feel as ready, resilient, and connected as possible.
6. Provide emotional and practical support when the service member is away.
7. Meet as many practical needs as possible.

Should the chaplain get involved? Definitely! It's also a great program for the chaplain's spouse to participate in. There is no obligation for the spouse, of course. But it is an opportunity to make friends, help others, and let your light shine for Christ.

KEITH'S STORY:

I grew up a military brat. If you ask me where I am from, I can't really tell you because I am from a lot of places. I was born in Norfolk VA, and lived a number of years there. But I have no roots there because my family no longer lives there. I lived in Panama, the Philippines, South Carolina, and Virginia as a Navy Brat. So, it is hard to say where I am from.

Several years ago, we "retired" and moved to Tennessee, where our kids live. When we got there, people just assumed that we moved from somewhere else in the state. My only personal connection with Tennessee is that I went to Carson-Newman University way back when. So even in retirement, having roots and fitting in is difficult because of being a Navy brat, combined with my own military career.

There are a lot of jokes about being a military brat, or a military family. For example, you know you are a military brat when . . .

1. Every time your family drives through the gate, you salute and say, "Have a great day SGT!"
2. You call your friend's parents "Mrs. and Major" or "Colonel and Mister."
3. You have a daddy/mommy deployment doll.
4. You think it's weird that your school friends' dads or moms don't deploy.
5. You know the seating plan on airplanes . . . and the reason for it.

6. Even as a preschooler, you don't yell "It's a plane! It's a helicopter!" Instead, you yell "It's a C-130! It's a Chinook!"
7. No matter where you are, at 5 p.m. you stand still, put your hand over your heart, face the flag, and wait for the music.
8. Your soccer and baseball coaches show up, not in a sports uniform, but in a military uniform.
9. You point excitedly at any building on any military base and proudly shout, "That's my daddy's house!"

And my all-time favorite:

10. You know that before every movie, the National Anthem plays and everyone stands up with hand over heart.

Of course, the list goes on and on.[2]

Our recommendation is that within a week of arriving at your new unit, you contact the leaders of the Family Support Network, make an appointment to meet them in person, and let them know you are there to encourage them and support them. Your role as a chaplain is not to lead the group, but to be an encouragement and support, offering your help so they can be more effective in meeting needs for the families of the command.

In doing so, you are functioning as an effective staff officer, becoming more visible to a wider group of people, and by establishing relationships, you're planting seeds that will almost always bear fruit later on.

---

2. Military Spouse, "35 Ways You Know."

CHAPTER 16

Pluralism and Religious Liberty

AMERICA'S FOUNDERS HAD EXPERIENCED the abuses of political and religious powers in the European monarchies, so they attempted to create a new nation that prevented the duplication of those problems. That is why from the very beginning, the United States was not a monarchy, and there would be no official religion. Instead of kings who reigned for life and whose heirs would inherit the throne, we would be governed by elected officials with limited terms of office. And instead of a state religion, the government would be prohibited from establishing an official religion, and it would guarantee the free exercise and expression of religious worship and practice for everyone.

Understanding this Constitutional mandate from the start, it is fair to say that even though the United States may have been founded on many biblical ideas and ideals, and even though many, if not the majority, of our citizens were Christians, America itself was not created to be a Christian nation. Our Constitution prevents us from having a state religion, while at the same time guaranteeing freedom of religious expression for people of every faith and culture. This is the situation in our military, and this is what every good chaplain understands.

Pluralism is foundational, yet it is one of the more difficult issues for many chaplain candidates, chaplains, and even some endorsers to understand and discuss because we're accustomed to working and ministering in a local congregation where almost everyone we interact with is from our own denomination, with identical doctrine and similar worship style. For many pastors, the only time they work with someone outside of their faith tradition is when there's a Community Thanksgiving Service or other city-wide program.

But as a military chaplain, every single day you'll see service members of different faith traditions. You'll routinely interact with and minister to Jews, Catholics, Muslims, Latter Day Saints, Protestants of many varieties, and those with no faith whatsoever. Some chaplains flourish in this kind of pluralistic environment, while others flounder, stick out like a sore thumb, or feel like a fish out of water. Clergy who come into the military with little ecumenical or inter-faith experience might experience some culture shock. Others might have to learn real fast what it means to be a genuine Christian who is faithful to the Bible and Christian lifestyle, while at the same time working and living side by side with agnostics, atheists, Hindus, cussers, smokers, alcoholics, and blatant sinners.

We are never asked to compromise our own personal faith. But at the same time, we have to respect and tolerate everyone else. In fact, part of the chaplain's job is to make sure each person in the military is afforded the same religious freedom, regardless of what they believe.

In 2013, former Army Chief of Chaplains, MG Don Rutherford, wrote a letter that was included in his *Strategic Roadmap for the Army Chaplain Corps*. Part of his message said:

> A foundational principle of our nation is our country's reliance on the grace of God. From the very inception of our United States, the preeminent value of the free exercise of religion and the non-establishment of religion has been a bedrock of our Democracy. This tradition stands enshrined in the First Amendment to the Constitution and in the enormous body of documentation penned by our Founding Fathers. To help preserve and defend our right of free exercise is the special mandate bestowed upon the Army Chaplain Corps by the American People.[1].

Chaplain Rutherford, who is a Roman Catholic priest, goes on to refer to today's military as "the most religiously diverse organization in the world." This is the environment we are called to minister in when we become military chaplains in the twenty-first century.

---

1. Rutherford, *Strategic Roadmap*, 2013, 4.

PAUL'S STORY:

Early in my career, I was assigned to an infantry battalion. The day I showed up and started meeting some of the soldiers, the Sergeant Major introduced himself and asked, "Hey chaplain, do you have your gotcha cards?"

"No, Sergeant Major. I've never heard of a gotcha card, and don't know what it is, so I'm pretty sure I don't have one. What is it?"

"The chaplain we had a couple years ago, every time he heard one of us cuss or swear or use the Lord's name in vain, he'd pull out a business card, but all it said in big bold letters was 'gotcha.' So, when the guys heard we were getting a new chaplain, they started wondering if you were going to be like the last one."

"I bet you guys hated him."

"Yes. We. Did."

"Tell you what. I don't plan on having any gotcha cards printed up, so you can relax. Cuss if you want. I'm here to love you guys."

Apparently, several soldiers were listening, because as soon as I made that statement, a cheer erupted from around the corner.

"You're gonna fit in fine here, Chaps. Nice to have you aboard."

The first year I was with that battalion, I simply loved them, spent time with them, and let the Holy Spirit do his job, and twenty-five of those guys got saved, converting to faith in Christ.

In that same unit, I participated in a two-week training exercise, and was housed in on-base lodging with an officer who practiced a type of New Age meditation. He was a bit uncomfortable being forced to spend time with a Christian chaplain, thinking I would condemn him or preach at him every time we were in the room together. Instead, I treated him with kindness and respect, and told him that when he wanted to spend some time meditating, I would leave the room so he could have some time alone.

Several days into the exercise, I noticed that he was grumpy, grouchy, and angry. So I asked him if he'd been doing his meditation lately. He stopped in his tracks, looked at me, and replied, "No, I haven't. No wonder I'm out of sorts and barking at my soldiers. Thanks for caring for me, chaplain!"

Later that year when we had our annual holiday family activities, I was asked to pray before lunch was served. Because it was not a Bible study or a worship service, I prayed a meaningful prayer, but did not mention the name of Jesus. After I concluded, a lieutenant approached me and said, "I am Jewish, and I want to thank you for being my chaplain."

KEITH'S STORY:

When I was stationed in Germany, one of the chaplains whom I respected held an Ash Wednesday Healing Service. I must admit that I had never attended an Ash Wednesday Service. It just wasn't something this Southern Baptist preacher ever did. However, when I attended that service, I was deeply moved by the Spirit as believers of different faith traditions came earnestly seeking the touch of God in their lives. Each time the Chaplain anointed another parishioner with ashes, God moved! It was an amazing, eye-opening worship experience for me, one that I will never forget. To this day, I try to participate in an Ash Wednesday service every year.

Because chaplains come from a variety of backgrounds, we have to be comfortable with traditions that are unlike our own. That's one of the reasons most faith group endorsers are members of an organization that falls loosely under the Department of Defense. The National Conference for Ministry to the Armed Forces (NCMAF) has a Code of Ethics that all endorsers agree to adhere to. This includes about 200 different groups. The code of ethics says:

> I understand as a chaplain in the United States Armed Forces that I will function in a pluralistic environment with chaplains of other religious bodies to provide for ministry to all military personnel and their families entrusted to my care. I will seek to provide for pastoral care and ministry to persons of religious bodies other than my own within my area of responsibility with the same investment of myself as I give to members of my own religious body. I will work collegially with chaplains of religious bodies other than my own as together we seek to provide as full a ministry as possible to our people. I will respect the beliefs and traditions of my colleagues and those to whom I minister.[2]

The Department of Defense (DOD) needs denominations and endorsers to provide clergy who fully understand how to function in a pluralistic environment, and who are able to minister authentically and faithfully while respecting those who differ in their beliefs and values.

---

2. "The Covenant and Code of Ethics for Chaplains in the Armed Forces," *NCMAF*, http://www.ncmaf.net/library/the-covenant-and-code-of-ethics-for-chaplains-of-the-armed-forces.

Some endorsers do a better job of this than others, just like some chaplains do a better job than others.

KEITH'S STORY:

Recently, I attended the Air Force Chaplains Basic Course Graduation at Maxwell Air Force Base. The current Air Force Chief of Chaplains was the guest speaker, and I had an opportunity to talk with him privately for a few minutes. I asked if there was one message he would like me to pass on to my students and chaplain candidates. His answer stuck with me: "Remember that chaplain ministry is not about us (the chaplains). It is about those we serve."

That, my friend, is worth repeating. It's not about us. It's about those we serve.

Serving as a chaplain for twenty-eight years, and then as an endorser for over fifteen years, I have seen chaplains who made the ministry all about themselves. They emphasized their rights, their agenda, and their message. Interestingly, those who serve in this way are usually the very ones who have problems, because they tend to rub people the wrong way. And their self-centered approach to ministry is often ineffective. I have even seen some endorsers who thought this way.

You have to keep in mind that when you become a military chaplain, it is no longer all about being a minister from your denomination or faith group. Yes, you will be expected to hold to your church's tenets of faith and practice. You will continue to live a godly lifestyle. And you'll even pay your ministerial dues or tithes as required. But you'll also be expected to serve, respect, counsel, and minister to all kinds of people, from all kinds of religious beliefs.

To do this, we typically balance the concept of "Perform and Provide." A chaplain performs direct ministry to service members of the same or similar faith groups, but not for people of different religions. When there are religious needs for those of other faiths, a chaplain "provides" or facilitates the meeting of needs. This might be done by offering religious literature, providing a place to meet and worship, or arranging a clergy or practitioner from that faith group to come in and minister.

In 2013, the Southern Baptist Convention wrote a statement on pluralism and what they expected of their chaplains. Part of the message said:

Pluralism and Religious Liberty

> SBC chaplains serve in a pluralistic setting but expect, under U.S. Department of Defense guidelines, that the rights and freedoms of chaplains will be protected so they may preach, teach and counsel in accordance with the tenets of their denominational faith group and their own religious conscience. In addition, chaplains are expected to treat all service members, regardless of rank or behavior, with Christ-centered dignity, honor and respect while assisting the institutional leadership in its religious mission requirements and responsibilities as guaranteed by the First Amendment to the United States Constitution.[3]

Many Protestant denominations that send clergy into the military have similar documents. Otherwise, they probably wouldn't be sending their ministers to serve in the military. The Assemblies of God military chaplaincy department says:

> Chaplains are ever-present in the lives of the . . . men and women they serve. Because they are held to the same rigorous standards, chaplains become a trusted member of the military family. New recruits turn to chaplains for encouragement and guidance as they adjust to military life. Officers of all ranks confide in chaplains during times of crisis and question, allowing chaplains a powerful place of influence among those who serve our country. Routine duties: lead worship services and Bible studies, teach classes on morals and ethics, counsel and support military members, represent Christ to all cultures and religions, serve in settings as diverse as the military presence around the world.[4]

Notice the last part of the statement: "represent Christ to all cultures and religions, serve in settings as diverse as the military presence around the world." Even though you are required to serve and facilitate ministry in a pluralistic environment, you will never be asked to compromise your personal religious tradition or faith group. In fact, one of the mantras of military chaplaincies is "cooperation without compromise." You will work alongside other chaplains whose faith tradition is not like yours. They might not share the same sacred texts that you do. You might disagree totally with their theology and worship, but nonetheless, they are chaplains just like you are.

---

3. Carver and Travis, "Southern Baptist Endorsed Chaplains," para. 1.
4. *Chaplaincy Ministries*, https://chaplaincy.ag.org/This-Is-My-Church/Military.

This always leads me to think about the common bond that we have with chaplains of all faiths. We might be many, but we are united by our work and the commitment to serve those in uniform.

When I befriended a retired Army rabbi, we became friends and he mentored me in many significant ways. One time when we were talking about praying or using the name of Jesus, he told me he would be offended if I didn't use the name of Jesus. He expected Christians to be loyal to their beliefs, just like he expected Jews to be loyal to their faith and traditions. I am confident that this rabbi would agree that it isn't about us. It's about those we serve.

As we think about Religious Accommodation and Religious Liberty in the military, our minds return to the First Amendment of the Constitution, which says: "Congress shall make no law respecting an establishment of religion, or prohibiting the free exercise thereof." As Thomas Kidd says in his book *God of Liberty*, the first amendment "both keeps us intensely religious and religiously free."[5]

The military strongly believes in the religious liberty and accommodation of its members. In fact, DOD Directive 1300.17 says:

> The U.S. Constitution proscribes Congress from enacting any law prohibiting the free exercise of religion. The Department of Defense places a high value on the rights of members of the Military Services to observe tenets of their respective religions. It is DOD policy that requests for accommodation of religious practices should be approved by commanders when accommodations will not have an adverse impact on mission accomplishment, military readiness, unit cohesion, standards, or discipline.[6]

The Army reinforces the DOD policy about accommodation and religious liberty in Army Regulation 600–20, paragraph 5–6:

> The Army places a high value on the rights of its soldiers to observe tenets of their respective religious faiths. The Army will approve requests for accommodation of religious practices unless accommodation will have an adverse impact on unit readiness, individual readiness, unit cohesion, morale, discipline, safety, and/or health. As used in this regulation, these factors will be referred to individually and collectively as "military necessity" unless otherwise stated. Accommodation of a soldier's

---

5. Kidd, *God of Liberty*, 55.
6. DOD Directive, 1300.17.

religious practices must be examined against military necessity and cannot be guaranteed at all times.

The other branches of the Armed Forces have similar statements in their regs, policies, and instructions, because religious liberty and accommodation are extremely important to the fabric of the military and its service members.

The bottom line is that chaplains in the military are more productive and bear more fruit for the kingdom of God when they stick to the positive side of ministry and the message of the gospel: love God and love people, be a friend to all, avoid condemning anyone, be gracious and respectful to people of all faiths and traditions, remain true to your own values and beliefs, and trust the Holy Spirit to be at work in people's lives. Chaplains who take this approach tend to be healthier, happier, promoted faster and further, and lead more men and women to faith in Christ.

Guest Anecdote Number Eight

Pluralism at its Finest

In the early Spring of 1997, I was a newly assigned CH (MAJ) at the United States Army Reserve (USAR), 77th Regional Support Command (RSC), located at Fort Totten, Queens, NY. I was the first chaplain assigned as an Active Guard/Reserve (AGR) to that Command. At that point, I had collateral duty as the Garrison Chaplain at Fort Hamilton, Brooklyn, NY, extending through the 30th of September of that same year. At the time of my arrival in New York, I was the lone "full-time" active-duty chaplain in the five-borough area.

Early one evening I receive a phone call at my home telling me that an Army Solider, stationed on a remote tour in Korea, was returning home on emergency leave, to Brooklyn, NY. The overview of the story was that her husband and two children were dead, and that this soldier, a Shi'ite Muslim, wanted a Shi'ite Imam to perform the funeral rights for her deceased family members.

My first thought was, "What in world am I going to do"? I had been in New York about two months and did not have any known, available resources. (This was before wide-spread home internet use.) So, my next move was to get out the phone book and to call local Mosques, to see if they could be of help. I made several calls, but the two that answered said that they were Sunni and could not help. Nor did they have any references to a Shi'a Mosque.

Guest Anecdote Number Eight

The next morning, I went to my office in the chapel at Ft. Hamilton. Providentially, two USAR chaplains were doing Rescheduled Training (RST) at the chapel. One was CH (LTC) Thomas Malloy, a Roman Catholic Priest, and CH (LTC) Doniel Kramer, an Orthodox Jewish Rabbi. I told them about the situation, and they got to work.

Later, the grieving soldier and her assigned escort NCO arrived at the chapel and she told me the backstory that led the tragic events. The soldier was from Iran. Upheaval and persecution transpired and she, her husband, and young son found themselves living in the Iraqi desert, in a camp for Iranian refugees. Her second child, a girl, was born during this time. Meanwhile, they applied for asylum and were granted entry into the US, where they settled in Brooklyn.

Life in Brooklyn was hard, as her husband could not find steady, sustainable employment. She said they lived with very little financial means. However, her husband refused to let his wife look for work; he had very hierarchical views on the marriage and felt that his wife should obey his commands. Finally, the woman took matters into her own hands. She enlisted in the US Army, primarily because it would provide a steady income and medical benefits. The soldier's husband was extremely unhappy about her joining the Army. Throughout Initial Entry Training (IET) and Advanced Individual Training (AIT), he constantly wrote letters to her, telling her to get out of the Army. She felt that he was so adamantly opposed to her serving in the Army because it made him look bad in his own culture with the perception that she was the primary breadwinner, and secondly that she would not obey him. The soldier had hoped for a Continental United States (CONUS) assignment following AIT, but instead found herself on a one-year, unaccompanied tour to Korea.

While in Korea, the letters continued. Finally, the situation took an evil turn. The husband suffocated the two children with a pillow, placed them in bed as through they were sleeping, and then hung himself. Across his chest he placed a sign with the words "I Love You" written on it.

Meanwhile, as I listened to this tragic, horrifying story, CH Kramer found a Shi'ite Imam to perform the funeral rights. He located one by contacting the Iranian Consulate at the United Nations. Together with CH Malloy, they located a cemetery and funeral home where the appropriate rituals could be performed.

A few days later I again spoke with the soldier and her escort NCO. The escort cried as the soldier described the ritual washing of the dead children before burial. As with my other meeting, I asked if it were appropriate to pray. She welcomed it, and I prayed a prayer of comfort and the Almighty's grace to be upon this shattered soldier, her family, and yes, the escort NCO, who undoubtedly never faced anything like this before.

Looking back, I felt proud to be associated with such fine men who demonstrated the best of what the Army chaplaincy represented. Where else, beside the chaplaincy, would you find an Orthodox Jewish Rabbi call the Iranian Consulate at the United Nations find a Shi'ite Imam? Where would you find a Roman Catholic Priest assisting in the efforts, or a Protestant chaplain providing pastoral care to a soldier, born in Iran, of a different faith tradition, from those chaplains that assisted her? This left an indelible mark on my life and I think, in a moment of deep tragedy, demonstrated the finest elements of the Army Chaplain Corps.

CH (COL-Ret.) Ron Casteel, US Army

CHAPTER 17

Personal and Professional Growth

OPPORTUNITIES ARE LIKE CRISES. Without warning and with no time to prepare, you have to respond. Yes or no, stay or go, do or die. You never know when you might be thrust into a situation that demands immediate, professional, knowledgeable action, which is precisely why we recommend that every year throughout your career you should add to your training, knowledge, and skill set, making sure you get some sort of certification in the process.

The military offers classes, seminars, and courses year-round. The Chiefs of Chaplains provide opportunities for advanced training specific to ministry and chaplain activities. In addition, chaplains can request some civilian training programs. Sometimes you'll have to foot the bill yourself, but more often, the military will pay for your training. The bottom line is that the more certifications you have, the better prepared you will be when opportunities and crises present themselves—and they will.

Keith's first duty assignment was at Fort Bragg, NC, where he was assigned to the 530th Supply and Service Battalion. It was the largest unit in the army at the time, almost one thousand people strong, and it existed to support the 18th Airborne Corps. One day, he was called to the Installation Chaplains Office and told they wanted him to go to jump school. That terrified him, and he didn't want to go. So . . . he didn't!

Keith regretted that decision the rest of his career, even to this day. Jump school would have opened many doors of ministry. Instead, his fear prevented him from taking advantage of a great opportunity.

In 2007, Paul was the chaplain at a small Forward Operating Base (FOB) in Iraq. They had quite a few casualties, and many situations that required Critical Incident Stress Management (CISM) intervention. One day a rocket made a direct hit on the medical clinic. He spent a couple hours with the medical team that day.

Several years earlier, he had completed the CISM training that the Army made available to chaplains. CISM offers a range of crisis intervention methods that usually include individual counseling, group debriefing, and post-incident referral for those who were either involved in a crisis or who watched someone else suffer or die. A chaplain will usually be a member of the response team rather than leading the team, but at Camp Echo there were only two who were CISM trained—Paul and the psychologist—and the psych was gone for a couple of weeks, so it was just Paul.

Keep in mind, the CISM training was never required for military chaplains. It was a voluntary seminar, but fully funded by the military. When he heard that it was available, he quickly signed up. That certification definitely opened doors, empowered him to help people in desperate circumstances, and even allowed him to lead a few people to faith in Christ.

Each of the military services has an education career path that is supposed to develop chaplain skills and leadership. The training begins with a basic officer training school, followed by the chaplain's basic course. This begins the professional educational track for each chaplain. Along the way, there are advanced officer courses that focus on mid-management leadership and supervision abilities. There are other schools that focus on developing advanced leadership abilities and honing those skills. Finally, there is a senior level school that teaches strategic leadership skills for senior level chaplains.

The previous paragraph encompasses an entire twenty-five to thirty year military career. If you attend all of these schools, you are probably being promoted on schedule and doing well in your career. The goal of every chaplain is to attend these courses, and you should make it your policy to request orders to complete the next course the minute you become eligible.

KEITH'S STORY:

I was in the Army, and attended every one of the schools listed above. They are challenging, but they will enhance your professional growth and move you towards your next promotion. They made me a better chaplain. However, there were other educational opportunities that were just as important in my career progression.

For example, years ago I attended a two-week Pastoral Coordinator training. Basically, it was designed for those chaplains who would become fund managers and chaplain resource managers at their installations. A lot of chaplains hate this aspect of being in the ministry, thinking it really isn't ministry. However, there aren't many ministries that can survive without adequate funding and financial management. Managing the money correctly helps other chaplains at the installation level.

A friend of mine also attended this training. He loved Resource Management, and later in his career he was selected to attend Syracuse University and receive a Master of Business Administration. This opened the door for him to work in the Pentagon as the senior chaplain managing the resources and money for the entire Army Chaplains Corps. His work directly supported and enhanced the ministry of every chaplain in the Army. There's no way to measure the impact he had on the kingdom of God.

There are other career-enhancing opportunities that the military offers to its chaplains. Chaplains can choose Clinical Pastoral Education (CPE), which is designed to help chaplains in hospital ministry. Some are offered Family Life Chaplain training, which is a master's degree in Family Life Therapy. Obviously, this training is designed to prepare chaplains to minister to families in need of help. Some chaplains can complete an advanced degree in World Religions or Ethics from various graduate schools such as Harvard, Duke, or Princeton. This training becomes a part of the total package to help the military as it develops strategic plans around the world.

When the war in Iraq and Afghanistan kicked off, there was a great need to educate the military on the importance of religion in the area of operations where the military was to deploy. The Department of Defense turned to its chaplains, who already understood the significance of religion in many cultures around the world, and the chaplains were able to provide the cultural and religious information our commanders needed to interact successfully with our coalition partners. Understanding their religious sensibilities helped our Armed Forces avoid offending the people.

The Navy's Advanced Education Program takes in around fifteen to twenty chaplains per year. Normally, eight go to CPE (split between

Portsmouth, VA and San Diego, CA), while the others go to civilian schools and war colleges for Master's level work. There are also career courses for LCDRs and CDRs. These programs are sometimes quite competitive, and the wise chaplain will request permission to complete the training as early as possible.

There is a Navy Chief of Chaplains Instruction regarding Advanced Education Programs. The instruction describes the eligibility requirements and application processes for each category.[1] The Air Force has its own version of the same kinds of education and training programs.

As important as these opportunities are to the chaplains in all the armed services, we can't limit this discussion to professional military training. There is another aspect of growth that is just as important as the professional, and that is personal growth.

KEITH'S STORY:

As I reflect back over my own career as a chaplain and then as an endorser, I've come to believe personal growth is more important that professional growth. Professional growth helps you in your public career, while personal growth helps you as a chaplain, parent, husband, wife, brother, sister, and friend. I suspect this is an area that is missing at times in all our lives.

Most endorsers offer retreats or conferences each year, and many of them are free to the chaplain. These conferences are designed to help the chaplain develop his or her personal growth and health. Some of the topics at these conferences include preaching, personal reflection, spiritual care/soul care, personal and professional mentoring, the minister's marriage and family, spiritual disciplines, overcoming temptation in the ministry, understanding your strengths and weaknesses, building trust, and many others. They all have one purpose: to enhance the personal growth of the chaplains and family members who attend.

The Billy Graham Training Center (The Cove) in Asheville, NC, offers a military chaplains retreat every year, right after Thanksgiving. It is fully paid for by donations from people who support the military. This retreat features a number of speakers whose singular purpose is to foster spiritual, emotional, and relational health and growth. We highly recommend that you attend this conference, or one like it, as often as you can.

1. COC Instruction 1521.1.

Another recommendation is that each chaplain should have a mentor. In fact, you might want to consider identifying two mentors: one for spiritual accountability, and one for professional development.

In addition to the mandatory career training the military offers, the additional training that we completed include certification programs like Suicide Prevention, Critical Incident Stress Management, Building Trust in the Workplace, Active Parenting, Personal Financial Preparedness, Premarital Counseling, Cross-Generational Ministry, Self-Care for the Professional, Personal & Professional Mentoring, Certified Life Coaching, additional masters or doctoral degree, Marriage Encounter, and several others. When people see that you have gone above and beyond to further your own qualifications, they are impressed. But what that translates to is that they trust you, they look to you for answers and guidance. And because your values and priorities are biblical and godly, you walk through new doors of opportunity and ministry.

Nobody shows up the day of a marathon without taking the time, the effort, and the expense to get ready. Deciding to do a marathon requires months of preparation. Physical training has to include running long distances several days each week. You modify your eating habits because nutrition can work for you or against you. You become an expert on things like foot care, appropriate clothing, and how to prevent chafing. You research the best shoes for your feet and the way you run. Just as important, you train your mind for the grueling ordeal of running 26.2 miles, because if you lose the mental game, you're already in trouble.

The same must be said for a chaplain who wants to prepare for serving in the military. You never know what you might face in your future. That's why it's important to continually add to your training, your learning, and your growing, both personally and professionally. The price of success is high, and you have to count the cost.

Is it worth it? We think so. But you have to decide for yourself. Remember, the more training you complete, the better prepared you will be when opportunities and crises present themselves.

Guest Anecdote Number Nine

Change in Plans that Worked Out Well

We know that all things work together for the good of those who love God.

Romans 8:28 (HCSB)

When Pam and I attended the Chaplains Advanced Course at Fort Monmouth, I received my RFO for Hunter Army Airfield. We were both extremely excited about returning to the south near our families. Toward the end of the course, however, I received a phone call from the Installation Chaplain. He said he wanted to have lunch with me. I thought, "Uh oh, something is wrong. Either something happened to Pam, or they want me to stay at Fort Monmouth."

I called Pam immediately and she was at home, fine and dandy. Now I was left with the prospect that they might ask me to stay at Fort Monmouth. It turned out that that was the case. They asked me to be the Resource Manager for the installation chaplains office.

The decision was not easy. Frankly, Pam shed some tears over staying in the northern part of the country. But we discovered it to be one of the best places of ministry that we served. I had to get extra training for the position. There were a number of courses I had to take. The Chaplains Branch had the Pastoral Coordinator course, and Fund Managers course. I also completed the Contracting Representative Officers course the Army offered.

All three of these courses helped me in the future and opened doors of ministry for me at other locations. They also proved valuable in my future civilian life. I used my experience and knowledge of resource management when I was the ecclesiastical endorser for the Southern Baptist North American Mission Board.

Dr. Keith Travis, Chaplain, Colonel, US Army, Retired

CHAPTER 18

Comparing Reserve and National Guard to Active Duty Chaplaincy

SHOULD YOU SERVE IN the Active Duty, the Reserve, or the National Guard? It's really up to you. If you're married, you should aim for unity between husband and wife as you approach this question. There are a lot of interservice rivalries and preferences, and people on Active Duty tend to disparage those who serve in the Reserve Components, but the truth is this: ministry can be outstanding no matter where you serve. People everywhere need Jesus, and a good chaplain can make a lasting impact anywhere. Therefore, the ultimate answer has to be that you go to the prayer closet to see what the Lord wants you to do.

The Navy, Air Force, Army, Coast Guard, and Marine Corps have full-time and part-time personnel. The full-timers are called Active Duty, and the part-timers are called Reservists or Reserve Forces. One way of distinguishing the two is by using the term "component." Full-timers serve in the Active Components of the various services. Part-timers serve in the Reserve Components, which consist of the Naval Reserve, Air Force Reserve, Army Reserve, Marine Corps Forces Reserve, Coast Guard Reserve, Air National Guard, and Army National Guard. Those who serve in the above-mentioned forces are usually paid, and they may earn a retirement if they serve twenty or more years.

But there's a volunteer level of service that you should at least be aware of. Each state has the prerogative of establishing a State Defense Force. Not all have done so, but those states that maintain these all-volunteer forces use a variety of names: State Defense Force, State Guard,

State Guard Reserve, or State Military Reserve. The Civil Air Patrol is another volunteer force, as is the relatively new Coast Guard Auxiliary. People serving with these volunteer forces are not paid and do not earn a retirement, but chaplains in these organizations have a genuine ministry and a great opportunity to impact people on behalf of the Kingdom of God.

A lot of chaplains begin their military service in one of the Reserve Components, and later decide to apply for Active Duty. Others start full-time in one of the branches of service and then move to part-time in one of the Reserve Components. Because of the lateral mobility within the Armed Forces, it might be helpful to have a basic understanding of some of the differences.

People in the Reserve and National Guard are referred to as "citizen soldiers." In other words, they balance two separate careers at the same time. They are often called "weekend warriors," referring to the times they put on the uniform for the weekend drill or battle assembly. The Reserve Components comprise a large part of the military in all the armed forces, and increasingly are called on to augment the operations of the Active Duty military.

The same is true for chaplains in the Reserve Components. Clergy who want to continue in their civilian careers while serving their country have a fantastic opportunity to do this in the Guard or Reserve. The qualifications are usually the same, but you're not required to be away from home as much.

If you serve full-time, that's your job, your ministry, and your life. You wear the uniform every day. You eat, sleep, and dream military. Active duty personnel hear many times the exclamation, "Uncle Sam owns you twenty-four/seven." If you're in the Reserve or Guard, on the other hand, your duty is usually weekend ministry once a month, plus a couple weeks per year. It's not usually your main job or ministry.

With the deployment cycle of the military, it is not easy being a Reserve/National Guard chaplain. Reserve Component chaplains can be activated, mobilized, or deployed, and when that happens, you suddenly become an Active Duty chaplain, with full pay and benefits, and you may have to leave your civilian job and ministry while you're mobilized or deployed. Many Reserve and Guard chaplains are wearing a right shoulder patch, which means they were deployed to a war zone. Deployment presents a challenge to the delicate balance between church life and military life that must be maintained. Many churches are prepared to see their pastor or staff member be deployed for *six months or a year*, but it is hard on the congregation. Many churches fire their pastor or staff member because they were deployed. One pastor, upon receiving orders for deployment, was told to move his family out of the parsonage.

This activation often causes hardship for the employer, and chaplains who are pastoring a church have to be aware of the pros and cons. If your congregation is supportive, being a Reserve chaplain can be a wonderful opportunity for gaining experience, ministerial training, and a chance to expand or extend your ministerial impact. But some pastors have been fired by their churches because they were activated for a number of months or a year.

At times, there is a sense that if you serve in a Reserve Component you are less of a chaplain than if you were full-time. You might hear the words, "Oh, he's only a Reservist," or "He's just a National Guard chaplain," as if these clergy were not as capable or not as good, as if the value of a life or a soul was somehow worth less in the reserve forces than in the full-time forces.

But if your goal is to represent the Lord Jesus Christ to people who need a savior, then anywhere you choose to do that is valid and worth pursuing. If you want to win souls and disciple people, that can be done full-time or part-time, wearing any uniform. There is no shame in serving the Lord in one of the Reserve Components.

It is true that most Active Duty chaplains understand the military system a lot better than Reservists because they live and breathe the system every day, as opposed to Reserve/National Guard chaplains who only see the military on their weekend drill/battle assembly. But this is not always the best way to judge the effectiveness of a chaplain. We must remember the military is looking for pastors in uniform, who are sent out or loaned to the military from the local church. So, for both Reserve Component and Active Duty chaplains, there should be a healthy balance of pastoral duties, military bearing, and knowledge.

Some Reserve Component chaplains have a hard time finding a church position because of their affiliation with the military. Many churches will say they are patriotic, but the simple truth is they do not want to see their pastor or staff member called away. While it is true that most Reservists' civilian jobs are protected by law (Uniformed Services Employment and Reemployment Rights Act: USERRA),[1] the same is not

---

1. Veterans Employment and Training Service.

true for Reserve chaplains whose full-time job is in a congregation. You cannot afford to forget this fact.

Many churches joyfully send their pastors to war. They bless them and their families, and celebrate with them when they return because they consider the pastor's military service to be part of the missionary outreach of the local church—and it is! Some churches continue to pay the benefits for their minister. In other words, they continue to contribute toward their civilian retirement and medical coverage.

Since the Reserves and Guard have their drill or battle assembly on a weekend, it is important that the chaplain negotiate with the commander and the church board. Will the church allow me to be gone for the weekend, to include Sunday? On the other hand, will the unit leadership allow me to miss Sunday morning drill so I can be at my civilian church? Can I negotiate this so I can do both?

PAUL'S STORY:

I served in the Reserves and Guard for a while early in my career. I found that most commanders were willing to work with the chaplain to be able to do both civilian ministry and military ministry during the weekend. But this was not true across the board. I ran into a commander or two who said they were not willing to make it work. In that case, I had to find another place to serve. It takes effort on the part of the chaplain, but it goes back to the call. If God has truly called you to this ministry, He will make the path workable.

My first reserve unit was in the National Guard. After a couple years, my supervisor told me I should get into a combat unit if I wanted to be competitive when it came time for promotions. I searched around and found an infantry battalion that needed a chaplain and made an appointment with the commander, who was also a weekend warrior. The conversation went really well, and it looked like a perfect fit . . . until I mentioned I wanted to be at my church on Sunday morning of drill weekends.

"No, I need you here," the Lieutenant Colonel said.

"Well, sir. This is not negotiable. I will find another slot." I got up and walked out of his office. I was just a captain, which is an O-3 in the Army, but I had to know my values and commitments and be strong enough to stand up for them.

As I was leaving the building, I heard him yell, "Wait a minute, Chaplain. OK! I'll agree to it."

We worked out a plan where I would be with the unit on Friday evening, Saturday, and Sunday afternoon, but not Sunday morning. I was with that battalion over four years, had a fantastic ministry among them, and I only missed my church's Sunday services two weeks during the summer for Annual Training, and once in a while on the Sunday in December when the unit had its family holiday activities.

KEITH'S STORY:

I retired in 2007 from the Army, a few years before I thought I would, to become my denomination's faith group endorser. When I got there, the war in the Middle East was raging. Chaplains were in high demand. The surge came, and the military, particularly the Army, was taking any minister they could as a chaplain. Reservists and Guardsmen were being activated and mobilized by large numbers. Some of these "citizen soldier chaplains" were going to large bases to take over as pastors on the installations, while others were going down range with their units to support and defend the United States. They were providing counsel to family members, conducting military funerals, and performing death notifications. They were preaching and helping installation commanders and Rear Detachment Commanders deal with the issues that war brings. It was an amazing thing to witness.

PAUL'S STORY:

Active Duty chaplains actually have less stress and fewer hassles juggling their careers than Reserve Components. When I applied for and was approved for Active Duty, I resigned from my pastorate, sold my house, and started a new chapter in my life. After a few months, I got several calls from pastor friends who all asked the same question: "What's the difference in stress levels between being a pastor and being a chaplain?"

My answer surprised them. "Well, if the stress of being a pastor is 100, the comparative stress of serving as a military chaplain is about a twenty-five." America was not at war at the time, and during wartime there's a lot of stress, of course. But being a pastor isn't an easy job.

Active Duty chaplains are paid full-time, have complete medical coverage for themselves and their family members, and earn a pretty good retirement. In addition, they qualify for VA home loans and education benefits.

Part-timers are paid for each drill period. A typical drill weekend counts as four "drill periods," two on Saturday and two on Sunday. Annual Training and other time served will count as one drill period per day. Reservists can get low-cost healthcare coverage for themselves and their families. There's a possibility they qualify for the student loan repayment plan. They also qualify for VA home loans and education benefits. This is also true for chaplains. But the rules are tricky, and they change from time to time, so you have to do your homework and keep searching until you get the right answers.

PAUL'S STORY:

While I was pastoring and serving in the Reserve Forces, I started asking around because I wanted to complete a doctorate using the GI Bill. I was told by eight different people that chaplains didn't qualify for the education benefit. I could have given up, thinking they must be right. But the ninth person said, "Of course chaplains are entitled to the same benefits as anyone else." It's true that there are guidelines you have to follow, so you have to know the rules. I used the education benefit to get a doctorate, and then still had some eligibility remaining, and got another master's degree.

Under the current policies, Active Component chaplains will get one percent of their base pay put into a retirement savings account, plus the military will match up to four percent of your base pay that you put into your retirement savings plan. In addition, "members who otherwise qualify for a retirement based on longevity of service will receive a defined benefit that is 2% times the number of years of service times the member's highest thirty-six months of basic pay."[2] Simplified, this means Active Duty personnel get a retirement savings account plus at least 40% of the average pay over their last three years in the military. If you don't stay in twenty years, you get to keep the retirement savings account, but you won't get the pension. If you stay in twenty or more, you get the

---

2. Military Compensation, Retired Pay.

savings account plus a pension of 40% or more, depending on the total number of years served.

Reservists earn retirement points for each drill period or duty day. Fifty points per year qualifies as a "good" year, and if you get twenty or more "good years" you qualify for a retirement. The military has an elaborate formula for calculating your Reserve pension, based on number of years, number of points, and your rank when you retire. National Guard chaplains have a more complicated points and retirement system. If all your service is within the same state, it's not too difficult to figure out, but if part of your service is in the Guard and part of it in another component, not all your points will count for retirement. The key is keeping track of your service, your points, and your "good" years.

A significant retirement benefit for both Active and Reserve Component chaplains is the lifelong medical coverage. Again, the rules change from time to time, but this is a valuable benefit to be aware of.

National Guard personnel will do most of their duty within their own state or territory. They might go elsewhere for special training or education, but their service is almost always in-state. Reservists can live anywhere they want, and travel to their unit.

Active Duty folks will move every one to three years, wherever the military decides to send them. Before getting orders, you'll get to submit your requests for your preferred assignments, but there's no guarantee you'll get what you requested. A phrase we all have to get used to is "needs of the Army" or "needs of the Navy" or "needs of the Air Force," or "needs of whatever branch of service you serve with." What that means is, "You're gonna go where Uncle Sam sends you, whether you like it or not." Full-time service members usually understand this process.

This chapter appears to ramble a lot more than previous chapters. That's because the differences between the components are varied and vast. Our aim here is to alert you to the fact that differences exist and are significant, and to provide just enough information to help you as you discern the Lord's will for your chaplaincy career.

Ministry in the full-time military is a special opportunity that has fantastic benefits. Ministry in the Reserve Forces is also a wonderful experience, also with a lot of benefits. You have to discern the call of God on your life, then pursue that calling, while at the same time taking advantage of every benefit you have access to for yourself and your family.

CHAPTER 19

Managing Your Career

WHEN KEITH WAS A young chaplain candidate, someone gave him the best piece of advice he ever got during his military career: save a copy of everything you ever receive. And he did!

Every LES (pay statement), every travel voucher, every receipt, every piece of paper that has your name and social security number. Every TDY order, PCS order, and promotion order. Every award, every certificate, every commendation. Every evaluation (OER, FITREP, OPR), every counseling statement. Every leave form, every eyeglass prescription, every confirmation of enrolling in the next military schooling. Ordination, college and seminary transcripts. *Everything.*

The reason you have to do this is simple. Somewhere along the way, the military will mess up your official records file, and this will cost you financially or possibly ruin your career if you cannot correct the system.

A lot of people these days feel more confident because of computerization and digital records. However, keeping a copy of your originals is still good advice. If you were to scan your records and save them in multiple places—different computers, different buildings, different clouds, or different planets—then you might be able to get away with not having the paper copies, but you absolutely cannot afford to trust "the system" or other people to keep track of your career. It's up to you.

The Army has a tradition. When someone is teaching or training a group of soldiers and is covering something that is essential or crucial or that is going to be on a test, the leader stomps his foot. That's the signal: *do not miss this.* When we talk about saving your records, we are stomping our feet as hard and as loud as we can!

KEITH'S STORY:

When I reported to Fort Bragg, NC, for my first Active Duty assignment, I was a First Lieutenant (1LT) with more than four years of duty in the Army Reserve. Soon after being promoted to Captain (CPT), I received a call from the Army Finance office, indicating I owed them a large sum of money because I was being overpaid. They said that according to my records, I was being paid as a CPT with over four years of service, but that being brand new, I was actually a CPT in my first year. When I told them I had been commissioned in the Army Reserve and had served four years, their reply was classic: "Prove it!"

So, the next day I went back to finance and presented every paper they asked for and more. The advice to save all my records paid off big time. Not only then, but many times throughout my twenty-eight years in uniform.

Similarly, a brand-new Navy chaplain was approved for Active Duty after six years as a Reserve chaplain. The pay office made a mistake when they keyed in a "0" in the prior service box, which meant his pay records omitted his six years of service. After about a year serving full-time, he took his records to the pay office at his Naval base and filled out the appropriate forms to correct the record. A month or so later, he and his wife were stunned to find out not only were they getting a hefty lump sum back payment, but an immediate raise of more than a thousand dollars per month.

His pay category was corrected to "O-3 with over six years" of service. That six years on the record will make a difference for him and his family the entire time he is in the Navy. Plus, it will figure into his retirement, because retirement pay is based on the average pay during his final thirty-six months of duty.

An Army Major checked his annual statement of service one day and discovered that although he had been in the military more than ten years, the official record listed him serving only two years. How on earth they could agree that he was an O-4 but insist he had only served two years is anybody's guess. Is that even possible? He went home and gathered all of his LESs, copied them, and the next day took them to the personnel office. He had kept all of his official records at home in a cardboard U-Haul box, and was able to demonstrate his time in service

One chaplain signed into his very first unit. During the in-processing, the JAG told him that when he wanted to take leave, he needed to fill out the appropriate form and have it signed by the unit administrator, and then save the form. Being brand new, the chaplain didn't know that after the form was signed, he needed to take it to a different office for processing. Eight months later, the same JAG went to the chaplain's office to say the chaplain was being investigated for leave fraud. The chaplain took all of the leave forms to the unit administrator, showed him they were all signed, and asked what he did wrong. The administrator told him the leave requests were never processed. Fortunately, the unit chose to process the forms after the fact instead of prosecuting, because the JAG admitted that he had given the rookie chaplain incomplete guidance, but also because every form was signed by the unit administrator who was spearheading the investigation. It could have ended that young chaplain's career right there! Today, the leave request process is computerized, so the records are automatically saved. But it's still important to save all your records.

The point is that you are the master of your career. You need to maintain your records, paperwork, and files. You would be surprised to find out the number of good people who do not do this. Human error, technological glitches, and the proverbial "fire in the records building" will inevitably cause problems if you can't back up your own documents. At times, this may cost you a few dollars on a travel voucher, but sometimes it adds up to tens of thousands of dollars or more that you may be entitled to, but you're not going to get because you can't "prove it." Don't be that person!

Whenever you are facing a promotion board, or perhaps have applied for a special training opportunity or schooling, a selection board will look at your records, and they will determine your fate based on what they see in your file. Sometimes the decision will hinge on one single piece of paper that is either in your file or not. Make sure it's there.

One time Keith found out his awards were not correct, and that his skill identifier at the end of his military occupational specialty (MOS) was incorrect. He had to submit proof for these facts to be corrected two weeks before the promotion board, or he would have been non-select.

A huge issue for promotion boards is the official military photo. The military changes its policies from time to time on this matter, but if your branch of service includes official photos in the board process, you have to be sure that your photo is perfect, that your weight is right, and that your uniform with all its insignia is exact. You also have to hope board members won't use your gender or ethnicity against you. The best way to overcome any potential problem is to guarantee all your details are right.

KEITH'S STORY:

Some years back, I sat on an accessions board for the Army. Each candidate had a file with his or her life history up to that point, including a photo. One applicant submitted a photo of him standing in his driveway holding his cat. It was odd. I often wonder whether his recruiter told him to do another photo, or if he just blew it off. Either way, he was not selected, and it was because of the photo. I suspect he was told to make a change, but he took the easy way. The point is this: along the way you will have the opportunity to allow others to invest in your life. Listen to them. Let their experience and expertise help you navigate the waters of managing your career.

Which brings up another piece of advice I received: to develop a relationship with a mentor who would be honest with me about my career and how I was doing. Someone who could help me understand the words, phrases, and facts on evaluations, fitness reports, and what they mean. I managed to find several chaplain mentors in my career, and their help was immeasurable.

Another important consideration would be for you to use your ecclesiastical endorser in this way. Many endorsers are former chaplains who were quite successful, and they have an abundance of experience they are willing to share. They want you to be successful. You might consider sending your officer evaluations or fitness reports to your endorser and ask for some guidance. As an endorser, Keith did this for his chaplains whenever they asked. Paul was not an endorser, but was asked by his endorser to be a regional representative, and in this capacity, helped several young chaplains with promotion packets and with the wording on their evaluation support forms or FITREPS.

You might also want to develop relationships with senior chaplains in your own denomination or faith group. At most chaplain conferences, there are senior chaplains who take time to answer questions. These should be seen as learning moments to help you manage your career. Sometimes the Chief of Chaplains from one of the services will attend and provide a briefing on the current state of the chaplaincy and what it will look like in the future. When this happens, take notes. It is always important to take advantage of the moments that might give you an understanding about what things look like for the future of your career. Those who pay attention will have an advantage.

To a large degree, your career path and promotions depend on your annual evaluations. In some branches of service, a chaplain has an immediate rater plus a senior rater. In other branches, a chaplain has one rater. Our recommendation is that the first day you sign into your unit, make an appointment with your rater to get acquainted, get your job description, and discuss the rater's expectations of your performance. Some senior leaders will meet with you immediately, while others want to wait a few weeks. Do not let it go past the first month to have this conversation.

In the meeting, ask your supervisor what he or she expects from you. Then specifically ask, "What it will take to earn the best evaluation possible?" The reason for asking is because it is your intention to do a great job and earn it. You have the right to know what your boss wants and expects, but you probably have to ask for that information. While Paul was in the Army, he made it his personal goal that every week he would do something that specifically added to what his rater was looking for. But he didn't stop there. He intentionally went above and beyond to do more than what was expected. And of course, he kept a record of everything he ever did, and was able to quantify his service and ministry accomplishments.

Consider using a daily planner, journal, or calendar to record phone calls, appointments, visitation, funerals, weddings, planning sessions, and other activities. At the end of every month, count up the number of each item. This is crucial when it comes time to prepare your evaluation support form or to report what you've been doing. Those who know how to quantify their accomplishments always look better in their reports and evaluations. How many counseling sessions, phone calls, personal visits, Bible studies, and memorial services? The number of people who attended each type of event. Everything must be quantified.

Periodically, every person in the military will be tested on their physical fitness. Don't wait until the day before to think about it. Your best approach is to stay fit year-round. Yes, it takes a lot of time to work out four or five days a week. But that's the price if you want to stay in military ministry, and if you want to be promoted.

Another important factor in career management is to find out the different kind of duty assignments you need, so you can "check the blocks." Too many good people get bogged down and miss being promoted because they thought all they had to do was preach, visit, do the military ceremonies, and trust God for the promotions. It is definitely true that you need to trust the Lord. However, you also have to be wise and make the right decisions. A Navy chaplain needs ship duty, an assignment with the Marines, maybe a tour with the Coast Guard, and other specific kinds of duties. An Army chaplain needs to serve with a combat arms unit, Joint service, and an installation or garrison job. Air Force chaplains need to serve at an installation and a flight wing.

All chaplains might have to do a tour of duty without their families in a deployed setting. This could be on a ship, in a location like Thule Air Force Base in Greenland, or maybe in South Korea. You need to call your detailer or assignment officer, find out what your career path requires, and then plot your course. Ignoring this part of your career planning will put you at a disadvantage, making you less competitive when it comes to promotions and future assignments. Remember, if you don't get promoted, you and your family will feel the financial impact the rest of your life.

It is highly recommended that you start reading books and articles about leadership styles and methods because as you move up the ranks, you will gradually find yourself moving into supervisory, managerial, and leadership roles. Some chaplains want to stay in positions that allow direct ministry. However, the military is designed to promote you into leadership roles where you will train, supervise, and mentor others. You'll still have some opportunities to minister, but it may not be the same as earlier in your career. The longer you're in the military, the more you'll discover that leadership abilities will be rewarded, so you might want to prepare for that.

We could go on and on about the various ways to manage your career. Instead, we'll conclude this chapter with three lists.

1. Maintain these records: LES, awards, date of rank, orders, TDY documents, receipts, ID card, passport, ecclesiastical endorsement, ordination, university and seminary transcripts, leave forms, birth certificates for you and your family, marriage license, official photo annually and after every award or promotion, all physical fitness test results statements, military schooling certificates of completion, security clearance, annual online training certificates, family care plan, login and passwords for military systems, medical and dental records, anything that has your name and SSN, unit and chaplain corps directory, installation directory.

2. Keep track of these items: length of time in current rank, total number of days and years served, retirement points, training completed, next military schooling needed, date of your next promotion board, when your next evaluation is due, unit training calendar.

3. Learn how to: write a FITREP, OPR, or OER, give an official presentation in your branch of service, write a memo and a letter and know the difference, properly put insignia on your uniforms, shine your shoes and boots, put a signature block on your email, effectively use the software your unit requires, login to your email and command website from remote.

Your job is to manage your career, your official records, your physical condition, and your personal and professional relationships. Is this demanding? You bet. But it pays off every time in terms of promotions, personal fulfillment, and ministerial effectiveness.

Guest Anecdote Number Ten

Chaplain Moses

The chaplain has a unique position within the unit. There is a command climate and structure that encompass a unit mission. All the parts within the command are working toward that mission. However, the chaplain operating in that setting has a great deal of independence. Chaplains are the only such element of the command that operates this way. Most days, no one is telling the chaplain what to do.

I remember sitting in on unit briefings where the XO or Commander was providing leadership, directions, assignments to individuals, and finally turning to me and saying, "Chaplain, I assume you will go do chaplain stuff." No direction, and a hint that he really didn't know what I did.

Operating within that command structure, but with the independence and freedom I had, I remember one interesting night. I was assigned to an Armored Battalion and the troops were doing field exercises at Fort Hunter Liggett, CA. The tank companies within the BN were wargaming, with some being the Blue Force and others the Red Force. There was also a petroleum element that supported both the Red and Blue Forces and the Command element. Due to the wargaming, everyone was bivouacked at different locations throughout the base.

As the chaplain, I had a responsibility to everyone and operated very independently of all other elements. In order to make contact with as many of the soldiers as possible during our time in the field, I made it a practice to meet up with a different group each night at their bivouac sight. During one such night, I had joined the petroleum unit. My Chaplain Assistant and I arrived about dinner time, and as I pulled into the area that night, there was a large oak tree with a GP medium tent pitched off to one side. I drove up to the tree with the nose of the Humvee nearly touching it.

The night proceeded like normal. I ate a meal with the troops, sat around and laughed, and talked about events of the field exercise. Then when it was time to go to bed, my assistant and I just opened up some cots, placed them beside our Humvee, and went to bed.

Sometime late at night, I woke up, and there was a bright light shining from the other side of the tree. Wondering what it was, I got up and went around the tree, and belching out from the side of the tree was a flame, shooting out like a torch. So, my Hummer was up against the opposite side, the GP medium with troops sleeping in it was close to the other side, ninety degrees from my Hummer and the tree was belching fire. Since the unit was also a petroleum element, we had fuel trucks parked nearby.

I woke up the people in the tent, we grabbed fire extinguishers and sprayed them all into the side of the tree where the flame was shooting out, to no effect. I decided I should move my Humvee. So, I jumped in and started backing away, and as soon as I started backing up, the flame shot out from my side of the tree and the tree cracked and began to fall straight toward me. Needless to say, I backed faster and cleared the area just as the tree fell directly in front of me. A call had gone out to the post, and a fire truck showed up shortly after and put out the flaming tree stump.

I was the hero of the camp that night. Everyone started saying, "Moses may have had his burning bush, but the chaplain has a flaming tree." Everywhere I went the rest of our field exercise, everyone would ask me about the tree. They started calling me "Chaplain Moses." It was an interesting and adventurous field exercise, and the night of the flaming tree opened up all kinds of opportunities for me to visit and share scripture with the troops. Every night, when I bivouacked with another element, they wanted to know what happened, they wondered if God had woken me up, because I would have been smashed under the tree when it fell. It wasn't the type of situation I thought would open up opportunities for ministry, but it made the two weeks in the field one of the best productive ministry times of my career. I also earned a new nick name.

Chaplains often get called padre, pastor, or holy man. And as I got older, some called me "Pappy." But the most unique title I ever had was "Chaplain Moses." It was a night I will never forget.

CH (COL) Rob Noland, US Army Retired

Chapter 20

Why Chaplains Get in Trouble

KEITH'S STORY:

Fort Leavenworth is the home of several Army leadership training courses, as well as the military's most famous prison, and I visited this installation several times during my career. When I was there for the Command and General Staff Officers Course, part of the training was to tour the installation, including the prison. When the senior officer leading the tour saw the cross on my uniform he said, "Chaplain, we're glad you are here for the short tour. You may not know it, but your branch often visits us for the long tour." It took a while to realize what he was really saying: chaplains sometimes get in trouble and end up in prison.

We're not sure why this is. You would expect Christian leaders to be the least likely to run afoul of the law, the last ones to violate their ordination vows, and the most likely to conduct themselves admirably and with integrity. But too often we get into trouble, and it's usually our own fault.

We all have weaknesses. We understand human nature, and we are well aware of the scripture that says "all have sinned and fall short of the glory of God." But those who are called to the ministry and to Christian leadership are supposed to be held to the highest standards of behavior. We should know how to avoid or overcome temptation. After all, we teach it and preach it and disciple others. According to 1 Timothy 3, a Christian leader must be "above reproach, self-controlled, sensible, respectable, not an alcoholic, and not greedy." Furthermore, a good reputation among outsiders is essential.

Earlier in this book, we mentioned the most common disqualifiers for chaplains, and used the term SPAM, which stands for sex, pornography, alcohol, and money. There are other disqualifiers: insubordination, disobeying orders, not being at work when you're supposed to be there, losing a military computer, or violating your security clearance. Minor offences might keep you from being promoted, but the items on this list can get you tossed into jail or thrown out of the military. Plus, these behaviors dishonor the Lord Jesus Christ, who you are supposed to represent.

You get into trouble as soon as you take something that isn't yours, when you try to keep secrets, or when you fail to communicate your activities and your whereabouts. Criticizing senior leaders or posting political comments on social media can ruin your career. Hate speech, arrogance, or derogatory comments—whether in the realm of racism, gender equality and identity, or denominationalism—can derail your career

The way to avoid getting into trouble is threefold. First, make sure you live according to your biblical convictions and your ordination vows. These commitments are important your entire life, not just when you're young and starting out.

Second, establish accountability measures and allow key people in your life to hold you answerable for what is morally right, and what is helpful in your career. If you're married, don't keep personal secrets from your spouse, and never say part of your life is "off limits" to your husband or wife. In addition, establish professional and spiritual mentoring relationships. We all need someone we can turn to when we are tempted, when we're hurting, and when we're about to do something unwise.

And third, most of all, make sure your relationship with the Lord is current, vital, and fresh. Take time each day to read the Word, worship, and pray.

Many clergy, including chaplains, get out on the edge of life doing ministry, feeling they are alone with no one else around. We're sometimes deceived into thinking we can get away with doing something wrong, and that nobody will notice. But that's never the case. There's wisdom in Luke 8:17: "For nothing is concealed that won't be revealed, and nothing hidden that won't be made known and come to light." Numbers 32:23 echoes this truth: "Your sin will catch up with you." Or as a few other translations put it, "Your sin will find you out."

As an ecclesiastical endorser, Keith was always saddened to get a phone call from the Chief of Chaplains informing him that one of his chaplains was in trouble. As Christians, but especially as Christian leaders, we need to continually have the internal and external controls that will help us fend off the arrows of the tempter. The Lord called you and prepared you for a life of service and ministry. Don't disqualify yourself by doing something unethical, immoral, or illegal. As Paul's father used to say, "Five minutes of fun isn't worth ruining a career, a reputation, or a marriage."

1 John 2 begins by saying, "My little children, I am writing you these things so that you may not sin. But if anyone does sin, we have an advocate with the Father—Jesus Christ the Righteous One. He Himself is the propitiation for our sins, and not only for ours, but also for those of the whole world."

Perhaps we can paraphrase it like this: "My dear chaplains, we are writing these things to you so that you may not get into trouble in your military ministry career. But if you do, you still have an advocate with the Father—Jesus Christ the Righteous One. However, that might not be enough to keep you in the military and out of jail."

Chapter 21

Having Fun

KEITH'S STORY:

I like to travel, hike, and play golf, and being in the military lets me do all three. Because of this, I have had a lot of fun in my career.

During my first duty assignment, a representative of the Chief of Chaplains spoke at one of our training events and mentioned that they needed Captain chaplains in Europe. Then he asked for volunteers. When I went home that afternoon, I told my wife, "Guess what! We are going to Europe!" She was thrilled. Neither of us imagined this could be happening to us. We had a blast in Europe, and the fun never stopped after we returned to the States.

I have fond memories of taking my kids to family day celebrations. The Army always had "static" displays. The kids could crawl in and around tanks, HUMVEES, helicopters of all sorts, and other neat stuff. We have many wonderful memories as a family.

PAUL'S STORY:

When I was a kid, my Navy chaplain dad would come home from deployments with fantastic stories of adventure and fun. He told about hitching a ride on a "Holy Helo," the Navy helicopter that would take the chaplain from ship to ship to conduct religious services and meet with sailors. The chaplain hung from a rope under the chopper, swinging wildly because of the rotor wash, and bashing painfully against the side of the ship. He got bruised from time to time, but I saw the gleam in his eye when he talked about it. He loved it. When he was stationed in Okinawa, he and the rabbi teamed up to participate in the Marine Corps billiards tournament. The Jarheads hated the fact that the two chaplains won the tournament and took home their trophy, but they respected the chaplains and started going to church and sabbath services. Dad also talked about building the largest religious program in the Navy by focusing on Sunday School, Bible Teaching, and "Coffee Hour," which is what he called the fellowship time after Sunday morning worship. Sailors do love their gedunk.

When I became a pastor, I thought it was natural to have fun with the congregation, and thoroughly enjoyed being in the ministry. And after becoming a military chaplain, that expectation carried over.

During Officer Basic Training, they bussed us out to the field to do the confidence courses: climbing ladders, crossing beams, descending the ropes, attempting the three-person balcony climb, and more. It gave us a feel for what our soldiers have to do. It was a lot of fun, especially for those of us who didn't come away with an injury.

My first assignment was with a medical unit. While participating in a field training exercise, I met with the First Sergeant one day, and he told me that one of his soldiers died. When I asked who the soldier was, he told me the name of the guy was "Otto." Well, I knew Otto was the name of the alarm clock dressed in an Army uniform. Instead of a bugle playing Reveille first thing each morning, the First Sergeant held a microphone up to the clock to wake up the troops. When the alarm sounded, a voice shouted, "Rise and shine, you sleepyheads, rise and shine!" Somebody got tired of hearing that stupid clock shout "Rise and shine," so he made a noose and strung up poor Otto between two field tents.

"What do you do when a soldier dies?" the First Sergeant asked.

"I would do a funeral," I answered matter-of-factly.

His eyes got real big. "Would you?"

Two days later, still out in the field on the back side of an Army training base, we had a funeral complete with full military honors and protocol . . . for Otto the Clock. One of the soldiers was a carpenter. He used scrap lumber to build a scale model replica of a coffin. Six soldiers served as pall bearers, marching in step as they carried the coffin to the ritual. The Colonel gave the commander's speech. The First Sergeant provided a tearful eulogy. And the chaplain's funeral sermon was a poem about time. Each of us is allotted a certain number of days, and when our time runs out, we're called to give an account before the Great Clockmaker in the Sky.

A hundred soldiers laughed so hard they literally fell out of formation onto their hands and knees in the dirt. Some of them pretended to howl and cry, others had actual tears because they were laughing so hard.

My Bible college professors and ministerial textbooks didn't cover funerals for clocks, and seminary homiletics classes never trained me to write sermons as poems, but that event created a rapport with the soldiers better than anything I ever could have planned. For the rest of my time with that unit, I had an open door of ministry, and I led dozens of people to faith in Christ. That was fun.

A couple years later I was with an infantry battalion in Yakima, Washington. While visiting our soldiers at various locations, I asked my driver if he would go up and over a mountain instead of taking the road around it. He agreed, but soon stopped and said he wouldn't go further because it was too steep. I told him the Hummer was built for steep inclines, and suggested he proceed.

That's when he told me, "Chaplain, I'm not stopping because the vehicle can't make it. I'm stopping because it's too scary. I don't want to drive up this mountain!"

"I understand. Let's trade places and I'll drive."

"Do you have your license?"

"Yes, Sergeant. I do." Being a good NCO, he insisted that I show it to him.

Driving up that mountain was so much fun. We got to the top, got out, and looked around. We could see for miles in each direction. Coming back down was even scarier because it seemed we were looking straight down. It was exhilarating.

As a Brigade chaplain, I was asked to participate in the annual Thanksgiving Day football tournament. I used to play competitive football, so of course I wanted to play. Our team was doing really well, winning each game. Until we came up against the commander's team. That's when I discovered that the Colonel makes the rules . . . and changes the rules . . . even in the middle of a play . . . to give his team the advantage. Yes, he taught his guys to cheat in order to make sure he won the trophy. We lost that game and took second place. I was sore—both physically and emotionally. But that took second place to planting the seeds of ministry and life-changing discipleship.

When I was in Iraq, I spent an afternoon playing table tennis with the Roman Catholic chaplain from the Polish Army. I talk about this experience in my book, *Safest Place in Iraq*. That was so much fun, providing a needed break from war-time ministry, and entertaining a bunch of our soldiers in the process, because a lot of them gathered to watch the table tennis showdown.

At Fort Buchanan, Puerto Rico, the phone in my office rang one afternoon. The installation commander asked if I was interested in going with him and about a dozen others to Saint Thomas. We'd be leaving the next morning at 8:00 on a Blackhawk. Whenever the boss calls to ask if you want to go somewhere, the answer is always "yes." So, I said "Yes, sir. I'd love to do that."

When I climbed into the chopper at about 7:30 the next morning, I had no idea what an awesome day this was going to be. Seventy-six miles flying above the Caribbean, over and around small islands, beaches, and palm trees. One of the most beautiful experiences ever.

Mid-day, after inspecting the facilities, we got into a van and went downtown for lunch. We were all in uniform, and as we walked into the restaurant, the crowd erupted into a loud cheer. It felt really good to be respected and appreciated like that. Then we found out they were watching a World Cup soccer game on the big screens in the bar. They didn't even notice we had arrived.

The chopper ride back to San Juan took a slightly different route, but was even prettier because the pilot flew lower, and we could see through the clear water. It was one of those experiences you're glad you said yes to because it provides images that are etched into your memory for the rest of your life.

BACK TO KEITH:

Every Thanksgiving and Christmas we invited young soldiers who were away from home and single to come to our house for dinner. There were usually five to a dozen who showed up. We had a pot of mashed potatoes, a huge Virginia ham, the biggest turkey we could find, and of course all the trimmings. Those soldiers ate, and ate, and ate. Then we all sat around and enjoyed some good talk. It was fun being their extended family, providing a home away from home. And it enriched our family as well.

While stationed at Fort Monmouth, we did a lot of retreats with the chapel family. Every fall we would go up to an old farm that doubled as a retreat center, and spend the days on hayrides, activities for the kids, and daily worship and devotions. It was memorable fun.

While stationed in Germany, the Catholic Chaplain and I organized a family trip, combining the Protestant and Catholic congregations, to visit Rome and the Vatican. We even managed to arrange an audience with the Pope. Of course, my being a Baptist boy meant that the audience with the Pope did not excite me the way it enthused my Catholic brothers and sisters. But when we got there, the Pope started blessing the children. Our son was only a few months old, so we decided to have the Pope bless him. Unfortunately, about that same time our baby decided to mess his diaper. It was a terrible mess, and we figured that the Pope did not want to bless a stinky little boy. Still, we have so many fun memories from this trip.

While on my last duty assignment before retirement, my CG wanted to fly down to Patrick AFB, FL, to visit one of our outlying units. He asked if I would fly down with him and play in a golf tournament. I obviously said, "Yes Sir!" He told me I could bring anything I wanted. So, I brought along my driver and my putter.

As we got on the Mil Air Lear Jet piloted by two young Air Force flyboys, the General looked at me funny and said "Chaplain, do you think you could make it more obvious?"

I thought to myself, "Well shoot, sir, you told me to bring whatever I wanted." But I didn't have the nerve to say it out loud.

We flew down and took care of business, and then golfed in the tournament, which we won. He told me on the way home that I could bring any club I wanted on the next trip. I just grinned.

In 2003, I was the Deputy Installation Chaplain at Fort Bragg as the entire state (it seemed) was getting ready for Coca-Cola 600 race in Charlotte. NASCAR had asked for a couple of chaplains from Fort Bragg, and I was one of the two selected to represent the Chaplains Office. NAS-CAR treated me like I was hero. I was invited to Raceway Chapel, had lunch with one of the drivers in his RV, and visited the NASCAR television booth high above the track. They took us to the lap counter building down on the track, and finally, we ended up in the NASCAR booth where food and drink were served. It was an awesome experience that I will never forget, a day that will always be on my highlight film.

Fun with friends comes in many different flavors. It might be going out for eighteen holes of golf, a ten-mile run, young soldiers over for holiday dinner, driving a HUMVEE straight up a mountain, or a chopper ride over the Caribbean. Any way you look at it, having fun with your friends is important. Building long lasting relationships in ministry is something you'll never forget.

Psychologists tell us happiness makes life better, and that one way to add balance to life is to have plenty of laughter. This is definitely true in ministry. Too often, ministry is messy, requiring that the chaplain walk with service members and their families through the most difficult times of their lives. Sometimes, we are the ones going through the fiery trial or walking a dark lonely road. It's so much better when we can balance the dark days with the fun times.

Because life is short, our hope is that you will have fun, smile and laugh a lot, knowing that God is in control. It'll make your ministry experience more meaningful to you, your family, and the people in your unit. They are watching you to see if your life, your love, and your faith are genuine, and they want to know if it's true that Jesus can make a difference—if happiness is even possible. If you can show them that the joy of the Lord is genuine, you and your family will enjoy being in the ministry. The people you serve will be attracted to you and your God. You'll be more effective in your chaplain career. And you'll bear more fruit for eternity.

SECTION FOUR

Bearing Fruit as a Military Chaplain

CHAPTER 22

Incarnational Presence

THE PROPHET ISAIAH SAID the Messiah would be called "Wonderful Counselor, Mighty God, Eternal Father, Prince of Peace." John 1:1 says, "In the beginning was the Word, and the Word was with God." In Matthew's Gospel, Jesus is referred to as "Immanuel, God with us." Christ was "God Incarnate," and throughout his life and ministry that's how he ministered to the people. He personified the very presence of God Most High.

In many ways, we have built our entire philosophy of ministry around this one thought: "If God Incarnate came to live among us, and if he called us to be a shepherd to his people, then we are called to represent him and be an incarnation of his truth and his love among the people we serve." In essence, we would represent him the same way he represented the Father.

The bottom line is that the ministry of a chaplain is incarnational. We have the opportunity to live and breathe and walk with those entrusted to us, embodying the message of faith, hope, and love in the name of Jesus Christ. We literally are the representatives of the Lord, which is an awesome honor and responsibility.

KEITH'S STORY:

Someone asked me one time what I thought was the greatest quality for military chaplains. I responded, "By being there! This is the most significant aspect of military ministry—just being there."

A friend of mine served as the senior chaplain at a major command. One day he took a mop with him to work. Everywhere he went that day, he carried his mop. After hearing about this strange behavior, the commander called him into her office and said, "Chaplain, please tell me why you are carrying that mop around."

"Well, Ma'am," he explained, "this mop represents a crucial aspect of what I do as your chaplain. MOP stands for Ministry of Presence. I want to be there for your soldiers."

Being there gives you the right to bear the message and presence of Christ, the One your church sent you to proclaim. *Being there* gives you the right to minister to those you are serving. We could tell you story after story of chaplains who decided at some point they didn't want to be there. They didn't want to go to the motor pool, to the field, on the deployment, on the road march, to PT, the hospital, the prison, the officers call, or whatever. Because they made a decision not to be there, they were never invited into the personal lives of the men and women they were called to serve, and their ministry suffered.

KEITH'S STORY:

In a very real way, being a chaplain is all about being where your people are, doing what it takes to build relationships, and staying ready spiritually and mentally for any opportunity that arises. I remember the many road marches I took with soldiers, hefting a rucksack that weighed the same as theirs, and marching every step with them. Or running several miles with my troops at 4:00 in the morning. Most of my best memories of ministry did not take place in a chapel or in an office. They took place when I was sweaty, stinky, greasy, or just out walking around among the troops.

Why is this the case? Because just like the people in Anytown, USA, the men and women in the Armed Forces want to see a Christian leader who is genuine, who isn't afraid to face reality, not afraid to get dirty, work hard, or experience deprivation. If you can do this and still be consistent in your faith, morality, and joyful attitude, that's when they'll respect you enough to hear what you have to say. That's when your preaching and teaching become meaningful. That's when they'll come to you for counsel. And that's when they'll ask you to lead them to the Lord.

Did you catch that? *They* will ask *you* to lead them to a saving knowledge of Jesus Christ. You won't have to persuade them. They will already have seen the message portrayed in your life, and the Holy Spirit will be hard at work drawing them into the kingdom.

PAUL'S STORY:

The year before I went to Iraq, my son was there as an infantry officer. He told me, "Dad, when you go to Iraq, make sure you go wherever your soldiers have to go. They'll love you for it." His words confirmed what I had known and practiced as a pastor and then as a chaplain.

People respond to you personally and spiritually when you spend time with them in their setting, or in a context where they don't feel at a disadvantage. When I was pastoring in Southern California, I used to visit the workplaces of the people in the church. Most of them loved it. During the summers, we had a church campout near a lake. We went to ball games together.

Spending time with people where they like to hang out balances the ledger in the relationship. The church is where the pastor is comfortable, and many non-clergy are less comfortable, feeling they are at a disadvantage. On the other hand, where they work and play and eat is where they have an edge, so being there with them evens the playing field. This practice resulted in natural opportunities to talk, get to know each other, and open up.

Your ministry as a military chaplain will be different every time you go to a new unit. Sometimes you won't have any Sunday responsibilities. Other times you'll pastor a congregation much the same way you would minister in any civilian church. Some positions entail nothing but visitation and counseling. Others will focus on preparing budgets and plans.

When I got orders for one assignment, my new supervisory chaplain called to tell me that this position would be completely administrative. There would be no direct ministry. I would be training and supervising other chaplains who did the ministry, ordering their supplies, solving their problems, and writing reports and budgets.

"Yes, sir!" I told him. "I can do that."

But as I started getting acquainted with the other administrators, budgeteers, trainers, and problem solvers, they began asking if I would lead a weekly Bible study during lunchtime. Several chaplains asked me to preach at their worship services. And after developing relationships throughout the unit, many soldiers came to me for counseling. And then they started coming to my office to ask what it meant to be a Christian. I was able to preach, teach, counsel, and lead people to faith in Jesus Christ as Lord and Savior.

When I worked at a small FOB in Iraq, my goal was to visit every office and unit on base each week. It was an ambitious schedule, but as a result of that regular face-to-face interaction, I had a fantastic relationship with the people on post, even with those who had no intention of attending worship. The door was open whenever I needed to talk to a soldier and whenever I needed help. It was an amazing experience; serving and ministering there was meaningful and fun even during the war. Friendship really does lead to ministry. Investing in people pays off in many ways.

Here's a list of places a proactive chaplain might want to visit his or her people. You won't do all of them every week. Maybe not all of them at every assignment. But when you become a chaplain, you should be thinking about where the people in your command work and hang out, and ask the Lord to show you his plan for ministry at these locations.

Field Exercises	Air Control Tower	The Chapel	The Chow Hall
The Motor Pool	Staff Meetings	Medical Clinic	Ship's Library
Wardroom	Family Support Group	Officers Club	NCO Club
The Brig	The Front Gate	Social Events	Promotions
Retirements	In the Bunkers	PT Formations	Bible Studies
Basketball Court	Playing Racquetball	Funerals	Weddings
Counseling	Billiard Tournament	Classrooms	The Armory
Barbershop	Family Day Picnic	Prayer Breakfast	Homes
Barracks	Holiday Celebrations	Galley	Road March
Jump Zone	Firing Range	Graduations	Offices

PAUL'S STORY:

When I was assigned to an infantry battalion, I was visiting some of my people at various locations one afternoon during a training exercise when I came across a group of guys just sitting around doing nothing. There was a row tanks parked above a cliff on the right. My Chaplain Assistant and I got out of our vehicle and approached the soldiers, but we noticed they were not talking. They were silent, with a rather ashen look on their faces. When I asked them what was going on, here's the story they told.

"We were training all morning, and when it came time for lunch, we parked our tanks up on that ridge right there. Then we came down here to eat. Suddenly, one of the guys yelled "Airborne!" We looked up and saw one of the tanks literally flying through the sky, about to land on us. We scrambled every which direction to get out of the way. We didn't have time to think. Just scrambled, ran, dived, crawled, whatever we had to do to get out of the way as fast as we could. The tank landed right on top the table we were having lunch at. The front of the tank crushed the front end of that deuce-and-half. Crushed it like a soda can. Nobody was hurt. But every last one of us knows for certain this coulda been the end. Coulda been our day to die. Apparently, the parking brake cable snapped. The tank started rolling forward, picked up speed, and flew right off that cliff. The wrecker came and hauled it away an hour ago. Now you come along. Chaps, would you say a few words? Maybe pray for us?"

I spent a couple hours with the tank crew that afternoon. Talking some, but mostly listening to them. Four of them gave their heart to the Lord that day. In an unanticipated encounter, I had the privilege of leading them to faith in Christ . . . Just because I was there.

In the gospels, Jesus is presented as "Immanuel, the God who is with us." One of the primary themes of apostolic teaching was the incarnation. God became a human to live among us and model a life of purity, dependence on the Father, and overcoming evil in the world. A chaplain is called to have that same incarnational impact in the military. In a very real way, because the Lord lives in us, our presence in the military is the presence of the Incarnated One.

In his little book *The Living Reminder*, Henri Nouwen wrote about the incarnational ministry of presence.[1] Part of what he says is that when we are with someone, we are there as representatives of Christ. While there, we have to say something. If our presence and our words are done right, sometime our greatest impact happens after we leave. Jesus told his disciples in John 16:7, "It is for your benefit that I go away, because if I don't go away the Counselor will not come to you. If I go, I will send Him to you." The same principle can happen today, when we understand

---

1. Nouwen, *Living Reminder*, 59.

incarnational ministry. When we are prayed up and walking in the Spirit, spending time with people can prepare them for the direct work of the Holy Spirit long after we're gone. And it's the work of the Spirit that changes lives.

Guest Anecdote Number Eleven

The Hardest, Most Rewarding Thing I Have Ever Done

I firmly believe no other ministry that I have ever been associated with in my lifetime has afforded me the opportunities to be the hands and feet of Jesus quite like military chaplaincy has. Shortly after arrival to my first duty station, Fort Stewart, Georgia, I was called upon to visit a young couple in a hospital in Savannah, Georgia, who lost their precious twins at birth. Walking with them through the pain of child loss and presiding over the funeral afforded me the opportunity to bring the hope of the gospel into that treacherous situation.

Then there was the moment in 2013, standing next to a United States diplomat in a combat hospital on Forward Operating Base Apache in Afghanistan as she breathed her last, after succumbing to a road-side bomb. Simply being present in that chaotic moment as the doctors wrestled with losing this diplomat, all the while having to treat other injuries, gave me the opportunity to bring a sense of calm in the room as I not only stood by their side, but helped them treat the wounded.

As a result of the same road-side bomb that took the life of the U.S. diplomat, three other warriors lost their lives that day. Having the opportunity to bring hope into that tense situation as we conducted the hero flight and, subsequently, the Memorial Ceremony, will be a moment that I will not soon forget. Death, especially in a combat zone, has a way of rocking everyone to their core, and chaplains have the distinct privilege of speaking hope into such trauma.

Then there are moments, like in 2018, when I had the opportunity to preach at the oldest Army chapel in the Pacific, which is located on Kwajalein Atoll, and was built during World War II. Not many people know this location even exists. I wasn't aware of it until I became the battalion chaplain for the 311th Military Intelligence Battalion out of Camp Zama, Japan, and became knowledgeable of our soldiers at this particular location. I will forever be grateful for the opportunity to preach the Word of God in such a historic location.

Finally, there are moments like I experienced in 2019, shortly after arriving to my new position with 2nd Battalion, 7th Special Forces Group (Airborne). I was called upon to be a part of the next of kin notification team as one of our units had recently lost a soldier in combat. Words fail to describe what it is like to knock on the door of a spouse and inform them that their loved one will not be returning home alive. But God puts you in situations like that because you, as his representative, have the opportunity to bring a sense of peace as the pieces are falling apart.

These episodes are just a broad stroke of some of the experiences the Lord has blessed me with as I approach the decade mark in the military. When asked how I like being an Army Chaplain, which is quite often, my response has always been, and will continue to be, "This has been the hardest thing I have ever done, but it has been the most rewarding thing I have ever done, and I love it."

CHAPLAIN (CPT) DANIEL GARNETT, US ARMY

CHAPTER 23

Personal Life of the Chaplain

BEING A PASTOR, MISSIONARY, teacher, or evangelist takes a toll on the individual. The same is true for a chaplain. That's why how you manage your personal life is crucial. A lot of ministers focus on the professional preparation and the ministerial tasks, with the mistaken notion that if they do well in those areas, they are guaranteed to succeed. The truth of the matter is that there's another side of life that is much more important.

When the Apostle Paul discusses the qualifications of church leaders in 1 Timothy 3:1–13, there's only one professional qualification mentioned: "A church leader must be able to teach." Every other characteristic has to do with the personal life. They include your relationships, behavior, values, integrity, sobriety, and sexuality. Also mentioned are your diligence, self-control, friendliness, emotional stability, and attitude towards money and possessions. Your reputation matters, both in the church and among non-Christians. The same personal standards apply to a volunteer worker in a local church, a professional clergyperson, a deacon or elder, a Sunday School teacher, a small group leader, a missionary, a women's ministry leader, a worship leader, or a military chaplain.

In essence, how you conduct yourself is the single most important qualifier for ministry in the kingdom of God. If you get this part right, you have the right to serve in ministry. But if you're personal life isn't right, then you have no business trying to be a Christian minister or chaplain.

Your incarnational ministry as a chaplain will place you in situations and locations that don't look, feel, or smell like church. You'll smell the oil and grease in the motor pool, the sweat and body odor of the PT formation, and the smokey, gunpowdery air at the firing range. You'll hear language and stories that are sordid, kinky, and messed up. Some days you'll wonder why you signed up for this line of work when you could be back in your hometown fellowshipping with the people at your church.

You'll have to pray, stay in the Word, and be intentional about fellowshipping with godly people just so the filth around you doesn't take root and begin to corrupt your own thoughts, language, and behavior.

PAUL'S STORY:

About six months after joining my first unit, I was speaking in a Bible study group at a local church, when someone asked a question that had an obvious, no-brainer answer. I had to catch myself before answering, however, because after being with the soldiers in the field, what started to come out of my mouth was, "H*** no!" But I managed to control myself, and what I actually said was, "Of course not." I have heard some chaplains who end up talking and behaving just like their Sailors, Marines, Soldiers, or Airmen. So, we need to be careful. We have to know our values, and endeavor to stay pure.

We've already mentioned the acronym SPAM, which refers to four of the common pitfalls among the clergy: sex, porn, alcohol, and money. But some of the factors that contribute to the problems are the Fishbowl Effect, stress, anxiety, loneliness, and, because military people move around a lot, the feeling of homelessness, or lack of roots. Another interesting dynamic is the fact that people are always watching and critiquing the clergy. The same is true in the chaplaincy. People want to know if your lifestyle matches your message, and the only way to know is to observe and listen. Which is why the ministry of presence is crucial.

Our opinion is that people have a right to watch, scrutinize, and critique Christians, especially Christian leaders. They are right to criticize us. The biblical message is that Jesus Christ makes a difference in our lives, and since we represent the Lord, people have a right to know whether we're hypocrites, or we're living the way the Bible teaches us to live. Are we moral, kind, and consistent? Or are we no different than the world? Is our Christianity hit-and-miss? Are we selfish or mean-spirited? People are watching, and you'll earn a reputation based on what they see in your personal life as well as your public life.

As a chaplain, your life is not your own. You have to keep in mind that people are watching. They will see you how you deal with your family. They'll notice your daily actions, how you handle anger, frustration, anxiety, fear, and grief. You cannot hide these emotions forever. People will know.

While one chaplain was deployed, he did some things and went some places that he should not have. Those who were with him saw what he did, and word got around, as it always does. A Navy ship isn't a Norwegian Cruise Line or a Carnival Cruise where you can remain anonymous. It was a small and extremely cramped ship. Everyone knew where the chaplain was at all times. His life was not his own. It didn't take long for the Commander and Executive Officer to begin asking questions. The result of the investigation was that he was forced out of the Navy Chaplain Corps. His career was over because of his inappropriate behavior.

Another issue is the importance of socializing with people in your command. We have said that ministry follows friendship. In light of this truth, are you prepared to offer yourself in friendship? Are you willing to open your home in hospitality? Does your approach to ministry include a lot of visitation and spending time with people away from the office and the church? Doing so will open doors for sharing the gospel, speaking into people's lives, and leading people to Christ.

How you handle your marriage and family is another crucial factor in this discussion. You'll have a lot of opportunities to counsel individuals, couples, and families. But if your own marriage is a mess, or if you haven't taken the time or made the investment in your own family to make sure all is well at home, this could seriously erode your ability to speak into others' lives. You really should consider reading books on marriage and parenting. Attend marriage conferences or retreats with your spouse. Doing so will be wonderful for your own marriage and family. And it will provide a wealth of information you can draw on when ministering to others.

A good marriage doesn't happen automatically, even for Christians. A happy family home life doesn't come about easily. Success in these relationships requires intentionality, research, practice, commitment, consistency, and growth. Effective pastors and chaplains understand that they have to prioritize and protect their relationships at home.

In a paper presented at the 2013 American Counseling Association Conference, Michelle Aulthouse said,

> There is a clear and present need for counseling interventions for clergy families. Research has shown that long hours, lack of pay and benefits, lack of privacy, unclear boundaries between work and family life, and stress from relocation place a tremendous amount of stress on clergy and their families.[1]

The presentation was titled "Clergy Families: The Helpless Forgottens' Cry for Help," and it focused on the ways counselors can provide help and healing for hurting clergy families.

Wouldn't it be better for people involved in Christian leadership to take care of these matters before they became problems? God is gracious, loving, and forgiving. You don't have to be perfect, but if you can avoid the major pitfalls by being proactive in your personal life, then you don't have to sacrifice your marriage, lose your children, or ruin an opportunity to have a lasting positive impact on behalf of the kingdom of God.

It boils down to understanding your own strengths and weakness, and doing what it takes to stay healthy and productive over the course of your military career. So, in the manner of David Letterman's famous top ten lists, here are our . . .

TOP TEN WAYS TO SUCCEED AS A MILITARY CHAPLAIN IN THE TWENTY-FIRST CENTURY:

Number Ten: Develop good friendships, both in the military and in the church world.

Number Nine: Build a healthy life, including a life outside of ministry.

Number Eight: Balance the serious and the fun.

Number Seven: Practice daily spirituality and devotions: Bible reading, prayer, worship.

Number Six: Continue to grow and learn: mentally, spiritually, and relationally.

Number Five: Come up with a good strategy for self-care.

Number Four: Allow someone to provide accountability in your personal life and ministry.

---

1. Aulthouse, "Clergy Families," 9.

Number Three: Put family first: career of spouse, personal fulfillment of spouse and kids.

Number Two: Guard your heart.

Number One: Keep your promises.

Psalm 116:12 asks the question, "How can I repay the Lord for all the good He has done for me?" The psalmist answers the question in the next two verses: "I will take the cup of salvation and call on the name of Yahweh. I will fulfill my vows to the Lord in the presence of all His people."

It is essential that you keep your promises, especially your promises to God, your spouse, and your kids. Don't be the person who says you'll do something, and then forget, or get too busy, or allow other priorities to get in the way. If you made a promise to God about your lifestyle, stick to it. If you told your spouse you'd take that trip, then make sure you go on that trip. If you told your kids you'd attend the recital or game, then make sure you are there on time and stay for the whole event. Keeping your promises reaps fantastic rewards; breaking your promises spells disaster.

In a nutshell, one of the most important things a chaplain can do is protect and fight for his or her personal life. You have to be intentional about your walk with the Lord, your personal relationships, and your emotional well-being. You're looking for a balance between the serious and the fun, the public and the private. If you can accomplish that, you have a good shot at building a life worth living—a life your family will be glad they're part of. And you'll improve your chances of a successful military career and a lifetime of effective, fruitful ministry.

CHAPTER 24

Spiritual Disciplines

PAUL'S STORY:

In January 2007, the pastor of the church Linda and I were attending asked the congregation to fast one day a week during the month of January as a way to start the new year with a spiritual focus. We signed up to fast on Wednesdays that month, and when I got orders to go to Iraq, I decided to continue fasting one day a week throughout the deployment. I am confident that making the sacrifice to fast and pray helped prepare me emotionally and spiritually for what I was to experience during that wartime deployment.

In addition to prayer and fasting, I selected a daily devotional book by Henry and Richard Blackaby, *Experiencing God Day-By-Day*, for my personal reading. I took a small mp3 player loaded with Christian music and worship songs. And I had my Bible. Each of these was a significant aspect of staying prepared emotionally and spiritually during the war, and helped me discern what God was doing in the lives of the men and women I served.

There are a number of really good books on spiritual disciplines that chaplains can draw from. One is *Conformed to His Image* by Kenneth Boa. Another is *Spiritual Disciplines* by Donald S. Whitney. And, of course, the classic by Richard Foster is *Celebration of Discipline*. These books can help chaplains expand their understanding and practice of the disciplines.

Spiritual Disciplines

Boa referred to the spiritual disciplines as "the product of a synergy between divine and human initiative, and they serve us as means of grace insofar as they bring our personalities under the lordship of Christ and the control of the Spirit."[1] According to Boa, the spiritual disciplines will impact the development of our inner being, which is being transformed by Christ. The apostle Paul stressed this same dynamic when he wrote, "Therefore, if anyone is in Christ, he is a new creation; old things have passed away, and look, new things have come" (2 Cor 5:17).

To refer to certain practices as "spiritual disciplines" does not mean other aspects of a chaplain's life are not spiritual or that they are less important. But as Richard Foster pointed out, practicing the disciplines is a wonderful way to put ourselves in a position to receive from the Lord what we need, and what the Lord wants to give us.

Whitney defined the spiritual disciplines as, "those practices found in the Scriptures that promote spiritual growth among believers in the gospel of Jesus Christ."[2] The word "practice" changes our perspective on spiritual disciplines, because it places them on a more "reachable" level, indicates that they can be accomplished every day, and that doing so can result in a healthy resilience and a dynamic spiritual life. For this to happen, however, we need to practice the spiritual disciplines consistently and frequently. Understood correctly, the spiritual disciplines are for our growth and for our blessing. They are instruments that help us increase in godliness. Whitney also says "the most important feature of any Spiritual Discipline is its purpose. That purpose is godliness."[3]

Some of the spiritual disciplines recorded in the Bible are prayer, meditation, fasting, silence, and solitude. Others include study, worship, service, and confession. And there are more. Each of the disciplines can be found in the Old Testament. Jesus Christ and the apostles continued them in the New Testament. Spiritual disciplines will help you keep Christ at the center of your life.

It might be helpful to keep in mind that if you are called to be a military chaplain, you won't be called to a monastic life, separated from others. Instead, the spiritual disciplines will equip you to serve others in community the way Jesus and his disciples did, while staying engaged with the people around you.

---

1 Boa, *Conformed to His Image*, 76.
2. Whitney, *Spiritual Disciplines*, 4.
3. Whitney, *Spiritual Disciplines*, 1.

KEITH'S STORY:

As a young student preparing to be a minister/chaplain, I understood the practice of spiritual disciplines. One that I did not hear much about in my church, however, was fasting. The first time I heard about fasting was during my senior year of college when I was doing an internship as the Minister of Outreach at a large church near our campus. The pastor taught us how he used the discipline of fasting to draw closer to God.

I must admit that as I moved into military ministry I didn't fast very often. However, at one particular installation, a chaplain who worked for me fasted regularly. It was one of the ways he prepared himself for the Lord to move more fully in his life. To this day he still fasts regularly.

The spiritual disciplines come easy for many military chaplains. I think this is because most military chaplains lead disciplined lives. Chaplains already do physical training. They watch what they eat because they have to weigh in. They often seek solitude by getting out and running on their own. Many of them use these times to commune with God. I remember wearing my weighted backpack and running through the German countryside talking to God and listening to him speak to me. I still do that today. My wife and I walk daily, and we use the time to commune with God, pray together, and discuss the Word.

What benefit can the disciplines offer to chaplains? The spiritual disciplines help develop resilience. Resilience is a buzz word that is often thrown around by everyone from chaplains to psychiatrists. There are undergraduate and graduate classes on the subject. In recent years, the connection between chaplaincy and resilience has been discussed in many doctoral theses.

Army Major General Bob Dees identifies resilience as the ability to "bounce back."[4] It isn't quite that simplistic, but a strong case can be made that with the constant practice of the spiritual disciplines, we are more able to "bounce back" from trouble, trauma, and trials because the power of the Holy Spirit becomes active and powerful in our lives. Eric Greitens, in his work entitled *Resilience: Hard-Won Wisdom for Living a Better Life*, says it differently, however. According to his research, people do not "bounce back" from difficult experiences. Instead, they find ways to integrate into their lives the lessons learned from the struggles.[5] Whichever way you look at it, one thing is clear: the spiritual disciplines

---

4. Dees, *Resilient Warriors*, 21.
5. Greitens, *Resilience*, 19.

make a difference in our lives, and this is also true in the life and ministry of a chaplain.

In 2 Corinthians 4:8–9, the apostle Paul writes about the difficulties in life when he mentions having trouble on every side, but not being crushed; being perplexed, but not driven to despair. Practicing the spiritual disciplines put him in a place where he could receive what he needed from God, and prepared him to handle whatever life threw at him. The inner power of God through the Holy Spirit helped him maintain a spiritual vitality that resulted in the marvelous impact we read about in the New Testament. The same can be true for us today.

Military chaplains may have to overcome a few obstacles when they attempt to practice the spiritual disciplines. For example, a Navy chaplain on a small ship might have difficulty practicing solitude. A chaplain who is deployed during war might find it hard to practice the discipline of silence. There are certain health conditions that might make food fasts impossible, but there are other kinds of biblical fasts. Our circumstances definitely impact what we can do. However, the important thing is that we faithfully pursue the practice of the spiritual disciplines according to the scriptures, as well as our own church tradition.

Doing so is important for all Christians, but even more so for pastors, chaplains, and other leaders. Not only are we called to lead by example. According to some scriptures, there may be times that prayers are not answered, and battles not won, without prayer, fasting, and the other disciplines the Lord is calling us to practice.

Chapter 25

The Ministry of the Chaplain

When we were pastors, our churches expected us to preach, teach, counsel, and lead others to Christ. When we became chaplains, or what someone has called "a pastor on steroids," the church expected us to preach, teach, counsel, and lead others to Christ. In other words, the mission of the church is the same wherever we serve.

As a military chaplain, you will find yourself doing all of these, plus being an ethicist, mediator, listener, and observer. You'll be involved in preparing budgets, planning programs, strategizing ministry, conducting weddings and funerals, and visiting the sick and imprisoned. You'll go places you never dreamed of going, face unexpected dangers, and experience a level of fulfillment unsurpassed in any other ministry or profession.

Depending on which service the Lord leads you to (Army, Navy, or Air Force) you may find that the ministry list grows and includes activities that don't seem like ministry. You might find yourself being a Jump Master, Ranger, or Special Forces Chaplain in the Army, all of which will require more preparation and education. In the Navy, you will more than likely assume ship duties that on the surface appear to have nothing to do with being a pastor. You might be a librarian, physical trainer, or a myriad of other jobs. The point is this: in all of these areas, God can use you. Can he use you as a financial counselor? Absolutely. Can he use you as a librarian on a ship? Absolutely. Can he use you as a Jump Master, Ranger, or Green Beret? Yes, he can. All of these endeavors are part of serving your command and its people. They are ways of being visible to a wider number of people, which equates to the incarnational ministry of presence, for they create opportunities to make contact with people who eventually will want to talk to you about the Lord. By participating in these facets of military life, you're paving the way for the fulfillment of your ministerial goals: preaching, teaching, counseling, and leading others to Christ.

The military needs pastors in uniform. But in the political and cultural climate of the twenty-first century, many politicians, military leaders, critics, and bean counters have a hard time justifying religious leaders in the Armed Forces because of manpower and budget issues. Therefore, they keep adding other duties. The Constitution and the Congregation want chaplains to be religious leaders, but the contemporary trend is to have you do something else. You have to know the differences. And, you may have to be both a religious leader and "something else."

It's important to remember that military ministry starts by "being there." Developing relationships is second because *ministry follows friendship*. Third comes the personal life of the chaplain. Your ministry style and effectiveness will inevitably be based on who you are, what you're made of, and the strength of your personal life. And fourth, your regular practice of the spiritual disciplines will help maintain your relationship with the Lord, which is the source of your spiritual vitality and anointing. This will empower you spiritually and allow you to discern how the Holy Spirit wants to use you to make a difference in people's lives. You will impact the command for morality and godliness, and truly be the incarnational presence God wants you to be.

Ministry can take many shapes. You will almost always be able to lead a weekly Bible study wherever you are assigned. The creative discernment will be where you do it, what time of day or week, and the approach you'll take. Some chaplains work in a chapel environment where the job is practically identical to being a civilian pastor. You'll preach, teach, visit, plan worship services, write the bulletin, train the ushers and greeters, and even have a monthly fellowship potluck. Some chaplains will organize small groups and a Religious Education program. You'll most likely have a Chaplain Assistant to help you.

Some chaplains never preach from behind a pulpit. Their ministry is largely one-on-one and involves visitation, counseling, conversations, staff meetings, and shooting from the hip. They might serve communion from the tailgate of a Hummer or a truck. They'll pray with soldiers or Marines while standing in the mud. An Air Force chaplain might find herself conducting worship services in the hangar at an air base.

Chaplains on a ship might have a room dedicated for church services, but some have to use the galley, library, or another shared space. This makes it a bit more cumbersome, but wherever you serve, be prepared to roll with the punches.

Being a chaplain involves a lot of non-ministerial tasks. As we discussed earlier, a chaplain is a pastor on one hand, and a commander's staff officer on the other. Doing the staff tasks well gives you the permission, the right, and the authority to do the ministry that you really want to do. You have to be ready, and you must be intentional.

PAUL'S STORY:

When I was a boy, our church had a scouting program called Royal Rangers, whose motto was "Ready for Anything." This has to become the mantra of today's military chaplains. You have a lot of different responsibilities and tasks, and you never know when the door of opportunity for ministry might open, so you have to be ready. Ready for Anything.

When I was conducting a Suicide Awareness and Prevention seminar for a Military Police company, I presented the material the way I was trained to do it. One of the statements from psychologists is that "one of the best preventions of suicide is a personal relationship." Someone who has a trusted friend to talk to has a good chance of working through the discouragement and pain of life, whereas someone who doesn't have a good friend might have to deal with the internal problems alone.

On this particular occasion, I added one sentence to the official material. "One of the best preventions of suicide is a personal relationship. This relationship may be with another person, or it could be a relationship with God." I told them I wasn't there to preach, but if anybody wanted to talk after the seminar, they would be welcome to do so. Then I finished the session and dismissed.

As I was hanging around talking with some people, a Lieutenant came up and asked if we could talk privately. I didn't have an office at that location, so I suggested we go outside. When we stepped out to the parking lot, we discovered it was raining steadily, but he wanted to continue.

"Chaplain, I was in the suicide session, and I want to talk with you about something you said. You mentioned it was possible to have a relationship with God?"

"Yes, Lieutenant. I did."

"Well, I have been thinking about suicide lately. My wife is divorcing me. I'm so stressed and hurting I'm not doing my job very well. My boss is on my case. I can't think straight. I need help. How do I have a relationship with God?"

I talked with him about Jesus, and presented the plan of salvation. He asked if I would pray with him to invite Jesus Christ into his heart. I asked him to repeat the prayer, phrase by phrase. Then I prayed for him. When we were done, I couldn't tell whether he had been crying or if the raindrops were running down both sides of his face.

So, I said, "LT, are you crying? Or is that the rain on your face?"

"Chaplain, I am crying because this feels so good. There might be some raindrops too, but I think it's mostly tears."

He threw his arms around me, asked me for a Bible, and promised to start going to church and find someone who would disciple him and help him become a strong Christian. Then he said, "Chaplain, I attended the suicide session only because it's a mandatory thing, and I had to be there with my soldiers. Thank you for coming today. You changed my life."

As the war was about to kick off in Iraq, one unit was having problems with communication. Their radios were not working, and they realized they could not communicate with each other. The commander called a staff meeting. The chaplain was there, of course.

It is important to note that sleep was at a premium at this point. Many of the officers and senior enlisteds had not slept well in several days. The commander came into the meeting and began to berate the staff, cussing and using foul language. After the meeting, the chaplain hung around and the commander walked over and said, "Chaps, it didn't go so good, did it?"

The chaplain answered honestly. "No sir, it didn't."

That was all that needed to be said. After a short pause, the commander asked the chaplain to pray. Miraculously or coincidentally, the radios began to work. Word got around, of course, and the chaplain got the credit because of his prayer. People started coming to the chaplain for prayer and discussion about the Lord. Similar stories could be told over and over again. Chaplains have the ability to change the course of eternity.

Often, this is done just by being there. During the war in Iraq, chaplains had an opportunity to lead service members to faith in Christ. After conversion, many of them wanted to be baptized. Some were baptized in the rivers and streams of Iraq, while others in water containers or boxes that were lined with plastic. Chaplains used their imagination to find places to baptize their flock.

It is unfortunate that chaplains are sometimes wounded in battle. Several chaplains have died during war operations, and many died later because of wounds they sustained while in combat. One chaplain who died in Iraq (the first in the Army since 1970) was chaplain Dale Goetz. He was killed by an IED. It was said that the men in his unit knew he prayed for them. They said they could feel the power of his prayers.

KEITH'S STORY:

As the war in Iraq was kicking off, I was in charge of training and preparing hundreds of Army chaplains to go to war. I also had opportunities to minister to other groups who were getting ready to deploy. A unit from Puerto Rico came through a mobilization site at Fort Bragg, and did not have a chaplain. There weren't any other Spanish speaking Protestant chaplains on the post, and since I had been a missionary in Latin America and spoke Spanish fairly well, I stepped in to provide ministry and lead this infantry unit in worship.

A young soldier who had been diagnosed with cancer was told he could not go down range with his unit, and asked if I would intervene for him. So, I called his doctor and talked with him. Amazingly, the military let him go to Iraq with his unit.

About a year later, I was giving a "Welcome Home" brief in a gymnasium on base when a soldier came running toward me. It actually frightened me because I wasn't sure what was going on. As he got closer, I realized it was the same soldier with cancer I had assisted the year before. He came close to me, almost chin to chin, and saluted. Then he said, "Chaplain, thank you for getting involved and helping me go with my unit to Iraq! Now I can go home and die, knowing I have served my country well."

One chaplain serving with the Marines has a wide-open door for ministry because he volunteered to manage the battalion's social media. Another chaplain offered to help the command staff plan special events because he was gifted in that area.

PAUL'S STORY:

While serving with an infantry battalion, I often went to the firing range with the troops, which sometimes happened on Sunday. This one particular Sunday, after worship services my NCO and I drove out to the live fire range. Since we had just finished church, we happened to have the supplies in our vehicle, and spread the word that we'd be conducting a brief worship service at the far end of the range.

As soon as they finished, about thirty soldiers showed up for church. We sang Amazing Grace and a couple other songs. I preached. We had communion. And then fellowshipped for a while before they had to get back to work. At staff meeting the next morning, the Battalion XO declared, "I have never heard Amazing Grace at a firing range. How'd you get so many guys to go to church out at the range, chaplain?"

But there's more to that story. I didn't always have an "altar call" at the end of field services, but on this particular day, towards the end of my homily, my Chaplain Assistant came up to me and said, "Chaplain, I think the Lords wants you to give an altar call for anyone who wants to get right with God." He happened to be a spiritually minded believer and I trusted his instincts, so I asked if anyone wanted to come up for prayer. Twelve soldiers came forward to ask the Lord into their lives.

There are many stories of chaplains who didn't do it right, who failed to connect with the people in the unit, who got into trouble, or missed the opportunity to change lives for the kingdom of God. What will it take for you to have a lasting positive impact with the people you serve? Only the Lord knows. But if you will focus on being an incarnational presence, taking care of your personal life, and staying faithful in the spiritual disciplines, we guarantee you the Lord will do his part and move by his Spirit, creating a path for you to speak into people's lives.

SECTION FIVE

Building the future of Military Ministry

CHAPTER 26

Understanding Culture

ANTHROPOLOGY IS THE STUDY of man, culture, the environment, and society. It undertakes a comprehensive examination of the past and the present in order to determine what differentiates us from other life forms, but also what differentiates us from one another. In essence, it's a study of what makes us human. Cultural anthropology is one of four sub areas, and its focus is,

> the study of culture and peoples' beliefs, practices, and the cognitive and social organization of human groups. Cultural anthropologists study how people who share a common cultural system organize and shape the physical and social world around them, and are in turn shaped by those ideas, behaviors, and physical environments.[1]

Christian clergy need to be aware of anthropological research if we want to remain on the cutting edge of ministry. It's important to know current attitudes and values on the popular level, as well as in politics and the military. It is crucial that we understand how culture is changing, how people feel and think, their ideals and fears. No longer can we assume everyone has the same value system or world view.

Interwoven throughout the fabric of this book is an understanding of the cultural change in American society and our military over the past twenty-five or thirty years. In fact, we can confidently assert that our culture is changing every single day. If we can grasp these intangibles,

1. Handwerker, "Construct Validity of Cultures," para. 1.

we have a good shot at staying relevant in our ministries, including the military chaplaincy.

Chaplains have the dual task of understanding American culture in general, and the culture in the military. Even more specific are the variant cultures of the Army, Navy, Marine Corp, Air Force, and Coast Guard. Looking through a finer lens reveals that every unit and command has a unique subculture. That's why you have to understand the big picture, and then be able to apply the principles in your particular context.

When we entered the military as chaplains, there was very little talk about the separation of church and state. We never worried about the Constitution and how it affected ministry to our troops. However, in the cultural climate of the twenty-first century, if you don't understand these issues, you will have problems ministering in the military. The constitutional discussion is here to stay.

On the other hand, there are thousands of changes in American society that equate to a cultural revolution. The following is not a paragraph, but a list of some of the changes and issues that are now part of our cultural fabric. The items listed are not all bad, nor are they all good. We just need to be aware of what they are because this is the ministry context we now face, day in and day out. If you encounter them in your ministry context, you might need to become familiar with the issues and make some adjustments to your approach to ministry.

Gender identity flux, women in ministry, women in leadership, pervasiveness of sex, common use of alcohol, pornography, gays and lesbians and other LGBTQ+ in the military, social media, Black Lives Matter, White supremacists, popularity of zombies, fantasy and science fiction, alternative religions, tattoos, the gig economy, diversity and the diminishing white male dominance, telecommuting, cussing in ordinary conversation as well as in public discourse, streaming services replacing television networks, worship bands replacing choirs, worshipping with lights low, casual attire at church, online education, doing away with hymnals, anti-denominationalism, the rise of independent chaplain endorsers, gun violence, same sex marriage, anything-goes mentality, veganism goes mainstream, music and movies go digital, climate change, rise of mental illness and insecurity, smartphones eclipsing land lines, decline of printed magazines and newspapers, online shopping replacing stores, questioning and rejecting traditional authority, openly defying police, divorce as normal, biracial marriage and family, marital unfaithfulness is expected, people have become a law unto themselves, and the erasure of Christianity's influence in society.

How will Christian chaplains approach ministry to transgenders. This was not an issue twenty years ago. How will we advise a commander who has no respect for religion? Will we condemn sinners or love them? How do chaplains minister in a pluralistic culture? How do we preach to people who have little or no biblical background and who don't accept the authority of the scriptures or the clergy? Can we work on the same staff with chaplains from other faith groups, or with people who call themselves Christians but whose standards and views aren't the same as ours? Is it even possible to succeed in the military as a team player without compromising our beliefs? Can we lead people to faith in Christ without violating the DOD guidance against inappropriate proselytizing? Should we give up even trying to be genuine Christians in the military? You have to come up with significant and appropriate responses to these questions. We would encourage you to discuss these matters with your endorser and denominational leadership. You're also welcome to contact us. We are committed to being available to civilian and military clergy who want to talk about ministerial effectiveness.

Perhaps you've heard it said that the Christian message never changes, even though the method of delivery does. This is true when we think about culture and politics. We are confident that the message of Jesus Christ has not changed. The Great Commission is still the mission. The Great Commandment is still to love God and your neighbor. The Great Call of God on your life must still be answered.

To engage the current culture, however, you must look for new opportunities for sharing the Good News, new ways of relating to people, and new methods of communicating. You will work in a sinful environment while maintaining your moral purity. You'll hear a lot of profanity without developing a foul mouth. And you'll be satisfied being a mere incarnational presence while waiting for relationships to develop and the right opportunity to speak.

In 2014, Jonathan Parnell wrote an article for *Desiring God* called "Three Tips on Being a Friend of Sinners."

> If Jesus was a friend of sinners, we should be too . . . This discussion can drift into a much bigger one about Christians and culture and all that. But instead of going there, let's just talk friendship for a minute. Friendship, which is not without its

implications, is more practical and relevant than a primer on the church's posture in society.[2]

Let's stop for a minute to let this sink in. Jesus was the epitome of sinlessness and purity. Yet, he was a friend of sinners. Perhaps that should be our starting point for ministry in an increasingly godless culture. It is true that in the military we will be eyewitnesses of some ungodly behavior. But those are the people we are called to befriend in the Name of Jesus. Like we have said several times, *ministry follows friendship*.

Whatever the cultural context you find yourself in, make it your first goal to establish friendship with the people. Get to know them. And while that dynamic is happening, pray for them and love them in practical ways. That's how you set the stage for effective, fruitful ministry regardless of the cultural dynamic you're facing.

---

2. Parnell, "Three Tips on Being a Friend of Sinners," *Desiring God*, https://www.desiringgod.org/articles/three-tips-on-being-a-friend-of-sinners..

CHAPTER 27

Controversy and Criticism

MIKEY WEINSTEIN IS WAGING a war against evangelical Christians in the Armed Forces. Ed Waggoner wants to disallow chaplains in the military who refuse to serve LGBTQ+ persons or who practice gender discrimination. Hans Zeiger and Kim Philip Hansen understand the importance of maintaining a military chaplaincy, yet they see a need for reform. Keith Travis and Paul Linzey acknowledge the problems and want to prepare chaplains who will be loyal to their church's mission and values, remain true to the Constitution, while at the same time honoring all people regardless of their faith background or lifestyle.

Weinstein was a Jewish legal officer in the Air Force who claims he was religiously abused by conservative Christians. According to his story, Evangelicals berated him, called him vulgar names, tried to proselytize him, and then shamed him. He indicates that his children had similar experiences. In addition to initiating numerous legal actions in an effort to end proselytization and religious abuse in the military, he wrote a book in 2006 entitled *With God on Our Side: One Man's War Against an Evangelical Coup in America's Military*. His Military Religious Freedom Foundation (MRFF) "is dedicated to ensuring that all members of the United States Armed Forces fully receive the Constitutional guarantee of religious freedom to which they and all Americans are entitled by virtue of the Establishment Clause of the First Amendment."[1]

Waggoner, a professor of theology at TCU's Brite Divinity School, is openly critical of the dominance of the Southern Baptist and Roman

---

1. Military Religious Freedom Foundation website.

Catholic chaplains in the military chaplaincy. Here's how he describes his book, *Religion in Uniform*, published in 2019.

> The first scholarly critique of the contemporary US military chaplain corps, this book shows why the chaplaincy is a failing public project, and what Americans can do about it. Waggoner argues political, military, and theological reasons to increase the chaplaincy's religious and moral diversity, to end bias and discrimination against women in the chaplaincy, to challenge the refusal of chaplains to serve LGBTQIA+ persons, and to stop the use of chaplains as religious ambassadors for global, full-spectrum military dominance. Religion in Uniform launches a new, critical and constructive discussion about US military religion for the 21st Century.[2]

At the time of this writing, Hans Zeiger is a State Representative in Puyallup, WA. While completing his graduate degree in Public Policy at Pepperdine University, he wrote a paper titled "Why Does the Military Have Chaplains?" The presentation in 2009 provided a rationale for the military chaplaincy, but in the process, admitted there are several unresolved controversies.

> Issues include the fair representation of denominations and faiths in the chaplaincy, the place of proselytizing by chaplains, the tension between a chaplain's religious beliefs and military force in the prosecution of war, a chaplain's free speech rights, and the role of chaplains in combat.[3]

Understanding the importance of resolving these complex problems, Zeiger concludes by saying, "Regardless of how these issues are handled by military leaders and policymakers, the place of chaplains alongside America's men and women in uniform will remain indispensable."[4]

Kim Philip Hansen seems to come to a similar conclusion in his book, *Military Chaplains and Religious Diversity*. Hansen acknowledges the historical and contemporary criticisms of the military chaplaincy, especially the complaints aimed at evangelical chaplains, but his approach as a sociologist is different from the lawyer, the theologian, and the politician. He spent time with dozens of chaplains, interviewing them about their work, what they liked and didn't like, and how they handled the

---

2. Waggoner's description of his book on researchgate.net.
3. Zeiger, "Why Does the Military Have Chaplains?"
4. Zeiger, "Why Does the Military Have Chaplains?"

controversies and criticisms. According to his research, military chaplains play an important role, not only because of their expertise, but because "they are directly involved in helping as many people as possible practice their religion as freely as possible because, like the nation they serve, their own corps is justified by how well it protects religious particularity."[5]

The authors of this book, Paul Linzey and Keith Travis, are evangelical former military chaplains who now teach seminarians who are training for military ministry. We witnessed many of the same scenarios and controversies described by the critics. We've seen the abuses, the excesses, and the problems. We've lived through many of the same situations, dealt with the challenges first-hand, and maintained our faith, our reputation, and our integrity. We know that much of the criticism is valid. We also know that good chaplains still have a valid place of service and ministry in the Armed Forces.

What are the controversies and criticisms? We've discussed a few of them already. Here's a broader list of the complaints we're dealing with in the military chaplaincy in the twenty-first century. We'll present a recommended strategy for how to handle these issues in the next chapter.

PROSELYTISM

Overtly trying to win people to one's own religion or ideology is frowned upon in the military. The political and practical reason for having chaplains in the military, however, is to fulfill the Establishment Clause and the Free Exercise Clause of the United States Constitution. These rights apply to everyone in America, including those in the uniformed services. As Hansen correctly points out, "While military personnel surrender some of their basic rights when they enlist . . . the right to free exercise of religion is not one they have to give up."[6] Restated and put into everyday terms, the Constitution says "you are free to be religious, and you are protected from others imposing their religion onto you."

RELIGIOUS ACCOMMODATION

Every commander tries to recognize and honor the religious practices and preferences among the people in the unit whenever possible. The

---

5. Hansen, *Military Chaplains*, 37.
6. Hansen, *Military Chaplains*, 37.

chaplain is an advisor to the commander in these situations, but the commander makes the final decision. Religious Accommodation issues may include time off for worship and holy days, wearing religious garments, whether to have a beard, religious dietary concerns, and other practices. The chaplain's role is to interview the service member, determine if the request for accommodation is genuine, and provide a written recommendation to the commander. Some chaplains don't want to cooperate with the Religious Accommodation requests of those who are not Christians, however.

PRAYING IN JESUS'S NAME:

Many Christian leaders teach their people to finish each prayer with the phrase "in Jesus's name, Amen." The idea comes from the New Testament. John 14:13–14 says, "Whatever you ask in My name, I will do it so that the Father may be glorified in the Son. If you ask Me anything in My name, I will do it." And in Matthew 18:19–20 we see, "Again, I assure you: If two of you on earth agree about any matter that you pray for, it will be done for you by My Father in heaven. For where two or three are gathered together in My name, I am there among them."

The military doesn't ask its chaplains to change the way they pray during religious events such as Bible studies, worship services, or prayer meetings. However, when a commander asks the chaplain to pray at a memorial ceremony, a promotion, or a staff meeting, there is an understanding that the event is not a religious event, and the chaplain is expected to pray differently. Some chaplains won't alter the way they pray at these nonreligious command ceremonies or meetings.

Chaplain Jim Denley is a retired Navy Captain, and now serves as the military chaplain endorser for the Assemblies of God. He likes to say it this way: "It is important to keep in mind that a chaplain with a good reputation and positive relationships in the command may be invited to provide a religious element within a nonreligious event." By understanding and respecting this nonreligious context, we are able to maintain an open door of ministry. This is what makes the incarnational ministry possible day after day.

GENDER INEQUALITY:

Some conservatives oppose anyone other than males serving in the military. And some faith groups don't ordain women or endorse them for military chaplaincy. Critics see Evangelicals as being out of touch with reality, and perhaps even acting illegally in this regard.

In Major Carol Barkalow's autobiography, *In the Men's House*, she recalls her experience as one of the first female cadets at West Point. On her first day as a plebe, she was asked by male upperclassmen why she was there. She answered that she wanted to be all she could be. She was merely repeating the recruiting slogan that was popular during at the time. One guy told her she should go somewhere else and be all she could be.[7] Gender bias is strong, and many educated, godly, professional women face abuse and disrespect every day.

Our recommendation is that you treat every person with kindness, respect, and love. Treat men and women the same way. You are certainly entitled to think women should not be in uniform, or that females should not be ordained or in leadership. But don't ever say that publicly or on social media. Wait until you retire from the military. Then you can say whatever you want. Until that time, you'll be doing yourself, other people, and the kingdom of God a favor by remaining positive, supporting others as best you can, and encouraging the women you encounter.

ANTI-DIVERSITY:

When the Department of Defense began considering whether to admit members of the LGBTQ+ community in the Armed Forces, many of those who provided the strongest opposition were Christian church leaders and chaplains. When the policy changed, a lot of evangelical chaplains refused to minister to the LGBTQ+ service members. Some even refused to provide counseling. Members of this demographic were not allowed to participate in many chaplain-led marriage and family events.

This anti-diversity posture isn't going to work anymore, however. Unless there are some radical changes, the direction that America is heading will increasingly include non-whites, non-Christians, non-males, and non-binaries, and if we are called to serve as chaplains, then we need to prepare to minister to whoever is there—to everyone who is

---

7. Barkalow, *Men's House*, 9.

there. We are still free to act according to our theology, our faith group, and our conscience. But within those guidelines, the more inclusive we can be, the more effective we'll be in ministry and the more successful we'll be as officers.

DIVIDED LOYALTIES:

Every chaplain represents his or her God, religious organization, endorsing agency, and the government. Every once in a while, these entities conflict with each other, and the chaplain is suddenly thrust into the position of having to choose which loyalty takes priority. How we navigate these divided loyalties can make or break our career, our ministerial effectiveness, and the future of chaplaincy in the Armed Forces. In the name of refusing to compromise, some chaplains bluntly and loudly defy any suggestion of doing or saying things differently than the way they want to.

Please understand from the start that when you accept a calling to be a chaplain, you agree to work, serve, and minister in a non-Christian, pluralistic environment. Within this context, there are a lot of Christians, and there's a lot of leeway to teach the Word, disciple believers, share your faith with nonbelievers, and let your light shine. Never compromise your morality or your theology.

On the other hand, make sure you look for ways to synthesize or blend your commitments. If you have trouble determining how to do that in a given circumstance, call your endorser, your chaplain supervisor, or a mentor.

SOURCE OF CHAPLAINS:

Historically, military chaplains have been provided by America's congregations: our churches, parishes, synagogues, wards, and mosques. Understandably, there's an expectation that chaplains will represent their faith groups while serving in the military. Today there are some independent endorsing agencies that are not connected with any church, denomination, or faith group. In addition, there is a push to bring nonreligious practitioners into the chaplain corps. When this happens, avoid the urge to criticize, argue, or lament publicly. Leave the fight to the Chiefs of Chaplains, the endorsers, and the courts. Your job is to love people, encourage and support the troops, and be there for them.

NONCOMBATANT STATUS:

American military chaplains are officially considered noncombatants. By law, by policy, and by international treaty, our chaplains do not carry or operate any weapons. The Chiefs of Chaplains have gone so far as to direct their chaplains to avoid firing weapons at the practice range with their troops. This is a controversial issue, however. There have been times during battle that a chaplain has picked up a weapon and used it in self-defense, and some have saved the lives of their soldiers or Marines. Others simply refuse to abide by the noncombatant policy.

We don't recommend that you do that. The night Jesus was betrayed, Peter picked up a weapon and injured someone. Jesus turned to him and simply said, "Put away your sword." Ladies and gentlemen, as a Christian, you represent the Lord himself, and he would say to you, "Put away your weapon." Our cause is not a physical fight, but a spiritual one.

FREEDOM OF SPEECH

All Americans have this right, including the freedom to talk about our religious beliefs. Some chaplains interpret this to mean they can say whatever they want, whenever they want, to whomever they want. Some chaplains have damaged their reputation by flaunting their freedoms, instead of discerning a better way to represent the Lord, the Bible, and the church.

As a general rule, it is better not to criticize, condemn, or taunt others. It is better not to argue, attack, or flaunt your freedoms. It is better to avoid the negative, and focus on the positive when talking about others or using social media. It is better to face conflict with kindness, wisdom, and reason than to charge in ready for battle. And it is better to let your behavior speak for you, rather than insist on using words.

SEPARATION OF CHURCH AND STATE

This key concept in America and in the military must be understood by everyone. Critics of the chaplaincy believe the mere existence of religious clergy in uniform is a violation of the separation principle. Some of our chaplains have failed to understand and respect this principle. It admittedly calls for a delicate balance among the Establishment Clause, the Free Exercise Clause, and the Separation Principle. Christians in the military do have religious freedoms, but we also have limits that must be honored.

In a Bible study, worship service, or counseling session with a Christian, go ahead and use religious language and talk about spirituality. But in a staff meeting, planning session, or other public setting, don't talk about the Bible or Jesus. When conducting a religious service go ahead and mention Jesus in your prayers. But in a command ceremony, promotion, or other gathering, when you pray, make it a generic prayer and avoid saying "Jesus."

STRATEGIC MILITARY USE OF CHAPLAINS:

One of the military's efforts internationally is to shape public perception of America, its people, its purposes, and its policies. Part of this effort has included the use of chaplains in key leader engagement, conversations with foreign religious leaders, and participating in humanitarian assistance and projects. In essence, critics say, we are providing a religious face for military dominance, and in so doing, exploiting religion for political and military aims.

This is an issue that will be decided at the highest levels, and should not be fought or argued by rank and file chaplains. Unless you are on a task force that convenes to discuss this issue, or you work at the Chaplain school, or you are the Chief of Chaplains, your role is to simply follow orders, love people, and make a difference where you can. Let those higher ranking than you speak to this matter. It's too easy to get sucked into a debate and make matters worse. The problem is complex.

The scriptures teach us to care for and help people, and humanitarian assistance is a big part of caring and loving. Helping communicate with key leaders is in some ways a natural for chaplains, because we are trained communicators. Plus, many of us have studied other cultures and religions and can help our command staff avoid some pitfalls. Yet, we don't want to become pawns of the political or military complex simply to further our secular national agenda. After all, we represent a higher kingdom and are called to be spiritual leaders, not political officers.

Because there is this built-in juggling act as we're walking the tightrope, it is better to let senior chaplains engage in this discussion. Those who are at lower echelons should focus on the ministry and the tasks that are assigned.

CIVILIANIZE THE CHAPLAINCY:

One ongoing controversy is how to provide for the religious needs in the Armed Services. Should chaplains be military officers? Or would it be better to hire civilian clergy? This is a question that has been around since the first days of the military. In fact, twenty-five years before the formation of the Continental Congress, George Washington was charged with protecting the frontier of the state of Virginia by Governor Robert Dinwiddie. Washington wrote several times to the governor concerning the need for a chaplain. His desire wasn't just for someone to provide religious services. They were already being provided by civilian pastors. No, General Washington wanted a chaplain who wore the uniform like the men that were being ministered to. The governor gave permission to have commissioned chaplains by 1775. But the question continues to surface: civilian or military clergy?

Most uniformed personnel indicate that they prefer to have military chaplains instead of civilian clergy. For them, it's a matter of trust and respect. They want someone who has been through similar training and hardship, someone who has been with them and who understands their life, and in some cases, has been wounded in action. There's a higher degree of respect and acceptance when the chaplain eats the same MREs, sleeps in the field, faces the same dangers, experiences the NBC training, and suffers through many of the same hardships of being away from home and PCSing too many times.

Another issue is the confidentiality that military chaplains can guarantee. Senior military leaders have stated that the Uniform Code of Military Justice (UCMJ) would not apply to civilian contract chaplains, meaning confidentiality could be lost if the military contracted civilian clergy to fill the role of the chaplain. Losing confidentiality would be terrible for the military.

CHRISTIAN DOMINANCE OF THE CHAPLAINCY

This became an issue when non-Christian faith groups began to increase in numbers in America and in the military, yet there weren't chaplains from those faith groups. Many Christians opposed allowing those religions to send their practitioners into the chaplaincy. Some still do. During the first century of American history, almost all military chaplains were Christians. The second century has seen the addition of chaplains from many other faith traditions, and that list continues to grow.

But the other side of the coin regarding Christian dominance has to do with the abuses and failures that have occurred when chaplains don't or won't or can't minister to the full range of religious, relational, and ritual needs of the people in the command. This must be addressed not only by individual chaplains, but by denominations, endorsers, the Chiefs of Chaplains, and ultimately by political leaders in Washington.

LEGITIMIZING STATE VIOLENCE:

Some critics believe the mere presence of clergy in the military is a tacit approval of the military enterprise, a blatant religious sanction of war. The words and actions of some chaplains seem to add fuel to the fire. However, this seems to be more a matter of perception than substance, because chaplains are in the military not to shoot and not to kill. We are there to provide for the spiritual and relational needs of our people, and to guarantee their right to worship no matter where the military takes them. It is important for chaplains to focus their efforts on spiritual leadership, to accommodate the religious needs of everyone in the command, and to clearly abstain from combat-related activities. Otherwise, we run the risk of adding validity to this criticism.

CHRISTIANS IN THE MILITARY:

There are many who believe Christians should have nothing to do with the military. They think it's wrong to be in uniform, and, therefore, wrong to have military chaplains. According to some, "The very fact that a Christian or a minister is even in the military is a tacit approval of warfare and killing, and that's not biblical." Those who feel this way have a right to their convictions, and should be strong enough to stand up for their beliefs. When people in uniform come to this conclusion, they can declare themselves to be Conscientious Objectors, and the chaplain is one of the first to interview them and verify that their convictions are valid and consistent. They can legally step away from serving in the military. We will support that matter of conscience.

There is no merit, however, to the claim that all Christians must have nothing to do with military service. The scriptures differentiate between the prerogatives of governments and those of individuals. Governments may incarcerate or punish; individuals may not. Governments may tax; individuals may not. Governments may impose and enforce laws; individuals may not. Governments may raise an army to defend itself, its people, and its interests; individuals may not. An individual presuming to act the same way the government acts would be considered a criminal or an outlaw.

There is another side to the discussion, however. The scriptures do teach us to turn the other cheek. And the Bible does teach us not to seek revenge. We are told by the Lord to love our enemies and pray for those who persecute us. This is not speaking to nations, however. The force of these passages is meant to be applied on the personal level. In the day-to-day life of the disciple, we are better off avoiding the fight, not striking back, and resisting the urge to be ugly in response. It simply doesn't apply to nations as a whole.

A nation does have the right and the responsibility to maintain a military or a police force, and good, godly, religious people can certainly be a part of maintaining the peace, protecting the homeland, and even waging war when the government sees fit to do so.

THE ROLE OF CRITICISM

Winston Churchill is often credited with saying, "Criticism may not be agreeable, but it is necessary. It fulfills the same function as pain in the human body. It calls attention to an unhealthy state of things." There is wisdom in Churchill's comment. Our critics can help us make some needed corrections and refinements in how we think about and practice military ministry in the twenty-first century.

Abraham Lincoln is believed to have said, "He has a right to criticize who has a heart to help." In light of Lincoln's perspective, perhaps we can see the critics of the chaplaincy not as enemies who must be battled, but as voices whose input can make us better. Or, as basketball player LeBron James has pointed out, "I like criticism. It makes you strong."

Yes, there are problems. Yes, there are controversies. Yes, there are criticisms, and many of them are valid. It has been said that in every criticism there is a measure of truth. If that is the case, we should take a good look at what our critics are saying and then go back to the Bible and see what the Lord would say to us.

Guest Anecdote Number Twelve

Understanding Culture

When "Don't Ask, Don't Tell" was overturned in the military, many senior leaders did not like the military being used as a social experiment. As I write this, the same thought process has come back up regarding the acceptance of transgenders in the military.

Our culture is changing often, almost on a daily basis. Recently, several chaplains contacted me wondering how our faith group (Liberty Baptist Fellowship) is responding to the issue of ministering to transgenders. This was not an issue twenty years ago. The old saying "times are a-changing" is something to think about in terms of culture, because culture is always changing.

As a chaplain serving in the military, how are you going to minister in a changing culture? This is an excellent question, and one that each individual needs to answer personally. I have seen some chaplains who could not adapt to a changing culture and were not effective ministering in the military.

Each February, the military chaplaincy celebrates the "Four Immortal Chaplains." If you've done any study in chaplaincy at all, this story rings a bell. The four chaplains (a Rabbi, a Methodist, a Catholic Priest, and a Dutch Reformed minister) all sailed together on the USS Dorchester. They embodied the pluralistic ministry of the chaplain. Even though culture has changed, the challenge of working and ministering beside a fully endorsed chaplain of a different faith group is something you must understand and accept. Frankly, some cannot accept it and, therefore, will not be able to stay in the military.

While teaching military chaplain candidates in the past year, I've heard some tell me they do not want to go into the military if so and so became or was reelected president. My reply is that a chaplain has to know the difference between being obedient to the President, Congress, Senate, the Department of Defense . . . and being obedient to the call that God has put on your life. If God has called you to be a chaplain, he will sustain you through cultural and societal changes. As Christians, we have to trust God to see us through all of the issues of culture, pluralism, politics, or whatever.

Understanding culture is paramount for chaplains in the military today who want to be effective and make a difference for the gospel. If we can do that, we should be able to work within the limits or bounds of culture while staying true to our theological and moral commitments. That's the example Jesus set for us.

CH (Col-Ret) Keith Travis

Chapter 28

Diversity

We happen to agree with Mikey Weinstein that all members of the United States Armed Forces should fully receive the Constitutional guarantee of religious freedom, and that there is no room in our military for religious abuse or intolerance. The Air Force Chief of Staff who directed his downtrace commanders to avoid promoting religious services was absolutely right. There must never be any coercion for or against religion, nor any message, whether blatant or subtle, that those who are of a certain religion are better or worse than anyone else.

We also think Ed Waggoner has a valid point when he directs the chaplaincy towards increased diversity, and we can't afford to ignore his recommendations. But there are nuances that make these issues more complex than an easy agreement or disagreement.

We understand that if we are going to meet the religious needs of all personnel in uniform, there needs to be adequate representation of all faith groups and demographics, but whether this will ever include atheists and humanists will depend on the decisions of the courts. If the judicial branch were to determine that these ideologies are the equivalent of a religion, even though they claim to have no God, or if the courts were to decide that they are not religions, but their values and behaviors are similar to those of religious groups and should be accommodated accordingly, then we eventually might see military chaplains from these groups serving in the military.

Some faith groups do not ordain women, and they have the right to hold to their convictions. Similarly, some faith groups do not ordain members of the LGBTQ+ community, and they have the right to maintain their theological and moral commitments. Yet, the fact remains that women and LGBTQ+ are allowed to serve in today's military. Not only must we find ways to meet their needs, but we also might find ourselves serving alongside chaplains who are female, nonbinary, or non-Christian. Doing so doesn't mean we approve of unbiblical lifestyles; it means we can get along with people who are different, who we disagree with. It also means we are big enough to love them and acknowledge their civil rights.

A corollary issue is that some faith groups will not allow their chaplains to conduct weddings or other sacred rites for members of the LGBTQ+ community. Most of the time, the traditional principle of "perform and provide" works well. Chaplains from differing faith groups and traditions work together to minister to and serve the people in the command. There are times, however, when there may not be someone in the vicinity who can perform the requested ministry, and that's when the spotlight shines negatively on those whose religious convictions prevent them from performing direct religious ministry.

Dr. Waggoner recommends that every chaplain should be willing to minister to all people, and those who aren't willing to do so should be disallowed from serving in the military.[1] This approach perhaps would go a long way towards putting an end to discrimination based on gender and LGBTQ+ identification.

A problem with Waggoner's recommendation, however, is that excluding chaplains and faith groups who don't ordain or endorse women, or who won't support and minister to LGBTQ+ personnel, is a step towards establishing a state religion and denying the free exercise of religion. In essence, Dr. Waggoner's well-intentioned recommendations, while aiming at providing and caring for a valid segment of people in the military, may be a violation of both the Establishment Clause and the Free Exercise Clause. Yet, the need to care for and provide for everyone in the military is real.

PAUL'S STORY:

A few years before "Don't Ask Don't Tell" was repealed, I served at a senior command. There were two women who I knew from a previous assignment, and considered them my friends. We had a lot in common

---

1. Waggoner, *Religion in Uniform*, 70.

and liked many of the same restaurants, movies, and games. In fact, my wife and I invited them over to our home for dinner several times, but they never came. One day I arrived at work a bit later than I normally arrived, and parked in a different place than usual. Across the parking lot, I saw my two female friends get out of a car, give each other a kiss, and take separate routes to enter the building through different doors. That's when I realized why they would not socialize with me and my wife. They knew I was a conservative Christian, and they couldn't afford to trust me. If I was aware of their lifestyle and reported them, they both could have lost their careers, so they couldn't take the risk. Their fear of potentially losing their livelihoods meant that I would never be their friend, and I would never be able to minister to them.

Several years later, after LGBTQ+ personnel were openly allowed in the military, I was serving at a different installation. One Sunday, two men attended the chapel. After worship, I was greeting parishioners at the door, when these newcomers approached. One of the men introduced himself to me and said, "Chaplain, my husband is having surgery this week. Would you pray for him?" After I agreed to pray, he turned to his husband and reported, "Sweetheart, the chaplain wants to pray for you." I laid hands on him and prayed. Then we talked a while before they went on their way.

Another critical issue has to do with racism in the military. A report published in May 2021 was titled "Deep-rooted racism and discrimination permeate U.S. military," and included this statement. "In interviews with The Associated Press, current and former enlistees and officers in nearly every branch of the armed services described a deep-rooted culture of racism and discrimination that stubbornly festers, despite repeated efforts to eradicate it."[2]

The same article cited the racial statistics among officers. According to their studies, "The breakdown of all active commissioned officers: 73% white; 8% each Black and Hispanic; 6% Asian; 4% multiracial; and less than 1% Native Hawaiian, Pacific Islander, American Indian or Alaska Native. And the diversity gap widened the higher individuals moved up in the ranks."[3] The demographics among chaplains are similar.

The imbalance among ethnicities in the officer ranks may be evidence of a larger systemic problem because being an officer requires a

---

2. Stafford et al, "Deep-Rooted Racism," para. 6.
3. Stafford et al, "Deep-Rooted Racism," para. 32.

college education, and a chaplain needs an additional three-year master's degree. These degree programs are expensive. Could it be that the policies, procedures, and actions that serve to prevent non-whites from amassing wealth might be part of the reason we have a higher percentage of white officers and chaplains, and why we have a low ratio of officers who are people of color? This issue might be worth further investigation because the discrepancy tends to breed a distrust of officers in general. Too often, this distrust applies to chaplains.

Yet there have been some improvements. Ronit Y. Stahl in her book, *Enlisting Faith: How the Military Chaplaincy Shaped Religion and State in Modern America*, talks about the struggles America's military chaplaincies have had trying to become pluralistic. She mentions that despite the weaknesses and failures we've encountered, we have made some progress. "A century ago, as the United States prepared to enter World War I, the military chaplaincy included only mainline Protestants and Catholics. Today it counts Jews, Mormons, Muslims, Christian Scientists, Buddhists, Seventh-day Adventists, Hindus, and evangelicals among its ranks."[4]

The process has been uneven, we're not proud of everything that has transpired over the past century, and there's more work to do and more changes to make. We have taken steps in the right direction, but as our critics have pointed out, we still have too many biases and shortcomings, and that is why we must learn to love all people and be willing to serve all our Soldiers, Sailors, Airmen, Coast Guardsmen, and Marines.

Over the past decade, all three military chaplaincies have worked hard to increase the number of female chaplains. For example, when Paul was in charge of Army chaplain recruiting in 2009 and 2010, the Army Chief of Chaplains, directed the team to actively recruit females. The Chief's office also hosted a series of conferences for female clergy. The intent was to foster a climate of acceptance and support for women in ministry, women in the military, and women as chaplains. There has been a similar emphasis on bringing in chaplains who are people of color.

The Chaplain Center at the United States Naval Academy is a great example of the new emphasis on meeting the needs of people of all faith groups. When new Plebes show up for their first summer, the chaplains find out the number of each reported faith group. Then they make a concerted effort at providing time, facilities, and leadership to accommodate

---

4. Stahl, *Enlisting Faith*, 4.

the religious needs. Throughout the year, the chaplains track the number of Midshipmen who participate in prayer services, worship opportunities, and fellowship events for each faith group. In addition, they provide counseling and other programs for all Midshipmen whether they identify as part of a faith group or no faith group.

In 2021, the represented faith groups at the Naval Academy included Catholics, Jews, Muslim, Hindus, Latter Day Saints, Christian Scientists, Buddhists, and Protestants of various denominations. In addition to the chaplain-led religious opportunities, there were more than a dozen extracurricular religious groups on campus that were allowed to provide for the free exercise of religion of the Midshipmen. The Mids can also go off the Yard and participate in the congregation of their choice. The other service academies offer similar religious opportunities for cadets of all faith groups.

The Naval Academy does continue the somewhat controversial practice of prayer before the noon meal in the dining facility. There have been complaints of this practice on the grounds that it forces the Midshipmen to participate in religion even if they don't want to. But the Academy justifies it with the reasoning that part of the mission of the institution is to train students for command positions in the United States Navy. According to this reasoning, the Midshipmen need a religious program that contributes to their moral and spiritual development, offers service and leadership opportunities, and gives them a chance to experience firsthand a healthy religious program that meets the needs of all personnel in the command.

This is crucial because in addition to their own personal spirituality, commanders at all levels must be aware of the religious needs of their sailors and Marines, and be prepared to respond to a variety of requests for Religious Accommodation. Therefore, it is of paramount importance that today's midshipmen experience a healthy, thriving religious program that impacts all naval personnel associated with the Academy. They need to know what a quality, chaplain-led program looks like so that when they are in the operational Navy or Marine Corps, they can ensure similar opportunities are in place for their personnel and families.

Diversity implies the inclusion of people of different races, cultures, faiths, gender identities, and color. Our nation consists of people from all around the world, every imaginable people group, and every ideology. And every citizen in the United States is supposed to be guaranteed the same freedoms, the same opportunities, the same respect, and the same deference. A few quotations from our history demonstrates this inherent belief in and commitment to equality.

THOMAS JEFFERSON IN THE DECLARATION OF INDEPENDENCE:

"We hold these truths to be self-evident, that all men are created equal, that they are endowed by their Creator with certain unalienable Rights, that among these are Life, Liberty and the pursuit of Happiness."[5]

PRESIDENT ABRAHAM LINCOLN IN HIS GETTYSBURG ADDRESS:

"Four score and seven years ago our fathers brought forth on this continent a new nation, conceived in liberty and dedicated to the proposition that all men are created equal."[6]

EMMA LAZARUS'S POEM AT THE STATUE OF LIBERTY:

"Give me your tired, your poor / Your huddled masses yearning to breathe free / The wretched refuse of your teeming shore / Send these, the homeless, tempest-tost to me / I lift my lamp beside the golden door!"[7]

MARTIN LUTHER KING JR. IN WASHINGTON DC, 1963:

"I have a dream that one day this nation will rise up and live out the true meaning of its creed: 'We hold these truths to be self-evident, that all men are created equal.'"[8]

This theme runs deep throughout our history, from the very beginning, through the darkest times, and remains in our national DNA today.

5. "The Declaration of Independence," https://www.mountvernon.org/education/primary-sources-2/article/the-declaration-of-independence-july-4-1776/.

6. "Gettysburg Address," http://www.abrahamlincolnonline.org/lincoln/speeches/gettysburg.htm.

7. "The New Colossus," https://www.nps.gov/stli/learn/historyculture/colossus.htm.

8. "I Have a Dream," https://www.npr.org/2010/01/18/122701268/i-have-a-dream-speech-in-its-entirety.

Diversity

Christian clergy, including military chaplains, cannot afford to become categorized as anti-diversity in any way. First, because we represent the God who created and loves all people, and we are called and ordained to reflect his values. Second, because if we get sidetracked arguing over Critical Race Theory, Black Lives Matter, LGBTQ+ Pride, feminism, partisan politics, or any other contemporary cultural movement, we will have lost our voice, our spiritual authority, and our raison d'etre. We need to lead the way and be the ones who treat people right, who champion the cause of Christ in loving and caring for all people, who don't accept the status quo when it is unjust or inadequate.

James 1:27 expresses the theme of caring for those who cannot provide for themselves when it says, "Religion that God our Father accepts as pure and faultless is this: to look after orphans and widows in their distress and to keep oneself from being polluted by the world." This is the heart of Christ in action.

The Gospels show Jesus spending time with outcasts and people of ill repute. So much so, in fact, that he was labeled "a friend of sinners." But that moniker didn't bother him. In fact, I can imagine our Lord smiling when hearing that accusation as if he were saying, "Friend of sinners? Of course I am a friend of sinners. That's why I came into the world. I love them. I care about them. I want them to feel comfortable spending time with me. That's why I hang out with them. And that's why I will hang on the cross for them."

And that should be the approach among contemporary Christians. Rather than being known for judgmentalism, we can be known for love, friendliness, and kindness. As Christians, as representatives of the God who is above all and Lord of all, we can be bigger than our differences. We can genuinely love people, like them, and spend time with them without always having to point out their sins, faults, weaknesses, or differences. And we can do this without ourselves falling into sin, without losing our theology, without losing our salvation, while maintaining a godly moral lifestyle and theological orthodoxy.

When the creation story in Genesis was written, many cultures believed their leader to be a son of god or a representative of god. Ancient civilizations in Asia, Africa, Europe, and the Americas held similar beliefs. Many religions believed only their leader had the divine image, and their ruler was almost always an upper-class male of the dominant ethnicity.

Genesis came along and said something quite revolutionary. Every human being is created in God's image. This includes women, people from all ethnic groups, the poor, and those from other cultures and lifestyles. That's what makes the religion of the Bible radically different from most other religions of the world. Right from the start, God decided there would be total equality. All human beings were to be treated fairly with equal opportunities, there being no glass ceiling or any kind of artificial limitations that restrict people groups who are less favored. There was to be no hate, no fear, and no bias. Nobody was to be superior or inferior to others.

Though the majority of cultures around the world have had some form of caste system that subjugated women, minorities, children, and the less fortunate, the plan of God was to move humanity away from that kind of thinking because all human beings are created in the image of God and continue to bear the Imago Dei. In essence, gender and racial equality were supposed to be established three thousand years ago.

PAUL'S STORY:

A few years ago, I was talking with a friend about how we as Christians should relate to sinners, specifically gays and Lesbians. The friend offered the old adage, "love the sinner, hate the sin," and was satisfied that he had covered the topic adequately. So I asked him if he'd read Dr. Gary Chapman's *The 5 Love Languages*. He said he had read and appreciated the book, but he began to squirm when I went further and asked which of the love languages he uses to express his love for gays: Words of Affirmation? Quality Time? Physical Touch? Acts of Service? Gifts?

The fact is, we like to talk about loving sinners, but when the rubber meets the road, we don't do it very well or very often. My friend had never expressed love to anyone from the LGBTQ+ community in any way whatsoever, and didn't like it when I suggested that the truth of the matter was that he didn't love sinners at all.

Ask yourself these questions: When was the last time you had a person of a different ethnicity into your home to socialize? When was the last time you went out to lunch with someone who was different than you? Is it even possible to love people and minister to them without spending time with them? How do you feel about people who are of a different faith, ethnicity, gender, or lifestyle? Do you ever spend time with them as a friend?

Dr. Martin Luther King, Jr. observed that "Love is the only force capable of transforming an enemy to a friend."[9] There is a lot of truth in his comment, and Christian chaplains would do well to start loving people more, and condemning them less.

We agree with Dr. Waggoner when he says Christian chaplains should emphasize the theology of love. Love for God and love for the neighbor is the hallmark of genuine Christianity. If we really believed that, Waggoner suggests, Christian chaplains and endorsers "will amend their chaplain policies and behaviors in order to love and serve others more faithfully."[10]

Whether Christian denominations and endorsers are willing to amend their policies remains to be seen. At the very least, we should accept the fact that all people must be treated with kindness and respect, even people of different color, gender, lifestyle, and religion. We should be willing to demonstrate genuine Christian love, which is what the Bible teaches. Plus, we should acknowledge that all people have civil rights that must be respected and protected, which is what America's founding documents declare. We are not suggesting that we change our views on morality and theology, but that we change how we treat people and how we talk about them.

Might those denominations and endorsers who don't support religious rites for LGBTQ+ be willing to consider allowing their chaplains to perform civil unions that are not religious weddings. Might this be an appropriate compromise for chaplains who in some ways are called to be civil servants with command functions, yet who are called to represent their faith group and its values? It's not our decision to make, but we believe it may be worth consideration by denominational leaders and endorsers. It's a tough issue.

Could we consider providing personal counseling for those whose lifestyle is different than our own? Is it possible to find ways to befriend them and bridge the gap, perhaps offering professional and relational acceptance?

In many denominations, chaplains are organized within the missions department. Understanding that chaplains are missionaries should

9. The MLK Memorial in Washington DC.
10. Waggoner, *Religion in Uniform*, 159.

lead us to take a totally positive approach to spending time with the people in our command, especially the sinners, the ungodly, those who are different from us, and those whose lifestyle is farthest away from what we consider to be the biblical ideal. You don't win people to Christ by condemning them or shunning them. You win them by spending time with them and loving them.

Too many of us have forgotten that we are called to humble ourselves and serve. The fact of the matter is that in essence, we stopped loving those who are unlovable or broken or different; we started condemning sinners instead of befriending them; and we became racial, religious, and political elitists, which is contrary to the attitude of our Lord. Somewhere along the way, we started asserting our own rights instead of laying down our lives.

If we can once again learn to love people, sinners might start to feel safe and at ease among us. And if sinners were to feel safe around us, like they felt in the presence of Jesus, then we might have a chance to let the light of Christ shine through us, and the incarnational ministry of presence would once again become a powerful force, changing hearts and changing lives.

CHAPTER 29

A Recommended Strategy

IN ANY ENDEAVOR, UNDERSTANDING the rules of the game is crucial if we're going to play the game effectively, if we're going to have a seat at the table and a voice in the discussion. Here are seven recommendations we think will help Christian clergy be successful in the military chaplaincy while bearing fruit for eternity and staying true to their biblical and ministerial calling.

RECOMMENDATION NUMBER ONE

We must understand biblical theology and apply it to military ministry. For example, in John 6:44 Jesus declares, "No one can come to Me unless the Father who sent Me draws him." If Jesus is right, it's not a Christian's job to persuade others to believe in Christ. That's the role of the Holy Spirit. The Lord often uses us to talk with others, share our perspective, and set an example, but he is the one responsible for bringing people to faith in Christ. Therefore, Christians in the military should accept the role of being an incarnational presence, letting the light of Christ shine through us, while we love and befriend others. This approach has been called friendship evangelism or lifestyle evangelism, and seems to be more effective in a pluralistic context than confrontational evangelism.

Another example of biblical theology is that God is the judge, and we are not. He has the prerogative of condemning unbelievers, but we do not. Interestingly, John 3:17 says "God did not send His Son into the world that He might condemn the world." If Christ himself did not come into the world to condemn sinners, then Christians serving in the Armed Forces might want to follow his example when talking to or about sinners, non-Christians, or anyone who doesn't live or believe like we do.

A third example is a biblical understanding of what it means to pray in Jesus's name. It doesn't mean to tack on the words "in Jesus's name" at the end of a prayer. If it did, then someone who cries out in desperation "God help me" would be met with silence from heaven. But God doesn't treat us that way. He hears every cry for help and every heart in need. It might also be helpful to keep in mind that there are no prayers in the Bible that end with "in Jesus's name, amen." Take a quick look at the prayers in the Bible and you'll notice there are some powerful prayers, but not a single one ending with our common finishing phrase. Also, when James 4:3 talks about why some prayers are not answered, he cites wrong motives as a reason, but he doesn't mention failing to say "in Jesus's name, amen" as a cause of unanswered prayer. Therefore, we need to take a fresh look at what it means to pray in Christ's name.

"Name" in the Bible refers to identity, authority, character, and relationship. To pray in Jesus's name, therefore, means we pray understanding who he is, we recognize and live under his authority, we know and reflect his character, and we are in a dynamic relationship with him.

When these conditions are in place, you don't have to say the words "in Jesus's name" at the end of each prayer to be praying in his name. You can pray with assurance because you know his identity, authority, and character, and you are in relationship with him. You are praying in Jesus's name.

Understanding our own theology helps us avoid three common pitfalls when ministering in the military. We don't have to pressure people or criticize them in order to win them to Christ. We can trust the Lord to draw them to himself, and he is good at his job. We never condemn people, tell them they are sinners, or tell them they're going to hell. God is the judge, not us. And we can pray, confident that we are praying in Jesus's name, even when we don't say those words at the end of the prayer.

This understanding is important because in the military there are two types of situations we might be praying in. First is during a religious event, and second is at a command event. During worship services, Bible studies, discipleship sessions, and visiting someone who is a Christian, we can pray however we want. There are no restrictions. You can say Jesus, Lord, Father God, Holy Spirit, Abba Daddy, or anything else you have in mind to say, just like you would at any church in America. And you can close your prayer with the traditional "in Jesus's name, amen."

When a chaplain prays at a command function, however, there is a huge difference, and the chaplain has to understand this. Command activities are not religious events. They are not part of the religious program. The commander has the authority to order all personnel to attend official functions. Therefore, even if the chaplain is asked to pray at the command event, the chaplain has to respect the diversity of the personnel in attendance. A good Christian chaplain will not say the words "in Jesus's name" when praying at a staff meeting, retirement, promotion, memorial ceremony, Family Day lunch, or Veterans Day commemoration, because these are not religious events. They are command activities.

A good chaplain also understands the difference between a memorial service and a memorial ceremony, a funeral service and a funeral ceremony. A service is a religious event, which means you can pray however you want, and a ceremony is a command event, which means you will honor and respect the religious freedom of those who are not Christians. So we learn how to pray to the Lord, to the Almighty, or to the Creator. We sometimes begin by verbally acknowledging that there are people of many faith traditions in the room, and we respect them all by asking them to think, meditate, or pray according to their own tradition, while the chaplain prays in his or hers.

Because we know our own theology, we will be praying in Jesus's name, even when not saying those words. We will be fulfilling the Great Commission and winning souls to Christ by loving people and trusting the Holy Spirit to speak to them. And we will avoid condemning and offending people, even when they know what our standards are. And they will know those standards because we are setting a godly example while spending time with them.

RECOMMENDATION NUMBER TWO

We need to take time to consider and understand the Establishment Clause and the Free Exercise Clause of the U.S. Constitution: "Congress shall make no law respecting an establishment of religion or prohibiting the free exercise thereof."[1] How should this statement impact the

---

1. Bill of Rights, *First Amendment*, https://www.archives.gov/founding-docs/bill-of-rights-transcript.

military chaplain? None of our actions should ever violate either of these dynamics. In fact, part of our job in the military is to be the expert who helps others understand and behave accordingly.

At the end of a chapter titled "Culture War in the Chaplain Corps," Kim Philip Hansen makes this statement: "Although the Chaplain Corps is full of men and women who work extremely hard with the best possible intentions, recent conflicts reveal that it remains a work in progress. If a Constitutional military chaplaincy is even possible, it will require a balance between the First Amendment's two religion clauses that has not yet been found."[2] There is a lot of truth in Hansen's comments. That's why we are making an effort in this book to find that balance so that godly men and women will be able to continue serving as ministers in the military throughout the twenty-first century.

It is important to understand that America is not a Christian nation and never was. It may be true that there has always been a Christian majority, but our founding fathers intentionally decided there would be no official religion. There would be no penalty for having a different faith than the majority, and no punishment for having no faith at all. Plus, there would be no coercion to get people to change their ways or their beliefs. This is the meaning of religious freedom in America. We are free to worship, think, and believe as we please, and we allow others the same freedoms.

In the same vein, America's military is not a religious organization. Though there are many in uniform who are spiritual, the purpose of the Armed Forces is to serve under the leadership and guidance of the civilian government. The military is an extension of our political process. The Pentagon doesn't determine its own course of action. It receives orders from the government and then carries them out.

Taking these facts into consideration should lead chaplains and church leadership to adopt an attitude of humility. We have every right to be confident and loyal to our beliefs. Yet, we must accept the presence of people with different faiths and lifestyles. This is true in every neighborhood, town, and city in the United States, and it is true in the military.

Religious freedom is real, yet non-establishment is crucial. In a pluralistic environment, freedom "of" religion implies freedom "from" religion, and everyone is encouraged to freely be who he or she wants to be. That doesn't mean we agree with them, but it does mean we accept

---

2. Hansen, *Military Chaplains*, 201.

them and support them. You might event want to ask people whose faith and lifestyle are different than yours how they would like you to serve them and meet their needs.

RECOMMENDATION NUMBER THREE

Don't ever forget that as a chaplain you are called to be a spiritual leader. The military may have other reasons for wanting you there, but you have to understand your real mission. Your *raison d'etre* is to live a godly life, be available to people who want to draw near to the Lord, and be a pastor to the people in your command.

Don't let anything or anyone sidetrack or derail your mission. To accomplish your goals as a spiritual leader, avoid controversy as much as possible. Be careful which bandwagon you jump on. Clear it with a mentor, supervisor, senior chaplain, or your endorser. Stay out of politics, even when you feel strongly about a party, candidate, or issue. Use social media for positive comments and to make people look good. No politics, no grumbling, no condemnation, and no criticism. We also suggest that you never complain. Even in an After Action Review, don't be the one to point out flaws or weaknesses in others. This will hinder your ability to minister as their chaplain. Your input during an AAR should only be positive comments and observations. Do not shoot at the range with your troops. And don't shoot in uniform.

Never get drunk. Never have sex with someone you're not married to. Never take money or stuff that isn't yours. Practice your spiritual disciplines. And be a friend to all. In essence, make sure your role is always as a spiritual leader, and don't allow anything to detract from that.

RECOMMENDATION NUMBER FOUR

Do your best to prioritize your marriage and family. It's too easy to get so focused on ministry, career, and programs that we ignore, neglect, or minimize the importance of the people at home. This is never acceptable. Too many good preachers, pastors, evangelists, missionaries, and chaplains have lost their spouse or their children because they were so caught up in the work of the Lord that they failed to be the husband, wife, mother, or father that God called them to be. Put birthdays and anniversaries on your calendar. Plan days off and holidays around your family. Be there for your kids' recitals and games. Remember that your spouse matters more than anything else in the world.

Keep in mind that according to Matthew 18:18–20, unity invites the presence of the Lord and activates the power of God. So, if you want the power and the presence of the Lord in your home, it's up to you to lead the way and set the example of prioritizing your marriage and family.

RECOMMENDATION NUMBER FIVE

Always be a team player, understanding that you are on several teams simultaneously. As a military chaplain, you always represent the organization that ordained you and the agency that endorsed you. It is essential to remain accountable to these entities. Attend your annual endorser or denominational conference. Place a courtesy call to your endorser every six months. And if the denomination or endorser asks you for a monthly, quarterly, or annual contribution and a report, send them cheerfully, giving thanks that they believed in you and sent you to serve in the military.

As a chaplain, you are also part of a Religious Support Team or Religious Affairs Team. There will be times you have to protect, support, and defend your Chaplain Assistant. Be prepared to do that. At times you might have to fight for your budget, vehicle, office, a seat at the table, or a line on the agenda. If you are willing to do this, you will be relevant. If you fail to fight for your team, you will become irrelevant. Guaranteed.

You are also part of the command staff and the leadership team. As such, you represent the commander at all times. A key principle is to make your boss look good. Make sure you never blindside the commander. Communicate often and thoroughly. If there's a problem, tell the boss personally, not in a staff meeting. The same is true of your relationship with your chaplain supervisor. Again, you are part of a larger team, and you are accountable for your behavior. Remember, if you do your part well as a team player, you will increase your ministerial effectiveness and open more doors for ministry, which is why you are in the military in the first place.

RECOMMENDATION NUMBER SIX

Be sure you understand the two roles of a chaplain, and excel in both of them. (a) You are a minister of the gospel, representing both Jesus

Christ and your church. (b) You are a personal staff officer of the commander, representing your military boss at all times, but also with access to speak to him or her about issues affecting the unit or the people in the command.

There are quite a few ways to pave the way for continued success, and a wise military officer will heed the following tips, and perhaps be ready to share them with others, whether they are enlisted, NCO, or officer. Add a skill or certification to your training every year. Do everything in your job description *plus* an additional two or three tasks that aren't listed. Submit reports and budgets on time. Keep a record of phone calls, appointments, visits, worship services, Bible studies, training events, and other accomplishments. Quantify these items for your evaluations and reports. Use a calendar or daily planner, and don't forget an appointment or a responsibility. Take the initiative to meet with your rater quarterly and your senior rater twice a year. When there's a staff meeting or an event, be there early. Send thank you notes. Guard your laptop and CAC. Careers and reputations have been ruined by losing them.

In addition, an effective chaplain in the twenty-first century is supportive of all people in the military, regardless of gender, religion, ethnicity, political affiliation, or other demographic factors. Love them. Demonstrate that love in ways they understand and accept. Remember, Jesus was a friend of sinners. They loved him and welcomed him into their homes.

RECOMMENDATION NUMBER SEVEN:

"And whatever you do, in word or in deed, do everything in the name of the Lord Jesus, giving thanks to God the Father through him" (Colossians 3:17).

Chapter 30

What's at Stake?

WHAT HAPPENS IF WE can't figure out how to minister in a pluralistic setting without compromising our own beliefs? What are the ramifications if we insist on concluding every public prayer with the phrase "in Jesus's name?" What's at stake if we don't understand the contemporary culture? What if we don't get it right?

Several years ago, when "praying in Jesus's name" first became an issue, some commanders at military installations made the decision to completely discontinue public prayer. No chaplains participated in retirements, promotions, memorial ceremonies, or other command functions.

A similar decision was made in several state prison systems. Florida, Virginia, Texas, Georgia, California, and a few other states decided to stop paying prison chaplains. They made the decision to operate their programs without clergy. That move was short lived, however, because the sudden absence of chaplains made the governors and prison administrators understand the significant impact the clergy had among the inmates and the staff. In essence, the prison system needs its chaplains, even if their value is intangible.

It is not too far-fetched to imagine a scenario in which a military leader says, "I can use my budget for better purposes than having a chaplain on board. I'd rather pay for beans and bullets. I can use the resources for more fighters. Besides, the chaplain causes too many problems, doesn't understand pluralism, and can't seem to figure out how to provide for the religious needs of the different faith groups represented in the command."

Some might think this would never happen. But if we don't get our act together, that's exactly what could happen. Military commanders are extremely pragmatic. If it works, do it. If it doesn't work, replace it. Plus, there is political and cultural pressure to put an end to religion in America's military, or to change it radically. This is why chaplains must understand today's climate and pay attention to how they go about their responsibilities and ministries. To put it bluntly, maintaining a chaplain corps is at risk. But there are other potential losses, as well, both on the large scale and the personal level.

A chaplain who doesn't fit within the twenty-first century parameters will face personal consequences. If problems appear while applying to get into the military, the candidate might not be accessioned. If the problems show up after the person is commissioned, he or she might not make promotions, which eventually will lead the military to discharge the chaplain from the service. This will directly impact the individual and the family because it means the former chaplain will be looking for a job.

If godly ministers are not allowed to remain in the Armed Forces, the only religious practitioners in the military would be those who are less moral, non-Christian, or of a different theological persuasion. This would be a tragic loss of an incarnational presence in an environment where it is badly needed. Not having a seat at the table, to use a familiar expression, would entail a significant loss of influence. We wouldn't be there to let the light of Christ shine in a dark place. Our moral and ethical input would be erased. Soldiers, Sailors, Marines, Coast Guardsmen, and Airmen wouldn't have access to a Christian minister—nobody who can answer their questions about God, eternity, or how to overcome temptation. There's another consequence. The Constitutional clauses about the establishment of religion and the free exercise of religion would be skewed or abandoned.

For these reasons, it is of paramount importance that Christian ministers who are called to serve as military chaplains understand how to survive and thrive in that environment; understand the regulations, policies, and guidelines; and adopt the recommendations presented in the previous chapter.

This means loving and befriending the LGBTQ+ members of the military and respecting women in leadership and in ministry. This means building a camaraderie among Muslims, Buddhists, atheists, and other non-Christians. It means avoiding condemnation in our conversations, teaching, and preaching. If you are new to this approach, it might feel like you're letting evangelism happen as a byproduct instead of an intentionality, and this may be hard to accept.

PAUL'S STORY:

I took classes in outreach and evangelism in Bible college and seminary. I am trained and certified in Dr. James Kennedy's Evangelism Explosion, and implemented it in my civilian church. I memorized the Romans Road to Salvation and other ways to share Christ with nonbelievers. I believe in the Great Commission.

But in the military, I have never told a sinner he or she is going to hell. Never have I condemned anyone. I've never told someone his or her religion was the wrong one or wasn't true. Yet, I have led hundreds of people to faith in Jesus Christ, both in the military and in the civilian sector. Their conversions were genuine, and most are living for the Lord to this day. My approach is to be a friend, love people, build relationships, support them, invest in them, and trust the Lord to speak to their hearts.

Right now, we have an open door of ministry in America's military. To keep that door open, we have to be able to love and accept all people. That doesn't mean we approve of sin. We don't have to change our value system. But there are appropriate ways and times to communicate our message, and there are inappropriate ways and times to express ourselves. We want you to do it right so that you may enjoy a long career in the chaplaincy, caring for a wide range a people, and representing the Lord Jesus Christ.

We have to stop fighting peripheral battles, and focus on what really matters. Stop thinking we need to speak out on every cultural, moral, or political issue we encounter, and stick to the larger mission. Stop using social media to condemn sinners or engage in partisan politics, and use it to encourage people, make connections, and build a rapport with people.

What's at stake here? Simply this: if we will maintain a respect for all people and love them, and at the same time agree to abide by the military policies and guidelines, we can build relationships and share our lives with a lot of people who, otherwise, may never encounter a Christian pastor. If we forfeit that position and relinquish our seat at the table, who will be there when military personnel are spiritually vulnerable or sensitive?

We want there to be a steady, ongoing, incarnational presence of Jesus Christ in all branches of our military. The day might come when we lose this privilege. But may we never lose it because we didn't understand what was at stake, or because we were at fault.

Benediction

A Prayer for Men and Women Serving as Chaplains

Lord of Creation, Lord of Hope, Lord of all Joy: Thank you for welcoming us into your kingdom, and for calling us to a life of serving and caring for others. We know full well that without your grace, your strength, and your presence we are unable to fulfill your call. So we ask, Lord, that you would guide our steps, empower us, and anoint us so we may adequately represent you to the men and women in America's Armed Forces.

Give us the ability to serve humbly, care tenderly, and love deeply. Help us daily to focus on your call to serve instead of being served, and to care for those who are hurting even when we ourselves are hurting.

In serving individuals, families, and our command, may our words and our actions reflect the sacrifices you offered during your life and on the cross. May our efforts bring honor to you, your name, and your cause. And may we be able to discern, by your Spirit, how best to meet needs and communicate the knowledge of our Savior.

In caring for those who are in need of your touch, Lord, help us bring a soothing, healing dynamic that can only come from you. May the hand we extend as chaplains be as the balm of Gilead to hurting people.

In our efforts to love others, we need your help to be selfless servants who are in tune with what you are doing in their lives, loving them in ways they understand, so that when they see the cross on our uniforms, they are drawn to you.

When we are overwhelmed by the enormity of the task you have called us to, reassure us of your presence. When we are discouraged, lift us up. And when our efforts seem futile, remind us that you are always on the throne and that our job is to be faithful, leaving the outcomes to you. We confess that we need the fruit of your Spirit in our daily lives, and we rely on the gifts of your Spirit if we are to be effective in ministry.

Help us to be mindful of the forces of light and the forces of darkness at work in our world. Give us a divine discernment so we will be aware of the traps that might ensnare us, the obstacles that can trip us up, as well as the opportunities and open doors you set before us.

Thank you for your faithfulness, Oh God. Thank you for your mercies, which are new every morning. And thank you for the anointing and the empowerment of your Spirit.

In Christ's Name we pray, amen.

Author Bio for Paul E. Linzey

WHEN DR. PAUL LINZEY became the Protestant Pastor at the United States Naval Academy in Annapolis, Maryland, in a sense, he was returning to "the Blue Side" and coming full circle because he grew up in a Navy family. His father and brother were Navy chaplains, and one of his sons is currently a Navy chaplain. His other two sons are Army officers.

A pastor before going into the Army chaplaincy, Linzey retired in 2015 at the rank of Colonel. After leaving the military, he taught full-time at Southeastern University in Lakeland, FL, and is still an adjunct professor of Practical Ministry and a mentor in their Doctor of Ministry program.

He is an award-winning author who has written articles for religious and military magazines, and was a contributing writer and editor for Life Publisher's *Warriors Bible* in 2014. Then in 2019 he published a book called *WisdomBuilt: Biblical Principles of Marriage*. His second book, released in 2020, is titled *Safest Place in Iraq*, and focuses on his experience as a military chaplain in Iraq during the war. Many of his devotional articles can be seen at CBN.org's online magazine.

Linzey completed the Bachelor of Arts in Religious Studies at Vanguard University in Costa Mesa, CA. Graduate degrees include the Master of Divinity from Fuller Theological Seminary, the Doctor of Ministry at Gordon-Conwell Theological Seminary, and an MFA in Creative Writing at the University of Tampa. He taught Creative Writing at Southeastern University, and has been a featured speaker at several writers conferences and workshops.

Several years ago, Linzey was invited to Budapest, Hungary, where he taught a three-week intensive course at the Hungarian Bible College and spoke in churches throughout the region. As a chaplain representing U.S. Central Command, he led a five-person team that spent a month teaching at the Royal Academy of Islamic Studies in Amman, Jordan, training their military chaplains and cadets. Throughout his adult life, whether serving in a church, the military, or the university, Paul has been involved in small group ministries, pastoral care, lay leadership training, and marriage/family seminars and retreats.

His interests include music, digital photography, movies and theater, sports, and family. He and his wife have three sons who are military officers, ten grandchildren, and a beagle. His theme scripture is 1 Thessalonians 2:8, "We loved you so much that we were willing to share with you not only the gospel of God but our lives as well, because you had become so dear to us." Linzey's website/blog is www.paullinzey.com.

Author Bio for Brandon Keith Travis

A NATIVE OF VIRGINIA, Keith Travis served as an Army Chaplain for twenty-eight years, retiring in 2007 as a Colonel. Keith is a graduate of Carson Newman College in Jefferson City, Tennessee; he received a Master of Divinity from Southeastern Baptist Theological Seminary, Wake Forest, North Carolina. He completed a Doctor of Ministry from Erskine Seminary in Due West, South Carolina, and a Master of Arts in Counseling from Liberty University. He also studied at the U.S. Army War College.

Dr. Travis was the faith group endorser for the Southern Baptist Convention for eleven years, and he and his family were missionaries with the Foreign Mission Board (IMB) in Costa Rica and Mexico for six years. In addition, he has served in several churches as pastor or associate pastor.

He is married to Pam Travis from Greensboro, North Carolina. They have been married for forty-one years. They live in Florida and have three adult children (including a son-in-law), and two grandchildren.

Keith currently serves as Associate Professor with John W. Rawlings Divinity School (Liberty University), as an adjunct with Gateway Seminary (Southern Baptist Convention), where he teaches classes on

Chaplaincy at the MDiv and DMin levels, and also serves as a mentor in the DMin program. He is also the Associate Faith Group Endorser for Liberty Baptist Fellowship. He can be reached at bktravis1@msn.com.

Bibliography

"50 Martin Luther King Jr. Quotes To Inspire Greatness In Your Child." *Waterford.org.* https://www.waterford.org/resources/25-martin-luther-king-jr-quotes-to-inspire-greatness-in-your-child/. Accessed 26 June 2021.

"Accommodating Religious Practices." *Army Command Policy*, AR 600, Paragraph 5-6. Headquarters, Department of the Army. 24 July 2020.

"AP report: Deep-rooted racism and discrimination permeate U.S. military," May 27, 2021. *PBS.org.* https://www.pbs.org/newshour/nation/ap-report-deep-rooted-racism-and-discrimination-permeate-u-s-military. Accessed 28 June 2021.

Assemblies of God Chaplaincy Department. "I Am A Chaplain. This is My Church." https://chaplaincy.ag.org/This-Is-My-Church/Military. Accessed 26 July 2021.

Aulthouse, Michelle E. "Clergy Families: The Helpless Forgottens' Cry for Help Answered Through Reality Therapy." *Counseling.org.* Presented at the 2013 American Counseling Association Conference, March 20-24, Cincinnati, OH. https://www.counseling.org/ knowledge-center/vistas/by-subject2/vistas-families/docs/default-source/vistas/clergy-families-the-helpless-forgottens-cry-for-help. Accessed 13 January 2021.

Barkalow, Carol. *In the Men's House: An Inside Account of Life in the Army by One of West Point's First Female Graduates.* New York: Poseidon, 1990.

Barna Group. "38% of U.S. Pastors Have Thought About Quitting Full-Time Ministry in the Past Year." https://www.barna.com/research/pastors-well-being/. Accessed 6 December 2021.

Benimoff, Roger. *Faith Under Fire: An Army Chaplain's Memoir.* New York: Broadway, 2010.

Bergen, Doris L., ed. *The Sword of the Lord: Military Chaplains from the First to the Twenty-First Century.* Notre Dame:University of Notre Dame Press, 2004.

Billy Graham Training Center at the Cove. https://thecove.org/. Accessed 26 July 2021.

Blackaby, Henry T. and Richard Blackaby. *Experiencing God Day-By-Day.* Nashville: Broadman and Holman, 1998.

Bloom, Jon. "The Centurion: Faith that Made Jesus Marvel." *Desiring God.* https://www.desiringgod.org/articles/the-centurion-faith-that-made-jesus-marvel. Accessed 8 March 2020.

Boa, Kenneth. *Conformed to His Image: Biblical and Practical Approaches to Spiritual Formation.* Grand Rapids: Zondervan, 2001.

Brekke, Torkel. *Military Chaplaincy in an Era of Religious Pluralism: Military Religious Nexus in Asia, Europe, and USA.* Oxford: Oxford University Press, 2017.

Bibliography

Brinsfield, John. *Faith in the Fight*. Mechanicsburg: Stackpole, 2003.

Brittanica. "Critical Race Theory." *Brittanica.com*. https://www.britannica.com/topic/critical-race-theory. Accessed 26 June 2021.

Carver, Douglas L and Keith Travis. "Southern Baptist Endorsed Chaplains/Counselors in Ministry Guidelines in Response to the June 26, 2013 Supreme Court Ruling on the Defense of Marriage Act (DOMA)." *North American Mission Board*, SBC: https://www.namb.net/wp-content/uploads/2020/06/ chaplaincy_guidelines_ DOMA1.pdf.

"Chaplain Corps Advanced Education Programs." *COC Instruction 1521.1*, Jan 2016.

"Chaplains in America's Navy." *Navy.com*. https://www.navy.com/sites/default/files/2018-03/chaplain-brochure_0.pdf. Accessed 25 July 2021.

"The Covenant and Code of Ethics for Chaplains of the Armed Forces." National Conference on Ministry to the Armed Forces, 16 November 2015. http://www.ncmaf.net/library/the-covenant-and-code-of-ethics-for-chaplains-of-the-armed-forces. Accessed 26 July 2021.

"The Declaration of Independence." *Mount Vernon*. https://www.mountvernon.org/education/primary-sources-2/article/the-declaration-of-independence-july-4-1776/.

Dees, Robert F. *Resilient Warriors: The Resilience Trilogy*. El Cajon: Creative Team Publishing, 2011.

"Diversity and Inclusion Definitions." *ferris.edu*. Ferris State University. https://www.ferris.edu/administration/president/DiversityOffice/Definitions.htm. Accessed 26 June 2021.

Drury, Clifford M. *History of the Navy Chaplains Corp, Volume Two, 1939-1949*. Exeter, UK: Revaluation, 2018.

Duttweiler, Raleigh. "What the Heck is an FRG?" *Military.com*. https://www.military.com/spouse/military-life/military-resources/what-the-heck-is-an-frg-family-readiness-group.html. Accessed 25 July 2021.

Elliott, James Isaac and Steven Curtis Chapman. "Burn the Ships." BMG Rights Management. Sparrow Song / Peach Hill Songs / Cabinetmaker Music.

Foster, Richard J. *Celebration of Discipline: The Path to Spiritual Growth*. New York: Harper and Row, 1978.

Fowler, Todd. *You, God, and PTSD*. Indianapolis: Dog-Ear, 2014.

Garamone, Jim. "Selva Discusses How Chaplains Should Interact with Commanders." *U.S. Department of Defense*. https://www.defense.gov/News/News-Stories/Article/Article /1776392/selva-discusses-how-chaplains-should-interact-with-commanders/. Accessed 6 December 2021.

Greitens, Eric. *Resilience: Hard-Won Wisdom for Living a Better Life*. Boston: Mariner, 2016.

Hansen, Kim Philip. *Military Chaplains & Religious Diversity*. London: Palgrave MacMillian, 2012.

Handwerker, W. Penn. "The Construct Validity of Cultures: Cultural Diversity, Culture Theory, and a Method for Ethnography." *American Anthropologist* 104.1 (2002): 106-122.

National Park Service. *Nps.gov*. https://www.nps.gov/orgs/1209/what-is-cultural-anthropology.htm#:~:text=Cultural%20anthropologists%20study%20how%20people,the%20concept%20of%20culture%20itself. Accessed 14 February 2021.

History of the Navy Chaplains Corps, Volume Two 1939-1949, NAVPERS 15808

Kennedy, Nancy. B. *Miracles & Moments of Grace: Inspiring Stories from Military Chaplains*. Abilene: Leafwood, 2011.

Kidd, Thomas S. *God of Liberty*. Audio Book. New York: Basic, 2021.

Konieczny, Mary Ellen and Christophe Bertossi. "Religious Conflict and the Chain of Command in the American and French Militaries." *Journal for the Scientific Study of Religion*. Department of Sociology, University of Notre Dame. (2017) 56(2):248–254.

Kraft, Emilie S. "Chaplains," *The First Amendment Encyclopedia*. https://www.mtsu.edu/first-amendment/article/909/chaplains. Accessed 25 July 2021.

Laing, John D. *In Jesus' Name: Evangelicals and Military Chaplaincy*. East Granby: Resource, 2010.

Laniak, Timothy S. *While Shepherds Watch Their Flocks: Forty Daily Reflections on Biblical Leadership*. Charlotte: ShepherdLeader, 2007.

LifeWay Research. "1 in 4 Pastors & Congregants Suffer from Mental Illness." https://lifewayresearch.com/2014/09/22/1-in-4-pastors-congregants-suffer-from-mental-illness/. Accessed 6 December 2021.

Linzey, Paul. *Safest Place in Iraq: Experiencing God During War*. New York: Morgan James, 2021.

———. "When the Ship Sinks." *CBN.org*. https://www1.cbn.com/ devotions/ when-the-ship-sinks.

Meyers, MG John G. Jr. *The Company Command: The Bottom Line*. Alexandria: Byrrd Enterprises, Inc., 1996.

The Military Chaplaincy (Vol-1): a Report to the President, 1950. University of California Libraries. 29 Apr. 2012.

"Military Compensation. Retired Pay." *U.S. Department of Defense*. https://militarypay.defense.gov/Pay/Retirement/. Accessed 26 July 2021.

Military One Source. "The Unit Chaplain: Roles and Responsibilities." *Military One Source*. https://www.militaryonesource.mil/family-relationships/spouse/getting-married-in-the-military/the-unit-chaplain-roles-and-responsibilities. Accessed 8 September 2020.

Military Spouse Team. "35 Ways You Know Your Kid is a Military Brat." *Military Spouse*. https://www.militaryspouse.com/military-life/35-ways-you-know-your-kid-is-a-brat/. Accessed 25 July 2021.

Moon, Zachary. *Coming Home*. St. Louis: Chalice, 2015.

Murray, Randy. "Army Chaplains Corps: Serving 'God and Country' for 234 years with 25,000 chaplains." *Army.mil*. Fort Stewart Public Affairs. https://www.army.mil/article/ 24086/army_chaplains_corps_serving_god_and_country_for_234_years_with_25000_ chaplains. Accessed 1 December 2021.

Nay, Robert. *The Operational, Social, and Religious Influences upon the Army Chaplain Field Manual*, 1926-1952. U.S. Army Command and General Staff College, 2008.

Nouwen, Henri. *Life of the Beloved: Spiritual Living in a Secular World*. Hertford: Crossroad, 1997.

———. *The Living Reminder*. New York: HarperOne, 1977.

Office of the Attorney General. *Federal Law Protections for Religious Liberty. Memorandum for All Executive Departments and Agencies*, October 6, 2017, Washington DC.

Paget, Naomi K. and Janet R. McCormack. *The Work of the Chaplain*. King of Prussia: Judson, 2006.

Parnell, Jonathan. "Three Tips on Being a Friend of Sinners." *Desiring God*. https://www.desiringgod.org/articles/three-tips-on-being-a-friend-of-sinners. Accessed 14 February 2021.

Perkins, Tony. "A Clear and Present Danger: The Threat to Religious Liberty in the Military." *Family Research Council*. https://downloads.frc.org/EF/EF15F47.pdf. Accessed 6 December 2021.

Pfanner, Toni. "Military Uniforms and the Law of War." *RICR Mars IRRC* March 2004 Vol. 86 No 853. https://www.icrc.org/en/doc/assets/files/other/irrc_853_pfanner.pdf. Accessed 25 July 2020.

"Religious Liberty in the Military Services." *DOD Instruction 1300.17*, September 2020. https://www.esd.whs.mil/Portals/54/Documents/DD/issuances/dodi/130017p.pdf. Accessed 26 July 2021.

Sawchuck, Stephen. "What Is Critical Race Theory and Why Is It Under Attack?" May 18, 2021. *Education Week, edweek.org*. https://www.edweek.org/leadership/what-is-critical-race-theory-and-why-is-it-under-attack/2021/05. Accessed 26 June 2021.

Schaick, Steven A. "Examining The Role of Chaplains as Noncombatants While Involved in Religious Leader Engagement/Liaison." A Research Report Submitted to the Faculty In Partial Fulfillment of the Graduation Requirements. Air War College, Air University. 17 February 2009.

Schwartz, Norton A. "Maintaining Government Neutrality Regarding Religion." *Memorandum for ALMAJCOM-FOA-DRU/CC*, 1 Sep. 2011. Department of the Air Force, Washington DC.

Sessions, Jeff. "Federal Law Protections for Religious Liberty." *Memorandum for All Executive Departments and Agencies*. 6 October 2017.

Stafford, Kat et al. "Deep-Rooted Racism, Discrimination Still Permeate US Military." HuffPost, 27 May 2021. https://www.huffpost.com/entry/racism-in-us-military_n_60affb01e4b0f2a82ee77724. Accessed 6 December 2021.

Stahl, Ronit Y. *Enlisting Faith: How the Military Chaplaincy Shaped Religion and State in Modern America*. Cambridge: Harvard University Press, 2017.

———. "How the US military embraced America's religious diversity," *Military Times*, November 12, 2019. https://www.militarytimes.com/news/your-navy/2019/11/12/how-the-us-military-embraced-americas-religious-diversity/. Accessed 28 June 2021.

Stetzer, Ed. "Marriage and Ministry." *HeadHeartHand*. https://headhearthand.org/blog/2016/02/18/check-out-831/. Accessed 6 December 2021.

U.S. Air Force Chaplain Center. Air University. https://www.airuniversity.af.edu/Eaker-Center/AFCCC/. Accessed 28 December 2021.

U.S. Army Chaplain Center and School. https://usachcs.tradoc.army.mil/courses/chbolc/. Accessed 28 December 2021.

U.S. Navy Chaplain School. https://www.netc.navy.mil/NCS/. Accessed 28 December 2021.

Veterans Employment and Training Service. *Uniformed Services Employment and Reemployment Rights*. Acthttps://www.dol.gov/agencies/vets/programs/userra. Accessed 26 July 2021.

Waggoner, Edward. *Religion in Uniform: A Critique of US Military Chaplaincy*. Lanham: Lexington, 2019.

Weinstein, Michael. Military Religious Freedom Foundation. https://www.military religiousfreedom.org/about/. Accessed 26 July 2021.

Welch, Mark A. III. "Air Force Chaplains Summit 2016." Youtube video. https://www.youtube.com/watch?v=7aCErxoiN8s. 02:06.

"What is Anthropology?" *American Anthropological Association*. https://www.americananthro.org/AdvanceYourCareer/Content.aspx?ItemNumber=2150&gclid=CjwKCAiAsaOBBhA4EiwAoo_AnIk3jvw4DCVJ1X1t5SCG4B3PcFuBQzraDNKEF2yaeiD34wbDLJd8HxoC8JYQAvD_BwE. Accessed 14 February 2021.

"What Is Diversity & Inclusion." *Global Diversity Practice*. ttps://globaldiversitypractice.com/what-is-diversity-inclusion/. Accessed 26 June 2021.

Whitney, Donald S. *Spiritual Disciplines for the Christian Life*. Colorado Springs: NavPress, 2014.

Whittington, Michael C. and Charlie N. Davidson, *Matters of Conscience*. Lynchburg: Liberty University Press, 2013.

Zeiger, Hans. "Why Does the US Military Have Chaplains?" *Pepperdine School of Public Policy*. https://publicpolicy.pepperdine.edu/academics/research/policy-review/2009v2/why-does-us-military-have-chaplains.htm. Accessed 13 January 2021.

Department of Defense Publications

DEPARTMENT OF DEFENSE / JOINT

Appointment of Chaplains for the Military Departments (DoD Instruction 1304.19)
Guidance for the Appointment of Chaplains for the Military Departments (DoD Inst. 1304.28)
Armed Forces Chaplains Board (DoD Instruction 5120.08)
Religious Affairs in Joint Operations (Joint Publication 1-05, Nov 2013) (jg 1-05)
Mortuary Affairs (JP 4-06 1996)
Joint Planning (JP 5-0, 2047)
Religious Accommodation
Accommodation of Religious Practices Within the Military Services (DOD Inst. 1300.17, Jan 2014)
Army Command Policy (AR 600-20 Chapter 5, Nov 2014)
Navy Accommodation of Religious Practices (SECNAVINST 1730.88, Mar 2012)
Air Force Culture (AFI 1-1 Chapter 2, Aug 2012)

CIVILIAN

U.S. Equal Employment Opportunity Commission (USEEOC Compliance Manual Section 12)
"What You Should Know About Workplace Religious Accommodation"(US EEOC, 2011)
"Best Practices for Eradicating Religious Discrimination in the Workplace" (US EEOC, 2008)
"Office of Personnel Management 'Fact Sheet: Adjustment of Work Schedules for Religious Observances'" (OPM, 2019)

ARMY

Army Chaplain Corps Activities (AR 165-1 June 2015)
Religious Support (FM 1-05, Oct 2012)
Religious Support and the Operations Process (ATP 1-05.01, May 2014)
Religious Support to Funerals and Memorial Ceremonies and Services (ATP 1-05.02 March 2013)
Religious Support and External Advisement (ATP 1-05.03, May 2013)

NAVY

Religious Ministry Within the Department of the Navy (SECNAVINST 1730.7D, Aug 2008)
Professional Naval Chaplaincy (SECNAV 5351.1 CH-1 2 July 2015)
Chaplain Advisement and Liaison (SECNAV Instruction 1730.10, Jan 2009)
Confidential Communications to Chaplains (SECNAV Instruction 1730.9, Feb 2008)
Privileged and Confidential Communications to Chaplains (SECNAVINST 1730.9A, Aug 2008)
Appointment of Officers in the Chaplain Corps of the Navy (OPNAVINST 1120.9, Dec 2005)
Religious Ministry in the Navy (OPNAV Instruction 1730.1E, Apr 2012)
Chaplain Appointment and Retention Eligibility Advisory Group (COCINSTR 1110.1H, May 2007)
Chaplain Corps Command Qualification Program (COC Instruction 1412.1, Dec 2012)
Chaplain Corps Advanced Education Programs (COC Instruction 1521.1, Jan 2016)
John H. Craven Servant Leadership Award (Chief of Chaplains Instruction 1650.1, Jul 2012)
Management of Alcohol in Command Religious Programs (COC Instruction 1730.3, Nov 2014)
Navy Chaplain Brochure (https://www.navy.com/sites/default/files/2018-03/chaplain-brochure_0.pdf. Accessed 4 December 2019)
Religious Lay Leader (NTTP 1.05.1 M, 2016)

AIR FORCE

Chaplain Corps (Air Force Policy Directive 52-1, Nov 2018)
Chaplain Corps Awards (Air Force Instruction 36-2811, Nov 2014)
Chaplain Planning and Organizing (Air Force Instruction 52-101, Jul 2019)
Chaplain Corps Readiness (Air Force Instruction 52-104, Jun 2019)
Chaplain Corps Resourcing (Air Force Instruction 52-105, Jun 2015)
Religious Professional Scholarship and Deferment Programs (AFI 52-106, Jul 2019)

MARINES

Religious Ministry Support in the US Marine Corps (MCWP 6-12, Dec 2001)
Religious Ministry in the US Marine Corps (MCRP 3-30D.3, April 2018)
Religious Ministry in the US Marine Corps (MCO 1730.6E, Jun 2012)
Coast Guard
Religious Ministries within the Coast Guard (COMDTINST 1730.4C Mar 2012)

United States Law

First Amendment to the Constitution of the United States: the Bill of Rights, 1791
Title 10, United States Code, Armed Forces, 1956 (as amended through January 7, 2011)
Title 14, United States Code, Coast Guard, enacted by Aug. 4, 1949
Title 17, United States Code, Section 105 (Supp. III 1979)
Title 32, United States Code, National Guard, enacted Aug. 10, 1956

Index

5 Love Languages, The, 220

Abington School District v. Schemp, 10, 114, 137, 151
above and beyond, 49, 114, 137, 151
abuse, 104, 122, 199, 201, 203, 208
Accession Board, Accessioning Board, accessioned, 21, 46, 47, 48, 51, 54, 150, 231
accommodate, accommodation, 113, 115, 116, 128, 129, 201, 202, 208, 213, 216, 217, 230, 239, 245
accountable, accountability, 53, 67, 69, 70, 103, 109, 137, 158, 180, 228, 250
Active Duty, 29, 36, 39, 41, 42, 50, 51, 55, 57, 109, 130, 140, 141–46, 148, 215
Active Parenting, 137
adapt, adapting and overcoming, 36–38, 53–54, 211
administration, administrator, 56, 101, 149, 171, 230
advanced training, 112, 131, 133, 134, 135, 136, 138, 240, 246
advising, advisor, xvii, 6, 54, 56, 91, 97, 109, 112, 197, 202, 246, 268
advocate, advocate for chaplains, 65, 119, 159
age, 29, 31, 43, 44, 47, 104
Air Force, Air Force Chaplains, xviii, 5, 14, 15, 16, 29, 45, 52, 55–56, 60, 61, 81, 83, 91, 100, 101, 114, 126, 136, 140, 146, 152, 164, 186, 187, 196, 199, 213

airborne, 133, 173, 176
Airman, 101, 103
alcohol, alcoholic, alcoholism, 19, 70, 77, 78, 123, 158, 178, 196, 246
Amalekites, 17
America, American, 4, 5, 6, 9, 18, 40, 76, 83, 88, 122, 123, 144, 195, 196, 199, 200, 201, 203, 204, 205, 206, 207, 208, 216, 219, 221, 225, 226, 231, 232, 233, 240, 241, 242
American Anthropologist, American Anthropology Association, 240, 243
American Counseling Association, 179, 239
American Indian, Native American, 5, 215
anger, 33, 38, 43, 119, 179
anthropology, 195
anxiety, anxious, 30, 37, 119, 178, 179
appear, appearance, 111, 231
Armed Forces Chaplain Board, 6, 245
Army Chaplains, xv, xviii, 3, 5, 6, 13, 14, 15, 16, 29, 33, 34, 36, 37, 39, 41, 42, 44, 45, 51, 52, 53–55, 65, 69, 76, 81, 82, 83, 86, 90–91, 93, 94, 100, 101, 103, 108, 114, 123, 128, 130–32, 133, 134, 135, 138, 139, 140, 143, 144, 146, 147, 148, 150, 151, 152, 157, 160, 161, 176, 186, 190, 196, 209, 216, 235, 237, 239, 241, 242, 245, 246
Assemblies of God, Assemblies of God chaplains, xv, 69, 71, 109, 127, 202, 239

Index

attitude, 55, 170, 177, 222, 226
Attorney General, 241
Aulthouse, Michelle, 179–80, 239
authority, 11, 14, 44, 53, 109, 188, 196, 197, 224, 219, 225

background check, 44, 46,
background of military ministry, 3–23
balance, 205, 226, 72, 74, 126, 141, 142, 165, 180, 181
baptism, baptize, 112, 190
Baptist
    Liberty Baptist, 48, 76, 211, 238
    Southern Baptist, xix, 27, 39, 48, 68, 69, 70, 76, 109, 125, 126, 127, 139, 164, 199, 237, 240
Barkalow, Carol, 203, 239
Barna Group, 79, 239
Basic Training, xv, 52–59, 68, 126, 134, 161
battle, 14, 17, 18, 38, 190, 205
    battle assembly, 141–42, 143
    battlefield, 3
    Battle of Midway, xx
    court battle, 10
Be, Know, Do, 94
beans and bullets, 89, 230
bearing fruit, ix, xviii, xxi, 39, 121, 129, 165, 167–76, 181, 198, 223
becoming a military chaplain, 25–61
being a military chaplain, 63–165
benediction, 233–34
benefits, xxi, xxii, 90, 145–46, 173, 184
Benimoff, Roger, 239,
Bergen, Doris, 3–4, 239
Bible, iv, xviii, 21, 40, 78, 87, 93, 123, 161, 178, 182, 183, 189, 206, 209, 210, 220, 221, 224
    Bible college, 78, 162, 232, 236
    Bible reading, 74, 78, 180
    Bible study, 66, 78, 87, 103, 104, 111, 124, 127, 151, 171, 172, 178, 187, 202, 205, 206, 224, 229
    Warrior's Bible, 235
biblical
    biblical foundation, xviii, 17–23, 178, 197, 223, 235, 239, 241

biblical theology, 122, 185, 222, 223, 224
biblical values, 94, 137, 158, 208
big three, the, 95
Bill of Rights, 8–12, 15, 225, 248
Billy Graham Training Center, 136, 239
Blackaby, Henry and Richard, 182, 239
Bloom, Jon, 19–20, 239
Boa, Kenneth, 182–83, 239
boom, 98–99
bounce back, bouncing back, 184–85
Boy Scouts, 6, 82
branch
    branches of service, 30, 48, 52, 109, 146, 149, 153, 157, 215
    chaplain branch, 139
    judicial branch, 213
Brekke, Torkel, 239
Brennan, William, 10
Brinsfield, John, 240
Britannica, 240
British chaplains, 4, 13
Buddhist, 4
"Burn the Ships," 31, 240
burnout, 66, 76, 77, 79
bury the dead, 14, 108, 111, 113,

call
    altar call, 191
    Call of God, divine calling, xiv, xix, xx, 19, 22, 27–34, 37, 50–51, 76, 79, 94, 114, 143, 146, 197, 212, 233
cancer, 190
cape, capella, capellani, chapelain, 4
care
    emotional care, 67
    for all, 16, 22, 47, 90, 105, 111, 115–16, 125, 126, 206, 214, 219, 233
    for the family, 36, 71, 125, 152, 180
    for the oppressed, 18
    for the wounded, 54, 97
    medical care, 47, 137
    pastoral care, 22, 57, 125, 132, 236
    self care, 72–80, 114, 137, 180, 191

Index

spiritual care, 56, 112, 136
career, xiv, xix, 28, 44, 53, 58
  military career, 65, 66, 68, 79, 82, 84, 85, 86, 89, 100, 102, 108, 109, 110, 118, 120, 124, 133–46, 147–53, 156, 157, 158–59, 160, 165, 179, 180, 181, 204, 227, 232
  ministry career, 58, 73–75
  spouse's career, 38, 118, 181
Casteel, Ron, xv, 132
Casualty Assistance, 30, 113, 144, 176
Catholic, 4, 6, 44, 67, 123, 131, 132, 163, 164, 200, 211
Celebration of Discipline, 182–83, 240
certificate, certification, 112, 133, 134, 137, 147, 152, 229
chain of command
  command chain, 11, 67, 68, 109, 241
  ecclesiastical chain, 67, 109
  technical chain, 67, 109
challenges, 39, 50, 65, 110, 114, 118, 119, 141, 200, 211
change,
  benefits, 145, 146
  climate, 196
  cultural, 65, 195
  lives, 189, 191
  message, 197
  methods, 69
  Permanent Change of Station (PCS), 118, 138, 147, 207
  personal, 28, 32, 51, 61, 138, 221, 226, 232
  Religion in the Military, 231
  VA benefits, 145
  way we pray, 202
chapel, 4, 93, 104, 111, 131, 164, 170, 172, 176, 187, 215
chaplain
  Chaplain Assistant, 47, 50, 93, 100–7, 111, 155, 173, 187, 191, 228
  Chaplain Advanced Education, 133, 134, 135, 136, 138, 240, 246
  chaplain as first responder, 15
  Chaplain Candidate, 33, 34, 50, 54, 55, 67, 122, 147, 212

Chaplain Moses, 154–56
Chaplain qualifications, xviii, 15, 19, 43–49, 52, 94, 103, 137, 141, 177
Chaplain Team, 54, 57, 61, 75, 100–7, 109, 113, 228, 236
chaplain types, 83
Chapman, Steven Curtis, 31, 240
CHBOLC, 53–55, 242
check the blocks, 151
Chief of Chaplains, 5, 15, 29, 43, 66, 67, 91, 109, 123, 126, 136, 150, 159, 160, 206, 216, 246
Christians
  in the military, xiii, xviii, 4, 19, 20, 21, 49, 65, 75, 78, 81, 87, 102, 122, 123, 124, 157, 159, 170, 172, 177, 178, 180, 189, 197, 202, 203, 204, 205, 206, 207–8, 214, 215, 219, 221, 223, 224, 225, 226, 231, 232
  Christian nation, 4, 11, 18, 122–23, 201, 217, 226
  conservative Christians, 10, 49, 199
Churchill, Winston, 209
CIMT, 54
citizen
  citizen soldier, 13, 141, 144
  citizenship requirement, 44, 45
  religious freedoms, 13, 217
  civic functionaries, 87
civil
  Civil Air Patrol, 14, 141
  civil rights, 214, 221
  civil servants, 221
  civil unions, 221
  Civil War, 5
civilian
  civilian casualties, 99
  civilian clothes, 60
  civilian education, 54, 133, 136
  civilian government, 226
  civilian ministry, pastor, 28, 41, 46, 53, 68, 139, 141, 142, 143, 171, 187, 197, 207, 232
  civilian volunteers, 5
  civilianization of chaplaincy, 3, 207
  civilians in the military, 3, 245

(civilian continued)
  civilization, 3
Clear and Present Danger, A, 9, 242
clergy
  accountability, 158
  chaplains in nonmilitary settings, xxi, 4
  different denominations, xx, 4, 5, 14, 48
  different nations, 4
  different religions, 3, 5, 14, 48, 75, 126
  ecumenism, 123
  education requirements, 44, 45, 108
  endorsers, 67, 108
  families, 74, 180, 239
  female (see women)
  immigrant, 45
  maturity, 45, 46, 48, 123, 125, 195, 219
  new to military, 58
  pitfalls, 178, 180, 206, 224
  pluralism, 122–29, 219
  self-care, 72–80
Clinical Pastoral Education (CPE), 58, 113, 135
cloak, 4
clock, 59, 161
Coast Guard, 15, 16, 57, 83, 100, 114, 140, 141, 152, 196, 247, 248
code
  dress code, 53
  of Ethics (NCMAF), 125, 240
  Uniform Code of Military Justice (UCMJ), 207
  United States Code
    Title 10, Armed Forces, 14, 108, 248
    Title 14, Coast Guard, 15, 248
    Title 17, Works produced by government personnel, 248
    Title 32, National Guard, 15, 248
coercion, 213, 226
command function, 6, 14, 16, 21, 67, 68, 87, 89, 90–91, 97, 100, 101, 103, 104, 105, 108–114, 119–120, 121, 154, 172, 179, 186, 187, 190, 196, 202, 206, 208, 214, 217, 221, 222, 224–25, 227, 228, 229, 230, 230, 233, 239, 241, 241, 245, 246
commander, 30, 66, 92, 95, 154, 163, 170, 179, 201–2
  chain of command, 109
  commander's authority, 11, 103, 225
  commander's staff officer, 11, 67, 86, 87, 90–91, 95, 100–1, 109, 110, 111, 112, 113, 143, 189, 197, 228
  commander's religious program, 11, 109, 201–2
  working relationship with command staff, 16, 94, 110, 111, 116, 189
commission, xiv
  Commissioned Officer Training, 54–55, 59
  General Commission on Army and Navy Chaplains, 89
  Great Commission, xiv, 19–22, 197, 225, 232
  losing a commission, 66
Company Command: The Bottom Line, The, 90–99, 241
communication, 56, 158, 189, 232, 233
  confidentiality, 207, 246
  with Accessioning Board, 29
  with commander, 66, 86, 90–91, 92, 95, 100–1, 109, 111, 112, 113, 116, 143, 154, 163, 170, 189, 197, 202, 228, 229
  with endorser, 65–71
  with key leaders, 206
  with military personnel, 69, 87, 90, 96, 119, 197
compassion, 4, 18
compromise, xiii, 123, 127, 197, 204, 221, 230
condemn, condemnation, 124, 197, 205, 223–24
confidence, 45, 58
  confidence course, 161
  self-confidence, 34
confirm, confirmation, 171
  of God's call, 32, 42

Index 253

Conformed to His Image, 182–83, 239
conflict
  church conflict, 46
  conflict and criticism, 46
  Constitutional conflict, 10
  interpersonal conflict, 33–34, 205
  "Law of Armed Conflict," 14
  military conflict, 6, 66, 241
  organizational conflict, 204
  religious conflict, 241
Congress, 5, 8, 9, 13–15, 52, 128, 212
  Continental Congress, 207
  State Representative, 200
conscience
  chaplain's conscience, 15, 127, 204
  Conscientious Objector, 113, 208–9
  Matters of Conscience, 8, 240
  personal conscience, 34
consequences, 8, 76, 231
Constitution, xviii, 8–12, 13, 15, 81, 86, 87, 100, 122, 123, 127, 128, 187, 196, 199, 201, 225, 248
  Constitutional authority and chain of command, 11
  Establishment Clause, 8, 12, 122, 128, 201, 225
  First Amendment, 13, 123, 127, 128, 248
  Free Exercise Clause, 8, 9, 10, 11, 122, 128, 201, 206, 214, 225
Construct Validity of Cultures, 195, 240
Continental
  Army, 13, 207
  Congress, 13, 207
controversy, xviii, 87, 199–210
  Christian dominance of chaplaincy, 200, 207, 213
  Christians in the military, 208
  civilianization of chaplaincy, 207
  freedom of speech for chaplains, 205
  humanitarian use of chaplains, 200, 206
  differences between religious events and command events, 202
  diversity, 200, 203, 217
  divided loyalties of the chaplain, 204
  free speech of chaplains, 200
  gender inequality, 203
  legitimizing state violence, 208
  LGBTQ+ in the military, 200, 203,
  noncombatant status of chaplains, 14, 101, 205, 242
  nonreligious chaplains, 213
  praying "in Jesus's name," xx, 125, 128, 198, 202, 206, 224–25, 241
  proselytism, 199, 201 (see evangelism, proselytism, lead people to faith in Christ)
  religious accommodation (see accommodate, accommodation)
  separation of church and state, 205
  strategic use of military chaplains, 200, 206
  unfair denominational representation, 200
  women in ministry (see women)
Cortés, Hernan, 31
counseling,
  counseling military family members, 144, 179, 186
  counseling for chaplains, xiv
  counseling military personnel, 13, 126, 127, 170, 172, 179, 186
count the cost, 39, 51, 79, 81, 137
court battle, court cases, 9, 10, 240
  Abington School District v. Schemp, 10, 114, 137, 151
  Protestant chaplains vs. the Navy, 10
  Katcoff v. Marsh, 11
  Lemon vs. Kurtzman, 9
  Marsh vs. Chambers, 10
  Prince vs. Massachusetts, 9
CPE, 58, 113, 135
credibility, 100
Critical Incident Stress Management, 112, 134, 137
Critical Race Theory, 219, 240, 242
criticism, critics, 21, 46, 187, 199–210, 216, 227
cross
  cross-generational ministry, 137

(cross continued)
   Jesus on the cross, 219, 233
   Red Cross, 82
   wear the cross, 22, 81, 86, 87, 157, 234
crusades, 3
culture, xviii, xxi, 3, 6, 95, 195–98, 215, 218
   Construct Validity of Cultures, 195, 240
   contemporary culture, xiii, 122, 135, 187, 196, 197, 219, 230, 231
   cultural anthropology, 195, 240
   cultural change, 65, 68, 69, 122, 195, 211–12
   cultural context of ministry, 53, 93, 95, 96, 122, 127, 131, 135, 198
   cultural diversity, 91, 96, 127, 131, 135, 206, 215, 217, 220
   cultural revolution, 122, 187, 196
   culture of each branch of service, 52, 55, 95, 96, 196, 197, 245
   culture shock, 123
   "Culture War in the Chaplain Corps," 226, 231
   godless culture, 198, 231

danger, 9, 38, 117
Clear and Present Danger, A, 9, 242
Dees, Bob, 184, 240
Declaration of Independence, 218, 240
delegated authority, 11, 109
demographics, 20, 203, 213, 215
denomination, xx, xxii, 4, 6, 48, 65–71, 93–94, 108, 109, 122, 125, 126, 127, 150, 158, 197, 200, 204, 208, 217, 221, 228
   anti-denominationalism, 196
   communication with denomination, 68
   denominational endorsement, endorser, xviii, 34, 48, 65–71, 72, 93, 111, 125, 144, 208, 221, 228
   mainline denominations, 44, 94
Department of Defense, DOD, xvii, xviii, xx, 15, 38, 47, 65, 67, 92, 125, 127, 128, 135, 203, 212, 240, 241, 245–46
deploy, deployment, 37, 76, 120, 135, 141, 142, 170, 182
deployment cycle, 141
   qualified, 56
   separation issues, 35, 36, 37, 38, 112, 118
Desiring God, 19, 197, 198, 239, 242
dime-a-dozen, 49
disappointment, 79,
discern, discernment, 7, 48, 53, 146, 182, 187, 233
disciples, discipleship, xvii, 18, 20, 21, 39, 94, 142, 157, 162, 173, 183, 189, 204, 209, 224
discouraged, discouragement, 188, 234
discriminate, discrimination, 10, 15, 199, 200, 214, 215, 239, 242, 245
diversity, 82, 127, 213–222, 240, 242, 243
   anti-diversity, 203–4, 213, 219
   cultural, 127, 196, 217
   ethnic, 127, 196, 215, 217
   gender, 127, 196, 203, 213, 217
   moral, 200
   religious, xx, 4, 54, 123, 127, 200, 213, 217, 225,
divided loyalties, 102, 204
divorce, 74, 189, 196
DOD, 15, 29, 38, 46, 47, 48, 67, 70, 109, 125, 128, 128, 197, 242, 245
doomsday surveys, 78
drill
   Drill and Ceremony, 55
   weekend drill, Reserve and National Guard, 141, 142, 143, 145, 146
Duttweiler, Raleigh, 119, 240

ecclesiastical endorsement, 65–71
   communication, 68–69, 70, 227, 228
   endorsement, xvii, 5, 34, 70, 76, 152
   financial support from chaplains, 70–71, 126, 228

Index

endorser, endorsing agent, xv, xvi, xvii, xviii, xix, xx, xxii, 20, 27, 30, 36, 37, 46, 47, 48, 67, 72, 77, 86, 92, 108, 109, 111, 125, 126, 127, 139, 144, 150, 159, 196, 197, 202, 204, 227, 228, 237, 238, 240
  perspective, 6, 20, 44, 48, 58, 67, 70, 76, 77, 87, 93, 95, 197, 122, 126, 136, 159, 203, 208, 211, 214, 221
  represent your endorser and faith group, xxi, 4, 6, 14, 48, 67, 69, 70, 76, 81, 86, 87, 93, 102, 108, 109, 204, 205, 221, 228, 229
education, xiv, xix, 104, 113, 146, 216
  Clinical Pastoral Education (CPE), 58, 113, 135
  loan repayment programs, 15
  military, 53–58, 134, 135–36, 186, 240, 246
  online vs. in-person, 45, 196
  requirements, 43, 44–45, 46, 52
  Religious Education program, 187
  VA benefits, 145
emotional readiness, well-being, xiii, xviii, 3, 33, 35–40, 51, 52, 60, 74, 78, 79, 117, 120, 136, 162, 177, 179, 181, 182
Enlisting Faith, 216, 242
entanglement, church and state, 8, 9
Establishment Clause, 8–12, 67, 123, 128, 199, 201, 205, 214, 225
ethnicity, 150, 158, 215, 219, 220, 221, 229, 239, 240, 242
evaluations (OER, OPR, FITREP), 57, 89, 113, 147, 150, 151, 153, 229
Evangelicals, 201, 216, 241
  anti-diversity, 203
  complaints against, 200
  lawsuit versus the Navy, 10
  war against, 199
evangelism, proselytism, lead people to faith in Christ, 93, 96, 124, 129, 134, 162, 169, 172, 173, 189, 197, 199, 200, 201, 204, 223, 232
Examining the Role of Chaplains as Noncombatants While Involved in Religious Leader Engagement/ Liaison, 242

example, 20, 40, 72, 90, 105, 185, 212, 223, 224, 225, 228
expectations, 35, 48, 53, 93, 94, 103, 109, 151, 161, 204
Experiencing God Day-by-Day, 182, 239

facilitate religious services, 3, 97, 127
failure, 72, 76, 82, 102
faith, 16, 19, 20, 21, 34, 48, 87, 91, 96, 122
  Chaplain Assistants, 103, 104
  express one's faith, 11
  faith background, 5, 199, 207, 208, 214, 216, 221, 225, 230
  faith group, xx, xxi, 4, 11, 14, 15, 20, 27, 44, 46, 47, 48, 57, 67, 69, 70, 71, 87, 94, 102, 108, 109, 111, 112, 125, 126, 127, 144, 150, 197, 203, 204, 207, 208, 211, 213, 214, 216, 217, 221, 230, 237, 238
  faith group endorsers, xx, 6
  faith in Christ, xvii, 49, 124, 129, 134, 162, 172, 173, 189, 197, 223, 232
  Faith in the Fight, 240
  Faith Under Fire, 239
  lose one's faith, 76
  minority faith group, 14
  multi-faith ministry, 54–55, 67, 123, 127, 132, 214, 221, 225, 226, 227
  no faith, 87, 96, 103, 217, 226
  practice one's faith, 10, 11, 20, 67, 90, 93, 123, 125, 126, 127, 128, 165, 170, 201, 203, 204,
  share one's faith, 16, 21, 22, 93, 94, 127, 169, 204
family, 30, 31, 33, 35–40, 50–51, 60, 66, 73, 74, 75, 76, 77, 80, 82, 88, 94, 96, 102, 104, 130, 132, 136, 142, 144, 145, 146, 148, 152, 160, 164, 165, 172, 196, 203, 231, 235, 236, 237
Family Life Chaplain, family counseling, 113, 135
family readiness, 50–51, 180, 181
(civilian continued)

(family continued)
    Family Readiness Group, Family Support Group, 100, 117–121, 124, 144, 160, 172, 225, 240, 241, 242
    Family Research Council, 9
    manage one's own family, 19, 35–40, 74, 114, 152, 163, 179, 181, 227–28
fasting, 75, 182, 183, 184, 185
faux pas, 86
Federal Law Protections for Religious Liberty, 241, 242
female
    cadets at West Point, 203, 239
    Chaplain Assistant, 102
    clergy, chaplains, 214, 216
    friends, 215
few good men, a, 22
finances, money, budgets, 28, 51, 118
    attitude towards, 177, 227
    endorser, 70
    religious program budget, 16, 135
    pay, 147, 148
    retirement, 118, 140, 141, 143, 145, 146, 148, 153, 241
    SPAM (sex, porn, alcohol, money), 70, 77, 158, 178
    training, 113
First Amendment, xiii, 8, 10, 11, 13, 65, 68, 123, 127, 128, 199, 225, 226, 241, 248
First Amendment Encyclopedia, 10
first responders, xxi, 15, 83
FITREP (see evaluations)
Flag Officers, 92
for god and country, 86
fort
    Fort Bragg, NC, xxi, 30, 92, 95, 133, 148, 164, 190
    Fort Buchanan, PR, 163
    Fort Hamilton, NY, 130
    Fort Hunter-Liggett, CA, 154
    Fort Jackson, SC, 50, 52, 53
    Fort Knox, KY, 44
    Fort Leavenworth, KS, 157
    Fort Monmouth, NJ, 138, 164
    Fort Stewart, GA, 13, 175
    Fort Totten, NY, 130
    Hunter Army Air Field, 138
Foster, Richard, 182, 183, 240
founding documents, founding fathers, 13, 123, 221, 225, 226
four aspects of humanness, 74–75
Four Immortal Chaplains, 6, 91, 211
Fowler, Todd, 240
Free Exercise Clause, 8, 122, 128, 201, 225
fruitful ministry or service, xviii, xxi, 39, 121, 129, 165, 167, 181, 198, 223
fun, 37, 77, 105, 159, 160–65, 172, 180, 181
funds, funding, funds manager, 14, 70, 135, 139
funeral ceremony and funeral service, 46, 48, 109, 144, 151, 172, 175, 186, 202, 225, 230, 246
    for a clock, 161–62
    Shi'ite, 130–32

Garnett, Daniel, 175–76
gays, 21, 196, 220
    homophobia, 65
    LGBTQ+, 21, 65, 102, 196, 199, 200, 203, 213, 214, 215, 219, 220, 221, 231
gender, gender identity, discrimination 87, 150, 158, 196, 199, 200, 203, 213, 214, 216, 217, 220, 221, 226, 229, 231
General Officers, 13, 15, 16, 85, 90, 91, 92, 106, 107, 164, 184, 207
Geneva Convention, 14–15
German U-boats, 5
GI Bill, 145
God of Liberty, 128, 241
godliness (see holiness)
good
    good chaplain, 21, 22, 76, 90, 92, 100, 101, 104, 109, 113, 119, 122, 140, 225
    good commander, 91
    good news, 18, 20, 197
gospel, 20, 21, 44, 61, 69, 93, 110, 129, 169, 175, 179, 183, 212, 228, 236

Gotcha Cards, 124
government, iv, xvii, 3, 5, 8, 9, 10, 11, 12, 15, 16
Maintaining Government Neutrality, 15, 16, 242
graduate school, xvii, 58, 113, 135, 184, 200, 236
graduation, 28, 126, 172, 242
Great Call, xiv, xix, xx, 19, 22, 27, 28, 29, 30, 31, 32, 33–34, 37, 50–51, 76, 79, 94, 114, 143, 146, 197, 212, 233
Great Commandment, 19, 21, 197
Great Commission, xiv, 19, 20, 21, 22, 197, 225, 232
Green Card, 45
Greitens, Eric, 184, 240
growth, personal and professional, 54, 81, 133–37, 179, 183, 240

Handwerker, W. Penn, 195, 240
Hansen, Kim Phillips, 199, 200, 201, 226, 240
hazards, 117
health, 47, 73, 74, 79, 80, 117, 128, 136, 185
　exam, 44, 47
　clinic, 134, 172
　coverage, 47, 49, 131, 143, 145, 146
　government overriding interest, 9
　records, 152
Heavenly Father, 21, 72, 102, 159, 169, 173, 202, 219, 223, 224, 229
helicopter, 99, 111, 121, 160
Helpless Forgottens, 108, 239
Hierarchy, 109,
historical perspective, xviii, 3–7, 10, 57, 82, 90, 200, 208, 218, 240
holiness, 18, 183, 187
Holy Helo, 160
Holy Spirit, 20, 21, 29, 53, 73, 124, 129, 171, 174, 183, 184, 185, 187, 223, 224, 225
home, 57, 160, 161
　away from home, 36, 37, 38, 77, 99, 112, 118, 141, 163, 207
　home internet, 130
　home loans (VA), 145

hospitality in home, 179, 215, 220
letters and call to home, 13, 78
phone calls at home, 130
records kept at home, 148
relationships at home, 51, 118, 138, 179, 227
returning home, 27, 30, 31, 33, 36, 50, 84, 86, 88, 99, 130, 164, 176, 190, 241
spirituality in the home, 228
visitation in homes, 20, 21, 90
homophobia, 65
honor, xiv, 83, 90, 127, 169
　confidentiality, 91, 207
　the dead /fallen, 13, 14, 54, 97
　the Lord, 22, 233
　the religious freedom of non-Christians, 225
　the religious practices and preferences of all people, 201
　the Sabbath, 72, 73, 75, 76, 115
hospital, 5, 30, 31, 56, 67, 83, 90, 103, 113, 119, 135, 170, 175,
hostility toward religion, 10
How the US Military Embraced America's Religious Diversity, 242
human, humanity, 4, 195, 220
　body, 209
　connection, 4, 119
　error, 149
　God became human, 173
　Image of God, Imago Dei, 220
　initiative, 183
　nature, 85, 157
humane, humanitarian, 22, 100, 110, 206,
Hummer, HUMVEE, 155, 162, 165, 187
Humphrey, Keah, 50–51
Hunter Army Air Field, 138

identity
　Christian chaplains, 23
　gender, 150, 158, 196, 199, 200, 203, 214, 217, 220, 221, 229
　Jesus's name, 224
　Old Testament people of God, 18
　spouse, 118

(identity continued)
    uniforms, 82
IED, 98–99, 190
imam, 3, 4, 44, 130–32
immigrating chaplains, 45
Immortal Chaplains of the Dorchester, 5, 6, 91, 211
In Jesus' Name: Evangelicals and Military Chaplaincy, 241
In the Men's House, 203, 239
incarnation, incarnational ministry, incarnational presence, xxii, 93, 95, 111, 114, 169–174, 177, 186, 187, 191, 197, 202, 222, 223, 231, 232
indicators of risk of burnout, 79
infant baptism, 112
influence, influential, 13, 53, 66, 87, 92, 100, 101, 109, 110, 127, 197, 231
infringement of free exercise of religion, 10, 11
insignia, 82, 84, 86, 149, 153
integrity, xv, 6, 48, 56, 157, 177, 201
interference of the government, 11
intimidated, intimidation, 58, 100
Iorg, Jeff, xiii-xiv
Islam, Islamic, 3, 4, 44, 130–32, 236
Israel, Israelite army, 17, 18

jail, prison, 157, 158, 159, 170, 230
Jericho, 17
Jesus, xx, 17–22, 40, 94, 99, 114, 158, 159, 165, 183, 189, 205, 212, 223
    amazed by Centurion's faith, 19
    example of self-care, 72
    first New Testament ministry to military, 20, 239
    friend of sinners, love for sinners, 21, 197–98, 219, 222, 229
    incarnation, 169–174, 232
    message of Jesus, 21, 102, 178, 197
    name of Jesus, xx, 125, 128, 198, 206, 224–25, 241
    people need Jesus, 140, 232
    staff meetings, 206
    we represent Jesus, 81, 86, 87, 93, 114, 142, 175, 228, 232

Jewish, rabbi, 3, 6, 75, 128, 131, 132, 161, 211
Jump School, jump zone, 186, , 133, 172
Katcoff v. Marsh, 11
Kennedy, Nancy B., 241
Kidd, Thomas, 128, 241
Kingdom of God/Heaven, xviii, xxi, 16, 19, 20, 69, 70, 73, 79, 88, 102, 105, 129, 135, 141, 171, 177, 180, 191, 203, 206, 233
Konieczny, Mary Ellen, 241
kosher, 115–16
Kraft, Emilie S., 10, 241

labor of love, xix-xx
Lainge, John D., 241
language
    *5 Love Lan*guages, 220
    foul, corrupt language, 178, 189
    language of the people we serve, 52, 93, 95–96
    religious language, 206
Laniak, Timothy S., 241
Latin America, 190
Latter Day Saints, 123, 217
laws, legislation, 5, 13–16, 86, 157
    civilian jobs for Reservists, 142
    establishment of religion, 8, 9,128, 225
    Geneva Convention, "Law of Armed Conflict," noncombatants, 14, 15, 205
    Jewish chaplains permitted, 14
    Mosaic Law, 21
    religious liberty, 241, 242
    Military Uniforms and the Law of War, 82–83, 242
    United States Laws, 248
lead me to the rock, 22–23
leave, leave fraud, 147, 149, 152
legal grounds, legal foundation, 13–16
Lemon Law, 9
Lemon v. Kurtzman, 9
LGBTQ+, 21, 65, 102, 196, 199, 200, 203, 213, 214, 215, 219, 220, 221, 231
Life of the Beloved, 241

Index

lifestyle
  Christian/moral, 20, 67, 94, 123, 126, 178, 181, 219
  Lifestyle evangelism, 223
  military, 38, 47
  non-Christian or secular, 21, 96, 199, 215, 221, 222, 227
lifetime
  friendships, 53
  ministry, 80, 175, 181
  serve the Lord, 79
  trip of a lifetime, 87
limitations
  artificial unfair limitations, 220
  limits and bounds of culture, 212
  of authority, 53
  nothing off limits to spouse, 158
  personal and professional limitations, xiii, 96
  religious freedoms and limitations, 9, 11, 206
Lincoln, Abraham, 209, 218
Linzey, Chris, 41–42
Linzey, Paul, xv, xvii-xix, 235–36, 241
Living Reminder, The, 173, 241
loaned to the military, 109, 142
love, 21, 53, 96, 102, 138, 171, 219, 232, 233
  5 Love Languages, 220
  big enough to love, 214, 219, 222, 233
  endorsers love chaplains, 71
  Great Commandment, 129, 197
  labor of love, xix-xx,
  love all people equally, 18, 20, 21, 22, 87, 124, 165, 169, 197, 198, 203, 204, 206, 209, 216, 222, 223, 229
  love my job, 42, 176
  sailors love gedunk, 161
  sharing the love of Christ, 20, 111, 179, 197,
  symbol of love and sacrifice, 22
  theology of love, 221
  transform an enemy to a friend, MLK, 221
loyal, loyalties, 74, 128, 199, 204, 226

Maintaining Government Neutrality Regarding Religion, 15, 16, 242
manage
  career, 150, 152, 153
  personal life, 19, 177–181
  social media, 190
  to work together pluralistically, 6
mandate
  biblical, 23
  Constitutional, 122
  from the American people, 123
  government, xvii
marathon, 137
Marines, 83, 100, 103, 140, 196, 217, 247
  billiard tournament, 161, 172
  chaplain training, 57
  infantry battalion, 98–99
  meeting with the USMC general, 92
marriage, spouse, 34, 67, 76, 118, 131, 179, 180, 203, 240, 242
  adultery, 159
  biblical principles of marriage, 235
  biracial, 196
  license, 152
  seminars and retreats, 57, 112, 136, 137, 236
  same-sex, 196
  unity, 28, 36, 74, 80, 179, 227, 228
Martin of Tours, 4
Matters of Conscience, 8, 243
Maxwell AFB, 52, 56–57, 59–61, 126
medical coverage, 47, 49, 131, 143, 145, 146
medical exam, 44, 47
memorial service, memorial ceremony, 46, 48, 109, 144, 151, 172, 175, 186, 202, 225, 230, 246,
  for a clock, 161–62
  Shi'ite, 130–32
mentor, xv, xxii, 41, 47, 53, 55, 56, 57, 66, 113, 128, 136, 137, 150, 152, 204, 227, 235, 238
Messiah, 18, 169
Midway, Battle of, xx
military
  Military Academy, West Point, 5, 13
  bearing, 61, 142

Index

(military continued)
brat, 120, 241
Military Chaplaincy (Vol I): A Report to the President, 241
Military Chaplaincy in an Era of Religious Pluralism, 239
Military Chaplains & Religious Diversity, 200, 240
compensation, 147, 148
lifestyle (see Lifestyle)
Military One Source, 96, 97, 241
photo, 86, 149, 150, 152
Military Religious Freedom Foundation, 199, 243
spouse (see spouse)
Military Spouse Team, 241
ministry, xiv, xviii, xix, xx, xxi, xxii, 4, 6, 11, 21, 40, 41, 71, 84, 92, 94, 119, 125, 129, 138, 139, 151, 184, 185, 186–191, 207, 232
  accountability, 69, 70, 109, 137, 157, 158, 180
  after leaving the military, 68, 69, 79
  background of ministry, 3–23
  call, calling, xx, 27–32, 33–34, 37, 94, 159
  context, 22, 42, 53, 68, 89, 102, 114, 127, 135, 137, 151, 152, 156, 163, 165, 171, 172, 175, 186–191, 195–98, 201, 204, 209, 211, 246, 247
  failure, 66, 76, 82, 136, 158, 159, 170, 239
  fun, 160, 165
  future of ministry in the military, 7, 195–232
  hindrances, 89, 103, 227
  incarnational, 93, 111, 114, 165, 169–174, 177, 186, 202, 222
  incredible, fruitful ministry, 16, 39, 79, 81, 97, 110, 114, 140, 144, 162, 174, 175, 181, 198, 234
  Jesus's ministry, 21, 169, 198
  love for ministry, xx, 42, 129, 176
  model, example, xv
  ministry follows friendship, xv, 53, 172, 179, 187, 198, 231

  ministry of presence, 87, 93, 98, 111, 114, 170, 173, 178
  not about us, 126, 135,
  perform or provide, 111, 112, 126, 127, 214
  recommendations, 203, 223–29, 232
  requirements and experience, 43, 44, 45, 46, 48, 108, 177
  Reserve and National Guard, 50, 140–46
  self-care in ministry, 72, 73
  spouse, 38, 41
  stress, burnout, 76–79, 99
  training, 52–58, 59–61, 133
  women in ministry, 87, 196, 216, 231
minority faith groups, 5, 6, 14
  atheist, atheists, 123, 213, 231
  Christian Scientists, 216, 217
  Jewish, Jews, Rabbi, 3, 4, 5, 6, 14, 19, 44, 67, 75, 106, 115, 116, 123, 125, 128, 131, 132, 161, 199, 211, 216, 217
  Muslims, Islam, imam, 3, 4, 6, 14, 44, 123, 130–32, 216, 217, 231
  Hindus, 123, 216, 217
  humanist, humanists, 213
  Buddhists, 4, 6, 14, 129, 216, 217, 231
  Latter Day Saints, 123, 216, 217
  Service Academies, 5, 13, 55, 216, 217, 235, 236
Miracles & Moments of Grace: Inspiring Stories from Military Chaplains, 241
Mission
  chaplain basic training, 52–58
  military as our mission field, 21, 108, 143, 186, 197, 199, 221
  military mission, command mission, 89, 90, 99, 119, 128, 154, 217
  mission of chaplains, Religious Support mission, 21, 54, 55, 56, 95, 102, 103, 104, 105, 106, 119, 127, 227, 232
  mission of this book, xxi

Index

missionary, 22, 33, 79, 95, 96, 143, 177, 190, 221, 227, 237
North American Mission Board, xvi, 76, 139, 240
money
  attitude toward, 177
  chaplain Resource Manager, 135
  denomination/endorser, 70, 71, 126, 143, 180
  for seminary, 28
  misuse of, 70, 77, 158, 178, 227
  military priorities, 16, 230
  pay issues, 5, 14, 82, 87, 119, 141, 145, 147, 148, 241
Monroe, James, 13
Montgomery GI Bill, 145
Moon, Zachary, 241
mop, 170
morale, 6, 95, 97, 100, 112, 128
Moses, 17, 154–56
move, relocate, PCS, 33, 36, 37, 38, 51, 117–18, 142, 146, 147, 178, 180, 207
MRE, 59, 60, 93, 111, 116, 207
muddy boots chaplain, 92
Meyers, John G., 90, 241

name
  call on the name of the Lord, 181
  chaplain's name, 33, 83, 84, 147, 152
  clock, 161
  "Father, Son, and Holy Spirit," 21
  Jesus, Christ, xx, 21, 87, 102, 125, 128, 169, 198, 202, 224–25, 229, 230, 233, 234, 241
  Lord's name in vain, 124
  meaning of "name" in the Bible, 224
  name tag, 83, 84
  nickname, 156
NASCAR, 164
National Conference on Ministry to the Armed Forces (NCMAF), xx, 125, 240
National Guard, xv, 5, 15, 29, 50, 55, 140–46, 248
nation's cloth, xxi, 83

Native Americans, 5
Naval Station Newport, RI, 52, 57
Navy, 100, 140, 146, 179, 186, 196, 202, 217
  chaplain, 66, 76, 81, 83, 89, 90, 100, 114, 118, 148, 152, 160, 161, 179, 185, 235, 240, 242, 245, 246
  Holy Helo, 160
  instruction, 57, 108, 129, 136, 240, 246
  Navy brat, 120
  Religious Programs Specialist, RP, 57, 98, 99, 101, 103
  Tiger Cruise, 87–88
  training, 52, 57–58
  uniforms, 84
Nay, Robert, 241
NCO, 30, 84, 101, 103, 104, 131, 132, 162, 172, 191, 229
Nelson, Robert, 98–99
neutral, neutrality towards religion, 10, 15, 16, 242
New Age, 124
Nimitz, Chester, 89–90
Noland, Rob, v, 154–56
nonbinary, 102, 214
non-Christians in the military, 87, 102, 177, 203, 204, 207, 214, 224, 231
noncombatant, 14, 101, 205, 242
non-select, not selected, 81, 149
North American Missions Board, xvi, 76, 139, 240
Northway, Lisa, 33–34
Nouwen, Henri, 173, 241
nurture the living, 54, 97

Oath of Office, 42
Officer Training School, 52–58, 59–61
Old Testament, 17, 18, 72, 76, 183
online, 45, 152, 196, 235
Operational, Social, and Religious Influences upon the Army Chaplain: Field Manual, 241
orders, 36, 37, 50, 51, 52, 115, 134, 142, 146, 152, 158, 171, 182, 206, 226
ordination, 34, 44, 47–48

(ordination continued)
   documents, 147, 152
   requirement, 44, 47–48
   vows, 71, 157, 158, 181

Padre, 4, 90, 156
paperwork, 42, 60,147, 148, 149
Parnell, Jonathan, 197, 198, 242
pastor, 21, 39, 41, 43, 49, 51, 156, 161, 171, 182, 184, 232, 235, 237
   Captain Interrogative, 39
   conflict in church, 46
   pastor in the military, 49, 58, 86, 90, 109, 186, 187, 188, 227, 232
   pastor on steroids, xxi, 186
   pastor to chaplains, 77
   qualifications, 19
   Reserve or Guard chaplain, 141–42
   role, xxi
   serving with military, 3, 5
   stress, 144, 177
   USS Dorchester, 6
pay, 147, 148
PCS, PCSing (see move)
Pentagon, 11, 29, 135, 226
perform and provide, 15, 108, 112, 126, 130, 131, 214, 221
personal fulfilment, 22, 73, 75, 105, 114, 118, 153, 186, 187
   of spouse and children, 181
personal life
   of chaplains, xiii, xiv, xix, 29, 30, 32, 36, 46, 66, 72–80, 81, 94, 114, 118, 120, 153, 158, 177–181, 182, 187, 191, 209, 231
   of military personnel, xiii, 170, 188, 217, 221
   of spouse, 118, 158, 181
   personal and professional growth, 133–37
personal staff officer of the commander, 11, 67, 68, 109
Pfanner, Toni, 82–83, 242
photo, 86, 149, 150, 152,
physical fitness, 44, 47, 55, 66, 103, 113, 151, 152
pitfalls, 178, 180, 206, 224

pluralism, pluralistic, xiii, 11, 42, 57, 113, 122–29, 130–32, 197, 204, 211, 212, 216, 223, 226, 230, 239
polish (see shoes)
policies, policy, xxi, 16
   duty rotation, 30
   LGBTQ+ in military (see gays)
   manuals and regulations, 82, 239, 245–47
   noncombatant status, 205
   religious accommodation, 128, 239
   uniform, 84
politics, 69, 195, 197, 212, 219, 227, 232
pornography, 77, 78, 158, 178, 196
Powell, Colin, 93
pray, prayer, 3, 6, 20, 77, 102, 103, 114, 202, 209, 225
   at command functions, 22, 87, 124, 202, 206, 225
   at religious services, 202, 225
   fast and pray, 75, 182, 184
   for others, 92, 132, 173, 187, 189, 198, 215
   in Jesus's name, xx, 87, 128, 202, 224, 230, 234
   Jesus's example, 72
   personal spirituality, 28, 32, 114, 158, 178, 182
   with others, 78
   with spouse, 39, 40, 41, 184
preach, xx, 14, 87, 93, 108, 124, 127, 152, 157, 172, 176, 186, 187, 188, 197
president, 11, 13, 86, 212, 218
priest, priests, 3, 4, 6, 17, 18, 44, 123, 131, 132, 211
Prince v. Massachusetts, 9
priorities
   military unit, 16
   personal, 74, 137, 181
prison (see jail)
pro deo et patria, 86
programs,
   chaplain led, 14, 16, 48, 109, 186, 217, 227

education and training, xviii, 45, 58, 71, 133, 136, 137, 216, 240, 246
   family support, 119
   student loan repayment, 15
   unit led, 112, 230
promises, 181
promotions, 135, 118, 143, 151, 152, 153, 172
   boards, 81, 82, 86, 149, 153
   list, 82, 86
   non-select, 10, 231
   order, 86, 147
   packet, 150
   pay increase, 119
   pin on new rank, 86
   praying at, 202, 206, 225
   records, 147, 152
   requirements, 113
Protestant, Protestants, 10, 14, 49, 67, 123, 127, 132, 164, 190, 199, 203, 215, 216, 217
provide (see perform)
PTSD, 66, 76, 240
Purple Heart, 22

qualifications, xviii, 15, 43–49, 52
   add to or further, 94, 137
   Christian leaders, 19, 177
   Reserve and National Guard, 141
   weapons, 101, 103

rabbi (see minority faith groups)
race, racism, ethnicity, 150, 158, 215–16, 219, 220, 221, 229, 239, 240, 242
rank, 117, 127
   centurion, 19
   chaplains rank and pay without command authority, 14
   intimidated, intimidation, 58, 100
   of authors, 235, 237
   promotions (see promotions)
   rank and pay structure, 5
   records, 152, 153
   retirement, 146
   significance of rank, 87, 113
   uniforms, 82, 84, 85, 86

rater, 151, 229
readiness (see family readiness and emotional readiness)
Ready for Anything, 35, 37, 38, 39, 104, 164, 188, 205
recommendations, 203, 223–29, 232
records, 47, 86, 147, 148, 149, 152, 153
recruiter, recruiting, chaplain recruiter, xvii, 39, 44, 45, 48, 150, 216
red
   Red Cross, 82
   red flags, 35, 49
   Red Force, Blue Force, 154
regulations (see manuals and regulations)
relationships (see working relationships and relationships at home)
relics, 4
religion, religious
   Religion in Uniform, 200, 214, 221, 242
   Religious Accommodation, (see accommodate, accommodation)
   Religious Affairs Team, Religious Affairs Airman, 91, 101, 103, 228, 245
   (see chaplain)
   Religious Conflict and the Chain of Command, 241
   Religious Education program, 187
   religious freedom, 9, 11, 13, 87, 100, 123, 199, 205, 206, 213, 217, 225, 226, 243
   Religious Liberty, 129, 241, 242
   Religious Liberty in the Military Services, 242
   religious practitioners, 231
   Religious Programs Specialist, RP, (see Navy)
   Religious Support Team, 53–55, 100–5, 106–7,113, 228, 246
reports, 68, 69, 71, 150, 151, 171, 228, 229
represent, representation
   America, the government, the Constitution, the president, 81, 86

(represent, representation continued)
  Christ, Kingdom of God, faith, hope, 18, 21, 22, 81, 86, 87, 93, 114, 142, 175, 228, 232,
  church, denomination, endorser, xxi, 4, 6, 14, 48, 67, 69, 70, 76, 81, 86, 87, 93, 102, 108, 109, 204, 205, 221, 228, 229
  commander, 228
  ethics, morality, 54, 57, 70, 97, 100, 112, 125, 127, 135, 170, 187, 204, 221, 240
  family, 94, 165, 181
  military, 86
  organization, corporation, 83
reputation, 19, 66, 100, 105, 115, 158, 159, 177, 178, 201, 202, 205
requirements, 43–49
Reserve, Reserve Components, 140–46
resilience, resilient, bounce back, bouncing back, 34, 56, 120, 183–85, 240
Resilience: Hard-Won Wisdom for Living a Better Life, 184–85, 240
respect, 11, 19, 52, 82, 87, 89, 103, 106, 107, 123, 124, 125, 126, 127, 170, 197, 203, 205, 207, 217, 221, 225, 232
retired, retired pay, retirement, retirement points, xix, 27, 46, 69, 111, 120, 128, 144, 145, 202, 235, 241
Revolutionary War, 5
risk
  burnout, 66, 76, 77, 79
  Chaplain Corps, 231
  criticism, 208
  LGBTQ+ career, 215
  losing chaplain positions, 104
role of chaplain, xviii, xix. xxi, 15, 89–97, 200, 201
  Family Support Group, 100, 119, 121, 172
  incarnational presence, 223
  noncombatants, 101, 205, 242
  religious rights, 12
  Religious Accommodation, 202

  Religious Support Team, 54, 100–5, 113, 228, 246
  spiritual leader, 227
  wearing two hats, 86
Rome
  army, 19
  battlefield, 3
  centurion, 19
  pope, 164
  Vatican, 164
Rosenthal, Robert, 106–7
Royal Rangers, 188
RP (see Navy)
Rutherford, Don, 123

sabbath, 72, 73, 75, 76, 115, 161
Safest Place in Iraq, xvii, 77, 163, 235, 241
Sawchuck, Stephen, 242
Schaick, Steven A., 242
Schwartz, General Norton A., 15, 16, 242
Scrutiny, scrutinize, 46, 178
Secretary of Defense, 6, 11
secular, secularism, xiii, 9, 11, 206, 241
self-care, 72–80 (see care)
Selva, Paul, 91, 240
seminary, xxi, 27, 28, 30, 33, 39, 43, 44, 50, 51, 108, 111, 162, 232, 236
  Barnett College of Ministry & Theology, Southeastern University, 235
  Gateway Seminary, xiv
  Rawlins Divinity School, Liberty University, 237
  transcripts, 147, 152
separation issues, 36, 37, 38, 112
separation of church and state, 8, 9, 196, 205–6
service academies, 5, 13, 55, 216, 217, 235, 236
Sessions, Jeff, 242
sex, 70, 77, 78, 119, 158, 177, 178, 196, 227
shame, 142, 199
ship, 66, 100, 111, 179, 185, 188

ship duty, 152, 186
ship to ship religious services, 160–61
ship visit, 57
Tiger Cruise, 87–88
USS Dorchester, 6
USS Yorktown, xx
When the *Ship Sinks*, 5, 241
shoes, shine, polish, 81, 84, 88, 153
God sees the heart, 81
nice shoes, General, 85
Marathon, 137
sinners, 123, 197, 222, 224
friend of, 197, 198, 219, 222, 242
God loves, 87
Jesus with, 21, 229
love the sinner, hate the sin, 220
social media, 70, 111, 117, 158, 190, 196, 203, 205, 227, 232, 241
socializing, 46, 179, 215, 220,
soul winning (see evangelism, proselytism, lead people to faith in Christ)
Southern Baptists (see Baptist)
SPAM (sex, porn, alcohol, money), 70, 77, 158, 178
spiritual disciplines, 74, 75, 136, 182–85, 187, 191, 227
Spiritual Disciplines for the Christian Life, 243
spiritual leader, leadership, 137, 158, 170, 171, 180, 187, 191, 205, 206, 208, 227
spouse, 35, 67, 77
career, 118, 181
death notification, 176
deployment, separation, 37
divorce, 227
Family Support Group, 120
matters most, prioritize, 181, 228
promises, 181
retreats, 179
saying goodbye, 117
secrets, 158
unity, 22
staff
command staff, personal staff, 11, 16, 67, 86, 92, 94, 100, 105, 109, 110, 111, 112, 121, 188, 190, 206, 228, 229
chaplain staff, chaplain team, 16, 105, 113, 197
chaplain's impact, 230
Chief of Chaplain's staff, 109
chow hall staff, 116
church staff, 59, 102, 141–42
endorser's staff, 48
hospital staff, 30–31
staff duty NCO, 30
staff meetings, 89, 110, 172, 187, 189, 191, 202, 206, 225, 228, 229
staff officer skills, development, 54, 56
Stahl, Ronit Y., 216, 242
State Defense Force, State Guard, State Military Reserve, 140–41
Strategic Roadmap for the Army Chaplain Corps, 123
strategic military use of chaplains, 200, 206–7
strategy, xxi, 72, 75, 91, 180, 223–29
stress, 46, 51, 59, 76, 77, 119, 144, 178, 180
struggle, struggling, 18, 23, 51, 111, 118, 184, 216
subject matter expert, SME, 11, 87
suicide, suicidal, 45, 57, 61, 76, 100, 112, 137, 188, 189
superior officer, 66
supervisor, supervisory, xv, 30, 57, 67, 109, 115, 143, 151, 152, 171, 204, 227, 228
Supreme Court, 9, 10, 240,
Sword of the Lord, 3, 239
systemic racism, 215–16

tank, 96, 98, 99, 154, 160, 173
tasks, xviii, 15, 22, 52, 54, 79, 97, 100, 108–114,
common core tasks, 55, 103
military tasks, 89, 103
ministerial tasks, 101, 177
missionary tasks, 96
specialized command tasks, 101
staff tasks, 188, 207, 229

team
  chaplain team, 54, 57, 61, 75, 100–7, 109, 113, 228, 236
  chaplain recruiting team, 216
  command leadership team, 228
  Critical Incident Stress Management team, 134
  football team, 118, 162
  medical team, 134
  notification team (see Casualty Assistance)
  Religious Support Team, Religious Affairs Team, 57, 100–5, 106–7, 113, 228
  team player, 105, 109, 134, 197, 228
  Team Travis, v
  teamwork, unity, 106–7, 113
temptation, 18, 38, 77, 136, 157, 231
theocracy, 18
theology
  diversity, 127
  educational degree, 43, 44
  of church and endorser, 30, 108, 112, 204, 219, 221,
  of love, 221
  understanding our own, 223, 224, 225
Tiger Cruise, 87–88
tithes, dues, 71, 126
Title 10 of the US Code, 14, 108, 248
Title 14 of the US Code, 15, 248
Title 32 of the US Code, 15, 248
Top Ten Ways to Succeed, 180
training (see specific training areas above)
transgender, 197, 211
trauma, 57, 176, 184
Travis, Keith, 237–38
trouble, 43, 53, 100, 110, 137, 157–59, 184, 185, 191, 204
trumpet, 17
trust
  building trust, 52, 81, 87, 118, 136, 207, 215
  Holy Spirit, God, 53, 129, 152, 212, 224, 232
  "the system," 147
two roles of chaplains, 86

uniform, 41, 52, 60, 93, 94, 106, 128, 141, 163, 213, 226
  alarm clock, 161–62
  different kinds of uniforms, 110, 121
  pastors in uniform, 109, 142, 187, 205, 207, 208, 227
  Religion in Uniform, 200, 214, 221, 242
  Uniform Code of Military Justice (UCMJ), 207
  wearing the uniform, 81–88, 105, 148, 149, 157, 200
  women, 203
Uniformed Services Employment and Reemployment Rights Act, 142, 242
Up Front and Leading, 110
USERRA, 142
USS Dorchester, 6, 91, 211
USS Yorktown, xx

VA Benefits (see GI Bill)
vacation, 73
values
  of faith groups, 70, 199, 221
  of God, 219
  of military personnel, 96, 195
  of nation, 11, 195
  of those who differ, 125, 195, 213
  one's own, 74, 87, 94, 125, 129, 137, 143, 177, 178
Vatican (see Catholic and Rome)
Veterans, 84
  benefits, 145, 146
  Veterans Day events, 225
  reemployment, 142, 242
vision statement. xviii
visit,
  family or military trip, 34, 51, 164
  from endorser, 65, 92
  visitation, 13, 40, 90, 151, 155, 172, 175, 187
  workplaces, 57, 90, 171, 172
volunteer chaplains, 140–41
vows to the Lord, 71, 157, 158, 181

Index

Waggoner, Ed, 199, 200, 213, 214, 221, 242
waivers, 43, 44, 45, 48
  age, ministerial experience, faith group shortage, medical
war, warriors, xiii, 91, 143, 144
  death or dismemberment, 117, 190
  Iraq, 104, 135, 144, 182, 189, 190, 235
  issues, 144, 209
  National Catholic War Council, 67
  Military Uniforms and the Law of War, 82, 83
  religious sanction of war, 208
  war college, 136, 237
  war movies, 117
  war zone, 141
  war-time ministry, 163, 172, 185
  Weinstein's war against Evangelicals, 199
  World War I, 216
  World War II, 176
Washington, George, 13, 207
weight, 47, 66, 149
Weinstein, Michael "Mikey," 199, 213, 243
Welch, Mark, 91, 243
West Point (see Military Academy)
When the Ship Sinks, 5, 241

While Shepherds Watched their Flocks, 241
White, Brandon, 59–61
Whitney, Donald, 182, 183, 243
Whittington, Michael C., 8, 243
winning people to Christ (see evangelism, proselytism, lead people to faith in Christ)
women
  abuse and disrespect, 203, 220
  chaplains, xiii, 22, 48, 87, 200, 214, 216, 226, 233
  gender inequality, 203
  Imago Dei, 219–220
  in the military, 22, 40, 127, 129, 170, 182, 200, 214, 216, 233
  in leadership, 196, 216, 231
  in ministry, 48, 87, 196, 213, 216, 231
  athletes, 82
world religions, 8, 113, 126, 127, 128, 135, 196, 206, 208, 213, 219, 220
World War I, 216
World War II, 176
world view, 52, 95, 96, 195

You, God, and PTSD, 240

Zeiger, Hans, 199, 200, 243

www.ingramcontent.com/pod-product-compliance
Lightning Source LLC
Chambersburg PA
CBHW050840230426
43667CB00012B/2082